THE GROWTH OF
WHITE-COLLAR UNIONISM

THE GROWTH OF
WHITE-COLLAR
UNIONISM

BY

GEORGE SAYERS BAIN

Research Fellow in Industrial Relations
Nuffield College, Oxford

OXFORD
AT THE CLARENDON PRESS
1970

Oxford University Press, Ely House, London W. 1

GLASGOW NEW YORK TORONTO MELBOURNE WELLINGTON
CAPE TOWN SALISBURY IBADAN NAIROBI DAR ES SALAAM LUSAKA ADDIS ABABA
BOMBAY CALCUTTA MADRAS KARACHI LAHORE DACCA
KUALA LUMPUR SINGAPORE HONG KONG TOKYO

PRINTED IN GREAT BRITAIN

FOR MY
MOTHER AND FATHER

PREFACE

T HE purpose of this book is to isolate the major factors which determine the growth of white-collar unionism. It attempts to do this primarily by accounting for the variations in the industrial and occupational pattern of white-collar unionism in Great Britain. This membership pattern was constructed during 1964, the year in which the research for this project began, and generally indicates the position as of the beginning of that year. The unions' records were not sufficiently detailed to allow a systematic pattern to be constructed for previous years. Since the object is to explain the 1964 pattern, the situation is generally described as it existed in that and earlier years. Major changes which have occurred since then are generally indicated in footnotes. But no attempt has been made to provide a completely up-to-date account. Nor has any attempt been made to give a detailed history of the growth of white-collar unionism in Britain. In general, description has been provided not for its own sake, but only in so far as it contributes to the analysis.

Anyone who undertakes a study of this nature accumulates a large number of debts. These become particularly numerous if, as in this case, the institutions which the investigator is examining are not those of his own country. I am particularly indebted to the officials of all the trade unions, trade union federations, companies, employer associations, and government departments who granted interviews, completed questionnaires, answered letters, gave access to documents in their possession, and provided unpublished data. Some of these officials were also kind enough to read sections of the manuscript and comment on them. Without their assistance this study would not have been possible. In view of the numbers involved, I hope they will excuse me if I thank them here without mentioning them by name. I also hope that those who disagree with my conclusions will not feel that in arriving at them I have failed to take their views into account.

By electing me first to a Research Studentship and later to a Research Fellowship, the Warden and Fellows of Nuffield College made it possible for me to devote my time to research, and for this I am most grateful. The Research Fellowship was partially financed out of a grant from the Leverhulme Trustees to the College for research into industrial relations, and I should like to record my thanks to them. My thanks are also due to two of the College's secretaries, Jenny Bond and Lyn Yates, who typed various drafts of the manuscript with great efficiency and unfailing good humour.

A considerable amount of this study's argument is supported by statistical data and analysis. I would like to thank Beryl Cuthbertson who helped to collect much of the basic data, Ann Black who patiently and efficiently steered it through the computer, and Emiel van Broekhoven who designed the regression programme which has proved so useful to myself and other social scientists in Oxford. My special thanks go to Bob Bacon who convinced me of the contribution which statistical techniques could make to this study, instructed me in their use, and guided me in interpreting the results.

Parts of Chapters II and III were originally published in the *British Journal of Industrial Relations*, iv (November 1966), pp. 304–35, and I am obliged to the editor of this journal for permission to reproduce this material. This same material as well as parts of Chapters VIII and IX appeared in *Trade Union Growth and Recognition*, a research paper I prepared for, and at the request of, the Royal Commission on Trade Unions and Employers' Associations; this material is reproduced here with the permission of the Controller of Her Majesty's Stationery Office. I am particularly grateful to the Royal Commission for giving me the opportunity to undertake the research upon which Chapter VIII is based, and to its secretariat and staff for all the help they gave me in carrying out this research.

I also benefited greatly from the comments of those who read all or part of the manuscript. They include David Coates, Robert Currie, Valerie Ellis, Alan Fox, Arthur Gillman, Jackie Johns, Archie Kleingartner, Donald Robertson, Inga Taylor (who also helped to correct the proofs), and Alex Wedderburn. They helped to correct numerous errors of fact and interpretation and to remove many infelicities of style. Those that remain are a result of my obstinacy rather than their lack of critical judgement.

My greatest debt is to my teachers. Clare Pentland, my first teacher of labour economics and industrial relations, inspired my interest in the theory of union growth. Hugh Clegg and Allan Flanders taught me most of what I know about industrial relations in Britain, provided much helpful guidance especially during the early stages of the study, suffered through several drafts of the manuscript, and made helpful suggestions on almost every page. To these three individuals, I owe far more than this brief acknowledgement can suggest.

Finally, a special note of gratitude is due to my wife not only for her sustained encouragement throughout my long preoccupation with this study but also for the many improvements she suggested.

The help of all these people was invaluable and greatly improved the finished product. For any shortcomings which may remain in spite of their efforts and for all the opinions expressed, I alone am responsible.

GEORGE BAIN

Nuffield College, Oxford
December 1968

CONTENTS

LIST OF FIGURES

LIST OF TABLES

KEY TO ABBREVIATIONS

ABT	Association of Building Technicians.
ACTT	Association of Cinematograph, Television and Allied Technicians.
AEU	Amalgamated Engineering Union. This union merged during 1967 with the Amalgamated Union of Foundry Workers to form the Amalgamated Union of Engineering and Foundry Workers (AEF). The designation AEU is used in this study as the merger did not take place until after the end of the period under review.
AScW	Association of Scientific Workers. This union merged during 1968 with the Association of Supervisory Staffs, Executives and Technicians to form Division A of the Association of Scientific, Technical and Managerial Staffs. The designation AScW is used in this study as the merger did not take place until after the end of the period under review.
ASSET	Association of Supervisory Staffs, Executives and Technicians. This union merged during 1968 with the Association of Scientific Workers to form Division I of the Association of Scientific, Technical and Managerial Staffs. The designation ASSET is used in this study as the merger did not take place until after the end of the period under review.
ASTMS	Association of Scientific, Technical and Managerial Staffs. See also AScW and ASSET.
BEC	British Employers' Confederation. This organization merged in 1965 with the Federation of British Industry and the National Association of British Manufacturers to form the Confederation of British Industry.
BISAKTA	British Iron, Steel and Kindred Trades Association. This union is also referred to as the Iron and Steel Trades Confederation.
BISMA	British Iron and Steel Management Association.
CAWU	Clerical and Administrative Workers' Union.
CBI	Confederation of British Industry.
CIR	Commission on Industrial Relations.
CSEU	Confederation of Shipbuilding and Engineering Unions.
DATA	Draughtsmen's and Allied Technicians' Association.
EEF	Engineering Employers' Federation.
FSMBS	Foremen and Staff Mutual Benefit Society.
IDT	Industrial Disputes Tribunal.
IOJ	Institute of Journalists.
ISTC	Iron and Steel Trades Confederation. This union is also referred to as the British Iron, Steel and Kindred Trades Association.
JIC	Joint Industrial Council.

NACSS — National Association of Clerical and Supervisory Staffs. This is the white-collar section of the Transport and General Workers' Union.

NATSOPA — National Society of Operative Printers and Assistants. This union merged during 1966 with the National Union of Printing, Bookbinding and Paper Workers to form Division I of the Society of Graphical and Allied Trades.

NEJTM — National Engineering Joint Trades Movement.

NFPW — National Federation of Professional Workers.

NPA — Newspaper Proprietors Association.

NUBE — National Union of Bank Employees.

NUGMW — National Union of General and Municipal Workers. In practice, this union is sometimes referred to as the General and Municipal Workers' Union (GMWU).

NUJ — National Union of Journalists.

NUPBPW — National Union of Printing Bookbinding and Paper Workers. This union merged during 1966 with the National Society of Operative Printers and Assistants to form Division A of the Society of Graphical and Allied Trades.

PKTF — Printing and Kindred Trades Federation.

SOGAT — Society of Graphical and Allied Trades. See also NATSOPA and NUPBPW.

TGWU — Transport and General Workers' Union.

TUC — Trades Union Congress.

USDAW — Union of Shop, Distributive and Allied Workers.

Great Britain—refers to England, Wales, and Scotland.

United Kingdom—refers to England, Wales, Scotland, and Northern Ireland.

All references to *Written Evidence* or *Minutes of Evidence* is to that given to the Royal Commission on Trade Unions and Employers' Associations under the chairmanship of Lord Donovan.

I

INTRODUCTION

THIS study attempts to discover the major factors which promote or hinder the growth of trade unionism among white-collar workers, particularly those employed in manufacturing industries, in Great Britain. There are two reasons for wishing to do this.

The first reason is practical. While the number of manual workers in Britain is declining, the number of white-collar workers is increasing so rapidly that they will soon be in the majority. If the trade union movement is to maintain its relative position in the power structure of this country and to continue to play an effective role in the industrial relations system, it will have to recruit these white-collar workers. If it does not or cannot, the best it will achieve is numerical stability within an increasingly narrow band of the occupational distribution, and its ability to advance even the interests of its manual membership will be seriously impaired. From the point of view of those who believe that an effective trade union movement is essential to the successful functioning of a democratic society, it is obviously important to isolate the factors which promote or hinder its growth among white-collar workers.

The second reason is theoretical. There is a fairly extensive literature on the theory of union growth.[1] Unfortunately, very little of it is useful in giving insights into the process of union growth among white-collar workers. Many of the theories are concerned solely with manual unionism. More important, many of the theories are not oriented to empirical research and are couched in such a way as to preclude any chance of verification. They are more in the tradition of social philosophy than social science and have as their objective the 'interpretation' of the labour movement. They are, as one writer has aptly noted, a 'heritage of curiously fascinating and conflicting admixture of restrained or explosive polemic, implicit or patent advocacy, muddied metaphor, mild expressions of faith, fiery depositions of dogma, and occasional

---

[1] It is not possible or necessary to review here the large literature, most of which is American in origin, on the theory of union growth. This has been done by John T. Dunlop, 'The Development of Labor Organization: A Theoretical Framework', *Insights Into Labor Issues*, Richard A. Lester and Joseph Shister, editors (New York: Macmillan, 1949), pp. 163–93, and Mark Perlman, *Labor Union Theories in America* (Evanston: Row, Peterson & Co., 1958). See also H. B. Davis, 'The Theory of Union Growth', *Quarterly Journal of Economics*, lv (August 1941), pp. 611–37; J. Shister, 'The Logic of Union Growth', *Journal of Political Economy*, lxi (October 1953), pp. 413–33; and Irving Bernstein, 'The Growth of American Unions', *American Economic Review*, xliv (June 1954), pp. 301–18. This is by no means a complete list.

flashes of brilliant insight, which make all the rest so much easier to take'.[1]
By attempting to provide generalizations about the growth of white-collar
unionism which are basically operational in nature, this study departs from
the traditions of much of the literature in this field. But by so doing, it hopes
to be able to make some contribution to both the substance and the method of
the theory of union growth.

The practical and the theoretical also explain why manufacturing has been
singled out for special attention in this study. On the one hand, manufacturing industries are the major 'commanding height' of the economy and offer
the trade union movement its largest untapped potential of white-collar
members. On the other hand, statistical data are more plentiful for this sector
of the economy than for others, and this makes it easier to test generalizations
about union growth.

SOME METHODOLOGICAL CONSIDERATIONS

Those who have written on the subject of union growth have often defined it
very broadly. Besides trying to explain the growth of union membership, they
have also tried to explain the development of union structure as well as what
has variously been referred to as union personality or character.[2] The present
study takes a much more restricted view of union growth and confines itself
to trying to explain membership growth only.[3] This is not because these other
aspects of trade unions are uninteresting or irrelevant to an understanding of
their behaviour. Rather, it is because there is no good reason for assuming
that the factors which explain the growth of union membership necessarily
also explain the development of union structure, personality, or character.
Granted this, these aspects of trade unionism are too complex to be explained
adequately within the confines of a study that focuses on the growth of union
membership, and too important to be explained inadequately.[4]

[1] Abraham J. Siegel, 'Method and Substance in Theorizing About Worker Protest',
Aspects of Labor Economics (A Report of the National Bureau of Economic Research, New
York, and published by Princeton University Press, Princeton, 1962), p. 27.

[2] See, for example, Irving Bernstein, 'Union Growth and Structural Cycles', *Proceedings
of the Industrial Relations Research Association*, vii (December 1954), pp. 202–46; G. W.
Brooks, 'Reflections on the Changing Character of American Labor Unions', *Proceedings
of the Industrial Relations Research Association*, ix (December 1956), pp. 33–43; Richard A.
Lester, *As Unions Mature: An Analysis of the Evolution of American Unionism* (Princeton:
Princeton University Press, 1958); Arthur B. Shostak, *America's Forgotten Labor Organiza-
tion* (Princeton: Industrial Relations Section, Princeton University, 1962); David Lock-
wood, *The Blackcoated Worker* (London: Allen & Unwin, 1958), chap. 5; H. A. Turner,
Trade Union Growth, Structure and Policy (London: Allen & Unwin, 1962); and R. M.
Blackburn, *Union Character and Social Class* (London: Batsford, 1967).

[3] Although this study does not try to explain the growth and development of union
structure, personality, or character, it does, of course, consider the impact which these
factors may have upon union growth.

[4] Blackburn (op. cit., p. 10) has argued that it is not useful or valid to consider the
membership of a union separately from its character. Whether or not it is useful, the reader
can judge for himself after reading this study. Whether or not it is valid, there is not room

As used in this study, union growth is a quantitative concept; it is something which can be measured. There are primarily two ways in which this can be done: in terms either of *actual* union membership or of the *density* of union membership. The density of union membership is given by the following formula:

$$\frac{\text{Actual Union Membership}}{\text{Potential Union Membership}} \times 100$$

This study uses this latter measure of union growth on the grounds of methodological expediency.[1] By using the density of union membership rather than actual union membership, one of the most obvious causes of union growth, changes in potential union membership, can be excluded from the subsequent inquiry into the factors which influence the growth of white-collar unionism.

There are basically two types of data on the density of aggregate union membership which might be studied in making inferences about union growth: time series data and cross-section data. Time series data consist of observations on the density of union membership at different points in time while cross-section data consist of observations on the density of union membership at a single point in time but over different occupations, firms, industries, or geographical regions. Ideally, both types of data should be examined. This study does this to some extent, but it relies mainly upon cross-section data— the occupational and industrial pattern of white-collar unionism in Britain.[2] This is simply because of the difficulty, if not the impossibility, of constructing a time series containing a significant number of observations on actual white-collar union membership, not to speak of the density of white-collar union membership, in manufacturing industries or even the economy as a whole. It is a monumental task, as Chapter III will reveal, to obtain such figures even for selected post-war years.

The occupational and industrial pattern of white-collar unionism in Britain is the dependent variable of this study. In attempting to isolate the explanatory variables which account for this pattern of membership, it is not possible to carry out controlled experiments such as those used in the physical sciences whereby each factor is varied in turn while all the others are kept constant.

to debate here. But it is the author's contention that Blackburn's view is mistaken, and this contention will be supported by argument in a study entitled *Social Stratification and White-Collar Unionism* which the author, together with David Coates and Valerie Ellis, is preparing for publication in 1970.

[1] The density of union membership has also been referred to as the percentage organized, real membership, degree of unionization, and completeness. These terms are used synonymously throughout this study, but the density of unionization is the term which is generally used as it is the accepted British terminology. Blackburn (op. cit., p. 16 n. 1) notwithstanding, density is not 'the incorrect term'.

[2] Figures are also provided on the geographical pattern of white-collar unionism, but not much attention is devoted to it in the following analysis partly because of the unsatisfactory nature of the data and partly because there is not sufficient quantitative or even qualitative information available on a geographical basis to help account for this pattern.

In one or two places in the following analysis, it is possible by means of quantitative techniques to study simultaneously the effects of a few important variables. But generally, the examination of variables is step-wise. That is, the effect of each factor on the dependent variable is considered separately with only the most general allowances being made for the fact that 'all other things' may not be equal or constant. There is consequently a danger that other variables which affect the growth of white-collar unionism may obscure or distort the influence of the factor under consideration. But in order to make any progress at all, this study, like most social science investigations, has had to adopt this procedure.

SOME CONCEPTUAL CONSIDERATIONS

Before a pattern of white-collar union membership can be constructed, two concepts—a 'white-collar employee'[1] and a 'trade union'—have to be defined.

However the term 'white-collar employee' is defined, it is unlikely to be entirely satisfactory as there are almost bound to be some borderline cases.[2] Nevertheless, this study suggests that it is useful to define 'white-collar employee' to cover the members of the following occupational groups: foremen, overlookers, and supervisors; scientists, technologists, and technicians; clerical and administrative workers; security personnel; professionals; salesmen, commercial travellers, and shop assistants; government administrators and executive officials; and specially 'creative' occupations such as artists, musicians, and entertainers.

In a study on industrial relations, the justification for treating these various occupational groups as a collectivity is that this reflects general industrial practice. In industry, as Burns has noted, 'the line between the management and the worker, the widest social barrier, is so drawn that it includes in management all but the rank-and-file workmen'.[3] The members of the occupational groups listed above generally see themselves as belonging more with management than with manual workers, and are generally regarded by manual workers as one of 'them' rather than one of 'us' and by employer-managers as part of the 'staff' rather than part of the 'works'. The definition of 'white-collar employee' used in this study is significant and useful precisely because it is thought to be so by industry itself.

There are a whole complex of factors which explain why the line between manual and non-manual workers should be drawn in this way. But one of

---

[1] In this study the terms 'white-collar employee', 'non-manual worker', 'blackcoated worker', 'salaried employee', and 'staff worker' are used interchangeably.

[2] For a history and analysis of the major attempts to provide a logically consistent definition of a 'white-collar employee' see Fritz Croner, *Soziologie der Angestellten* (Cologne: Kiepenheuer & Witsch, 1962), chap. 2, and by the same author 'Salaried Employees in Modern Society', *International Labour Review*, lxix (February 1954), pp. 97–110.

[3] Tom Burns, 'The Cold Class War', *New Statesman* (7 April 1956), p. 331.

the most important, especially in private industry, is the relations of authority within the enterprise. Regardless of the white-collar workers' position in society or in the authority structure of the enterprise, they are linked with employer-managers 'by being associated with that part of the productive process where authority is exercised and decisions are taken'.[1] Even in non-industrial sectors of the economy such as the distributive trades and national and local government, the white-collar worker is the person who takes your money in shops and gives you orders in offices; in Lockwood's words, the person 'on the other side of the desk who is somehow associated with authority'.[2]

This study has followed the Ministry of Labour[3] and defined a 'trade union' to mean 'all organisations of employees—including those of salaried and professional workers, as well as those of manual wage earners—which are known to include in their objects that of negotiating with employers with a view to regulating the wages and working conditions of their members'.[4] The Ministry lists all the organizations which it feels are covered by this definition in its *Directory of Employers' Associations, Trade Unions, Joint Organizations, etc.*, and it is these bodies which have generally been taken as trade unions for the purpose of this study. This might be objected to on the grounds that it excludes certain organizations commonly referred to as 'professional associations' and 'staff associations' which have similar functions to trade unions. While this is true, it does not create serious difficulties given the scope and purpose of this study.

Professional associations which engage in collective bargaining are covered by the Ministry's definition, and, in general, they are listed in the *Directory*. There are certain exceptions, the most prominent of which is the British Medical Association. It is not listed even though it bargains with the Ministry of Health over the pay and conditions of general practitioners employed under the National Health Service.[5] Moreover, collective bargaining is not the only method of job regulation. This can also be accomplished by means of unilateral regulation, and some professional associations such as the Law Society use this method rather than collective bargaining.[6] But most professionals who rely upon collective bargaining are employed in the public sector

---

[1] W. G. Runciman, *Relative Deprivation and Social Justice* (London: Routledge & Kegan Paul, 1966), p. 47.

[2] Op. cit., p. 132.

[3] The Ministry of Labour is now known as the Department of Employment and Productivity, but its former designation is used here because the change did not occur until after the end of the period under review.

[4] 'Membership of Trade Unions in 1964', *Ministry of Labour Gazette*, lxxiii (November 1965), p. 480.

[5] See Harry Eckstein, *Pressure Group Politics: The Case of the British Medical Association* (London: Allen & Unwin, 1960).

[6] See Allan Flanders, *Industrial Relations: What Is Wrong With the System?* (London: Faber, 1965), chaps. 2 and 3 for a discussion of the various forms of job regulation.

of the economy, while most of those who depend upon unilateral regulation are concentrated among independent fee-paid practitioners in the service sector of the economy. Few are to be found in manufacturing, the sector of major concern to this study. In private industry, as Prandy has pointed out, the major functions of professional associations are education and certification as opposed to professional protection and collective bargaining.[1] Even granted the omission of some professional associations which should have been taken into account in computing density figures, they would not be of much quantitative significance. In manufacturing, professional associations are largely restricted to scientists and technologists, and this group accounts for only 4 per cent of this sector's total white-collar labour force.[2]

Few internal staff associations or staff committees are included in the *Directory*, regardless of whether or not they engage in collective bargaining, but this is of small consequence for this study. What evidence there is suggests that the vast majority of these organizations are sponsored, influenced, or dominated by employers.[3] They are therefore more indicative of the behaviour of employers than of employees, and it is with the latter that this study is primarily concerned. Moreover, many of these organizations do not have to recruit members; in companies in which they exist all employees often become members automatically. Hence the concept of membership density cannot be fruitfully applied to them. While there may be some staff associations which are both independent of employers and required to recruit members, these would seem to be few and far between,[4] and the omission of any which might exist would not significantly affect membership density figures. Although organizations of employees which are sponsored, influenced, or dominated by employers are not considered to be trade unions, they are a device which employers use to discourage the growth of trade unions among their white-collar employees. As such they are discussed in Chapter VIII.

The criterion of correctness cannot be applied to a definition; specific purposes require specific definitions. It is not suggested that the definitions of 'white-collar employee' and 'trade union' which are used in this study are universally valid or useful. Nor is it suggested that they cover every borderline case. All that is claimed on their behalf is that they are useful for analysing the growth of trade unionism among white-collar workers in manufacturing industries.

---

[1] Ken Prandy, 'Professional Organization in Great Britain', *Industrial Relations*, v (October 1965), pp. 67–79.

[2] See Table 2.7.

[3] See *infra*, pp. 132–3.

[4] The only major exception to this is in banking and insurance. Here the membership of staff associations has generally ceased to be automatic and they have become more or less independent of employers, if still favoured by them. They are listed in the *Directory* and were taken into account in computing density figures.

TECHNIQUES

Most of the usual techniques of social science are used in this study including the examination of documents and direct observation by means of questionnaires and interviews. The details of the various documents and surveys are given in the text, footnotes, and appendices, and there is no need to elaborate further upon them here. But this study also uses quantitative methods to analyse a relatively large amount of data. Given that union growth is by its very nature a quantitative concept and that many of the factors which might explain it are also quantitative in nature, this should not be surprising. The use of quantitative data and methods is now common in most areas of social science, but they are not all that frequently employed in industrial relations and labour history. Some comment on their use in this study is therefore called for.

There are two widely divergent views of statistics which are currently popular. 'One view is that published statistics are themselves vested with some quality of meaning not unlike the qualities ascribed to numbers by the Pythagoreans, and that they enjoy such a degree of infallibility that they may be accepted without question.' The other and yet more popular view is that 'statistics can be made to prove anything and therefore, by implication, that in fact they can prove nothing'.[1] Neither of these views is subscribed to here. The statistics used in this study should enable the reader to gain a better understanding of the process of union growth. This does not mean that these statistics are completely accurate. They are not. And if the generalizations which are based upon them are to be properly evaluated, their shortcomings must be fully understood. For this reason, considerable detail on the source, method of calculation, and reliability of all the statistics used in this study is provided in Appendix A, and, to a lesser extent, in the text.

This is not the place to become involved in a lengthy discussion of the advantages and disadvantages of using quantitative methods in social science. This question has been very fully discussed elsewhere,[2] and little that is new could be added here. But it must be emphasized that the use of these methods in this study is not an unnecessary complication. On the contrary, they have given deeper insights into the effect of certain factors on union growth and

---

[1] W. J. Reichmann, *Use and Abuse of Statistics* (Harmondsworth, Middlesex: Penguin Books, 1964), p. 11.

[2] Almost every textbook on the methodology of the social sciences discusses this question. See, for example, Abraham Kaplan, *The Conduct of Inquiry* (San Francisco: Chandler Publishing Co., 1964). Economic history is a field in which the application of quantitative methods raises similar problems to those in industrial relations or labour history, and the reader might find the following references particularly useful: Alfred H. Conrad and John R. Meyer, 'Economic Theory, Statistical Inference, and Economic History', *Studies in Econometric History* (London: Chapman & Hall, 1965), chap. 1, and Robert William Fogel, *Railroads and American Economic Growth: Essays in Econometric History* (Baltimore: Johns Hopkins Press, 1964), pp. 237–49.

have permitted generalizations to be made with greater confidence than would have been possible by visual assessment alone.

What has been said so far regarding quantitative methods is not intended to give the impression that these are the only techniques used in this study. They are only employed where the factors under consideration readily lend themselves to quantification, and many of the factors examined in this study do not. Where this is the case, more qualitative methods of analysis are used. In fact, besides adding, subtracting, multiplying, and dividing, the only statistical technique used in the following pages is regression analysis. The way in which this type of analysis is used in this study is explained in Appendix B, but it might be helpful if a few more general comments are made here.

Regression analysis is simply a statistical method for investigating the relationship or degree of correlation between variables.[1] When this method is used to investigate the relationship between a dependent variable and a single independent or explanatory variable, it is referred to as a simple regression analysis. When it is used to investigate the relationship between a dependent variable and more than one independent variable, it is referred to as a multiple regression analysis.

The strength of the association between the variables is given by correlation coefficients which are calculated mathematically from the available data in the form of numbers. They are expressed in values ranging between -1 and $+1$. The nearer the value is to either of these extremes the stronger is the correlation between the variables. If the value is positive, then the correlation is direct; high values of one variable are associated with high values of the other. If the value of the coefficient is negative, then the correlation is inverse; high values of one variable are associated with low values of the other. The closer the coefficient's value is to zero, the less is the correlation between the variables. The 'significance' of the correlation coefficients generated by this study is judged at the usual level of 5 per cent. If a correlation coefficient or any other result is said to be significant at this level, this means that there is only one possibility in twenty of the result arising by chance.

If variables are not correlated and the data is reliable, then it is fairly safe to conclude that there is no causal connection between them. But if variables are correlated, even very strongly, it does not necessarily follow that there is a causal relationship between them. Correlations are sometimes observed between factors that could not conceivably be causally related such as soil erosion in Alaska and the amount of alcohol consumed in South America. To establish a causal relationship, it is not sufficient to show that variables are highly correlated. Something more is required: strong reasons for expecting them to be correlated. Although correlation must not be confused

---

[1] For an introduction to regression analysis see Reichmann, op. cit., chap. 10, and J. J. Moroney, *Facts From Figures* (Harmondsworth, Middlesex: Penguin Books, 1956), chap. 16.

with causal relation, the former often helps to provide the pointers to the latter.

Where regression analysis has been used in this study, the relationship between the variables is generally first investigated by means of more qualitative methods. In addition, an attempt has been made to translate the significance of the results into English which is free of statistical jargon. But in one or two places this has not proved possible, and the author can only apologize in advance to the less statistically inclined reader.

THE ANALYTICAL FRAMEWORK

Every scientific investigation has some analytical framework to guide the selection of relevant data from the infinite mass of available material and to help organize this data in a meaningful and coherent form once it has been gathered. The analytical framework used in this study is reflected by the organization of the chapters.

Chapter II gives an account of the extent and nature of the white-collar labour force. Chapter III describes the aggregate pattern of white-collar union membership which exists in Britain.

All the remaining chapters analyse the factors which this study considers worthy of examination in searching for an explanation of this pattern. Chapter IV considers such socio-demographic characteristics of white-collar workers as their sex, social origins, age, and status in the community. Chapter V examines the white-collar workers' economic position, and Chapter VI analyses their work situation. The role which trade unions and employers play in union growth is explored in Chapters VII and VIII respectively while the influence of the government and the social climate is investigated in Chapter IX. Chapter X draws the various parts of the analysis together, and tries to produce a few generalizations regarding the growth of white-collar unionism.

The analytical framework used in this study does not provide a separate category for the attitudes of white-collar workers towards trade unionism, and no systematic attempt has been made to ascertain what these attitudes are by means of questionnaires or interviews. This is not an oversight; it is deliberate. If this study were concerned with discovering why one worker in a given environment joins a trade union while another worker in the same environment does not, then the explanation would have to take these attitudes into account as an independent variable. In such an analysis all the environmental influences surrounding individual workers would be held constant, and it would be safe to assume that any differences in their attitudes were mainly attributable to differences in their personality structures. But this study is concerned with explaining the behaviour of groups rather than of individuals. It is not interested in explaining why the propensity to unionize varies from one individual to another, but why it varies from one occupational group or industry to another. In such an analysis it is safe to assume that the attitudes of workers towards trade unionism are not an independent variable, but are primarily dependent upon one or more of the factors analysed in Chapters IV to IX.

II

THE PATTERN OF WHITE-COLLAR
EMPLOYMENT

THE ECONOMY AS A WHOLE

THE growth of the white-collar labour force is one of the most outstanding characteristics of the economic and social development of the twentieth century. This growth is both absolute and relative; not only is the total number of white-collar workers increasing, but so also is the proportion of these workers in the labour force as a whole.

While the growth of the white-collar labour force has not been as large in Britain as in some other countries,[1] it has nevertheless been significant as Table 2.1 shows.[2] Between 1911 and 1961 the number of white-collar workers increased by 147 per cent, while the number of manual workers increased by only 2 per cent having actually decreased since 1931. The disparate growth of these two groups is reflected in the increasing relative importance of the white-collar occupations. The white-collar section of the labour force increased from 18·7 per cent to 35·9 per cent of the total between 1911 and 1961 while the manual share decreased from 74·6 per cent to 59·3 per cent. During this same period the remaining section of the labour force, the employers and proprietors, showed a slight tendency to decline, this decline being balanced to some extent by an increase in the number of managers and administrators.[3]

Occupational composition[4]

Although the white-collar labour force as a whole has increased enormously, there are significant differences in the growth of its constituent occupational

---

[1] See Guy Routh, *Occupation and Pay in Great Britain* (Cambridge: Cambridge University Press, 1965), p. 12, table 3 for international comparisons.

[2] Throughout this study comments on the source, method of calculation, and reliability of all statistical tables and graphs appear in Appendix A.

[3] This decline in the employer and proprietor group should be interpreted with caution. Although there is a legal distinction between an employer and a manager, in social science the dividing line is more imaginary than real, for an employer becomes a manager as soon as his business is incorporated. The trend towards the incorporation of business enterprises is at least part of the explanation for the decline in employers and proprietors and the increase in managers and administrators. On this point see Routh, op. cit., pp. 19–21.

[4] For a much more detailed occupational breakdown of the white-collar labour force from 1881 to 1931 see A. L. Bowley, 'Notes on the Increase in Middle Class Occupations', *Wages and Income in the United Kingdom Since 1860* (Cambridge: Cambridge University Press, 1937), Appendix E. For a Marxist analysis of white-collar labour force trends during 1851–1931 see F. D. Klingender, *The Condition of Clerical Labour in Britain* (London: Martin Lawrence, 1935), pp. xi–xxii.

TABLE 2.1

The Occupied Population of Great Britain by Major Occupational Groups, 1911-61

Occupational groups	Number of persons in major occupational groups, 1911-61 (000s)					Major occupational groups as a percentage of total occupied population, 1911-61					Growth indices of major occupational groups, 1911-61 (1911 = 100)				
	1911	1921	1931	1951	1961	1911	1921	1931	1951	1961	1911	1921	1931	1951	1961
1. Employers and proprietors	1,232	1,318	1,407	1,117	1,139	6·7	6·8	6·7	5·0	4·7	100	107	114	91	92
2. All white-collar workers	3,433	4,094	4,841	6,948	8,480	18·7	21·2	23·0	30·9	35·9	100	119	141	202	247
(a) Managers and administrators	631	704	770	1,245	1,268	3·4	3·6	3·7	5·5	5·4	100	112	122	197	201
(b) Higher professionals	184	196	240	435	718	1·0	1·0	1·1	1·9	3·0	100	107	130	236	390
(c) Lower professionals and technicians	560	679	728	1,059	1,418	3·1	3·5	3·5	4·7	6·0	100	121	130	189	253
(d) Foremen and inspectors	237	279	323	590	682	1·3	1·4	1·5	2·6	2·9	100	118	136	249	288
(e) Clerks	832	1,256	1,404	2,341	2,996	4·5	6·5	6·7	10·4	12·7	100	151	169	281	360
(f) Salesmen and shop assistants	989	980	1,376	1,278	1,398	5·4	5·1	6·5	5·7	5·9	100	99	139	129	141
3. All manual workers	13,685	13,920	14,776	14,450	14,020	74·6	72·0	70·3	64·2	59·3	100	102	108	106	102
4. Total occupied population	18,350	19,332	21,024	22,515	23,639	100·0	100·0	100·0	100·0	100·0	100	105	115	123	129

groups. Table 2.1 shows that the clerks have claimed most of the ground yielded by the manual workers. During the period under review, clerical occupations grew by 260 per cent and increased their share of the total labour force from 4·5 per cent to 12·7 per cent. The growth in the proportionate share of the other white-collar occupational groups has been more moderate: the share of shop assistants remained remarkably constant; that of foremen and inspectors increased from 1·3 per cent to 2·9 per cent; that of managers and administrators from 3·4 per cent to 5·4 per cent; that of lower professionals and technicians from 3·1 per cent to 6·0 per cent; and that of higher professionals from 1 per cent to 3 per cent.

The very broad occupational classification of Table 2.1 tends to obscure the extraordinary increase in the number of scientific and technical employees. Although the total number of such workers is relatively small, they are increasing more rapidly than any other component of the white-collar labour force (see Table 2.2). The Census of Population of 1921 was the first to consider draughtsmen and laboratory assistants sufficiently important groups to merit a separate classification. By 1961 the number of draughtsmen had increased by 376 per cent, professional scientists and engineers by 688 per cent, and laboratory technicians by 1,820 per cent.[1] If these high growth-rates continue, the occupational composition of the future white-collar labour force will be considerably changed.

TABLE 2.2

The Growth of Scientists and Engineers, Draughtsmen, and Laboratory Technicians in Great Britain, 1921–61

Year	Scientists and engineers		Draughtsmen		Laboratory technicians	
	Number	Growth indices	Number	Growth indices	Number	Growth indices
1921	48	100	38	100	5	100
1931	71	148	59	155	11	220
1951	187	390	130	342	69	1,380
1961	378	788	181	476	96	1,920

NOTE: All numbers are in thousands; for growth indices, 1921 = 100.

[1] For a more detailed discussion of the trends in scientific and technical manpower see the following publications of the British government: *Scientific Manpower*, Cmd. 6824, 1946; *Scientific and Engineering Manpower in Great Britain* (London: HMSO, 1956); *Scientific and Engineering Manpower in Great Britain 1959*, Cmnd. 902, 1959; *The Long-Term Demand for Scientific Manpower*, Cmnd. 1490, 1961; *Scientific and Technological Manpower in Great Britain 1963*, Cmnd. 2146, 1963; 'Survey of the Employment of Women Scientists and Engineers', *Ministry of Labour Gazette*, lxviii (September 1960), pp. 256–7; 'Survey of the Employment of Technicians in the Chemical and Engineering Industries', *Ministry of Labour Gazette*, lxviii (December 1960), pp. 464–7. See also Kenneth Prandy, *Professional Employees: A Study of Scientists and Engineers* (London: Faber, 1965), chap. 3.

Sex composition

The large and growing proportion of women in the white-collar labour force is one of its most noticeable characteristics as Table 2.3 demonstrates. Between 1911 and 1961 the proportion of women in white-collar jobs increased from 29·8 per cent to 44·5 per cent. Although there were relatively few women in the higher professions or the managerial and supervisory grades, by 1951 they formed a majority among the lower professionals,[1] shop assistants, and clerical workers. Table 2.3 indicates that the most significant substitution of women for men occurred among clerical grades during the First World War.

TABLE 2.3

The Percentage of Female Workers in Major Occupational Groups in Great Britain, 1911–61

Occupational group	1911	1921	1931	1951	1961
1. Employers and proprietors	18·8	20·5	19·8	20·0	20·4
2. All white-collar workers	29·8	37·6	35·8	42·3	44·5
(a) Managers and administrators	19·8	17·0	13·0	15·2	15·5
(b) Higher professionals	6·0	5·1	7·5	8·3	9·7
(c) Lower professionals and technicians	62·9	59·4	58·8	53·5	50·8
(d) Foremen and inspectors	4·2	6·5	8·7	13·4	10·3
(e) Clerks	21·4	44·6	46·0	60·2	65·1
(f) Salesmen and shop assistants	35·2	43·6	37·2	51·6	54·9
3. All manual workers	30·5	27·9	28·8	26·1	26·0
4. Total occupied population	29·6	29·5	29·8	30·8	32·4

Between 1911 and 1921 the number of male clerks increased a little more slowly than the occupied population while the number of female clerks increased more than three times. In general terms, the increased number of women in white-collar occupations is explained by the increased demand for white-collar skills in the face of relatively full employment, shorter hours, earlier marriage, mechanization of housekeeping, improved educational opportunity, and the particular attraction and suitability of many of these occupations for women.

[1] The high proportion of women among the lower professionals over the whole period is explained by the preponderance of the traditional female occupations—teaching and nursing—in this occupational group. Likewise, the decline in the proportion of women in this group over the years is largely explained by the influx of men into these 'female' occupations. Men accounted for almost two-thirds of the entire increase in the number of teachers between 1911 and 1961. Even in nursing, men accounted for almost 10 per cent of the total in 1961.

Industrial composition[1]

The changing occupational structure of any society can be explained by two related causes: technical changes within industries leading to changes in the type of skills required, and differences in the relative rates of growth of industries. So far, only the horizontal distribution of employment has been examined, but changes in the vertical or industrial distribution are also important.

Part of the increase in white-collar employment can be explained by the shift of total employment from the primary sector, and to a much lesser extent from the secondary sector, to the tertiary or service sector of the economy—that sector with the highest proportion of white-collar employment. As can be seen from Table 2.4, the primary or agricultural sector of the economy has steadily declined while the service sector has increased. During the period 1881 to 1951, gains in the service sector were made primarily at the expense of the agricultural labour force. Contrary to popular belief, neither the rise of white-collar employment nor the decline of manual employment can be explained by any serious contraction in the secondary or manufacturing sector, the traditional manual stronghold. Although manufacturing employment as a percentage of total employment has fluctuated, on balance it has held up remarkably well.

TABLE 2.4

The Percentage Distribution of the Occupied Population in Great Britain by Economic Sectors, 1881–1951

Sector	1881	1891	1901	1911	1921	1931	1951
Primary	13	11	9	9	7	6	5
Secondary	50	49	47	51	49	47	49
Tertiary	37	40	44	40	44	47	46
Total	100	100	100	100	100	100	100

While manufacturing employment as a whole has remained fairly constant, there are considerable differences between the growth-rates of one manufacturing industry and another. For example, the growth of the chemical industry which has a very high proportion of white-collar employees, and the decline of the clothing and footwear industry which has a very low proportion, have obviously worked in favour of increased white-collar employment.[2] One scholar who has analysed the effects of industrial change on

[1] Except for manufacturing industries (*infra*, pp. 16–20) no industrial breakdown of the white-collar labour force on the basis of the 1958 Standard Industrial Classification exists. The most detailed and reliable industrial analysis of the labour force on the basis of the 1948 Standard Industrial Classification appears in Routh, op. cit., appendix B.

[2] *Infra*, Table 2.6 and Table 3.2.

occupational distribution in much greater detail than is permitted by the scope of the present study concluded that

For both lower and higher professionals, the growth of industries has been more potent than their proportions within each industry; for clerical workers and foremen, the reverse has been true—it is their increased proportions within industries that have given the strongest impetus to their growth.[1]

MANUFACTURING INDUSTRIES

Manufacturing industries as a whole

The growing importance of white-collar workers within the manufacturing sector of the economy is demonstrated by Table 2.5. Between 1907 and 1963 the white-collar work force in manufacturing increased by 377 per cent, whereas the manual work force grew by only 32 per cent having actually decreased in numbers since 1954. The growth of white-collar occupations in manufacturing is also reflected in the fact that over this period their share of the labour force increased from 8 per cent to 23·8 per cent.

TABLE 2.5

Employment in the Manufacturing Industries of the United Kingdom, 1907–63

Year	Numbers (000s)			Percentage of total employment			Growth indices (1907=100)		
	White-collar	Manual	Total	White-collar	Manual	Total	White-collar	Manual	Total
1907	394	4,557	4,951	8·0	92·0	100·0	100	100	100
1924	512	4,345	4,857	10·5	89·5	100·0	130	95	98
1930	590	4,285	4,875	12·1	87·9	100·0	150	94	98
1935	696	4,679	5,375	12·9	87·1	100·0	177	103	109
1949	1,178	5,873	7,051	16·7	83·3	100·0	299	129	142
1958	1,673	6,108	7,781	21·5	78·5	100·0	425	134	157
1963	1,881	6,017	7,898	23·8	76·2	100·0	477	132	160

Individual manufacturing industries

The system of industrial classification has been changed so often since the turn of the century that it is not possible to obtain a picture of the changing composition of the work force in individual manufacturing industries over any length of time.[2] Table 2.6, however, shows the growing relative importance of the white-collar occupations in the various manufacturing industries between 1948 and 1963. This growth was most marked in the chemical industry and to a lesser extent in the engineering; vehicles; and paper, print-

[1] Routh, op. cit., pp. 41–2. Salesmen and shop assistants were not classified separately so it is not possible to determine from Routh's study the industrial effect on this group.

[2] For the percentage of white-collar workers in individual manufacturing industries in 1924, 1930, and 1935 on the basis of the pre-war industrial classification system, see *Manpower* (London: Political and Economic Planning, 1951), p. 38, table 6.

ing, and publishing industries. It was least marked in clothing and footwear; textiles; leather, leather goods, and fur.[1]

TABLE 2.6

White-Collar Employment as a Percentage of Total Employment by Manufacturing Industry in Great Britain, 1948–64

Industry	1948	1959	1964
Food, drink, and tobacco	17·7	18·8	20·2
Chemicals and allied	25·7	32·3	35·5
Metal manufacture	13·7	18·4	20·7
Engineering and electrical goods	..	28·2	29·8
Shipbuilding and marine engineering	..	14·8	18·3
Vehicles	18·1	24·1	26·6
Metal goods N.E.S.	..	17·4	19·0
Textiles	8·8	12·1	13·5
Leather, leather goods, and fur	13·0	13·8	14·3
Clothing and footwear	9·9	11·0	11·7
Bricks, pottery, glass, cement, etc.	10·9	16·0	17·7
Timber, furniture, etc.	12·8	15·7	18·2
Paper, printing, and publishing	18·5	23·0	24·0
Other manufacturing	..	21·1	23·3
ALL MANUFACTURING INDUSTRIES	16·0	21·1	23·1

Occupational composition[2]

The most outstanding characteristic of the occupational distribution shown in Table 2.7 is the overwhelming numerical importance of clerks in the white-collar labour force of every manufacturing industry. In manufacturing as a whole, clerks comprise approximately 50 per cent of total white-collar employment: their share ranges from a low of 31·6 per cent in shipbuilding to over 60 per cent in leather, leather goods, and fur; timber and furniture; and paper, printing, and publishing. The rest of the labour force is divided fairly equally between foremen (16·2 per cent); scientists, technologists, and technicians (17·8 per cent); and other white-collar workers (16·5 per cent). There are significant variations from these over-all trends in the different industries.

---

[1] For an analysis of the factors promoting the growth of the white-collar labour force see P. Galambos, 'On the Growth of the Employment of Non-Manual Workers in the British Manufacturing Industries, 1948–1962', *Bulletin of the Oxford University Institute of Economics and Statistics*, xxvi (November 1964), pp. 369–87; Seymour Melman, 'The Rise of Administrative Overhead in the Manufacturing Industries of the United States, 1899–1947', *Oxford Economic Papers*, iii (February 1951), pp. 62–112, and by the same author, *Dynamic Factors in Industrial Productivity* (Oxford: Blackwell, 1956), chaps. 10–14.

[2] Since the main purpose of the following discussion is to demonstrate the nature and extent of the potential for unionization in private industry, the managerial grades have been excluded from the analysis. In modern, large-scale private industry, it is the managers who generally control the operation of the business and direct the labour force. Functionally, therefore, they perform the role of employer and cannot be realistically considered part of the trade union potential. To date, only managerial grades in the public sector have shown any general desire to join trade unions.

TABLE 2.7

Employment in Various White-Collar Occupations as a Percentage of Total White-Collar Employment in Manufacturing Industries in Great Britain, 1964

Occupational group	Food, drink, tobacco	Chemical	Metal manuf.	Metal N.E.S.	Eng. elect.	Ship. M.E.	Vehicles	Textiles	Leather, fur	Clothing, footwear	Bricks, etc.	Timber, furn., etc.	Paper, print, pub.	Other manuf.	All manuf.
1. Foremen	18·1	13·2	20·4	18·1	11·5	31·0	14·0	31·6	23·4	22·8	21·5	22·0	12·4	17·8	16·2
2. All scientists, technologists, technicians	4·8	25·3	16·4	10·2	26·6	23·8	24·6	10·8	4·0	4·3	11·9	4·9	3·5	10·9	17·8
(a) Scientists, technologists	1·7	10·1	4·1	1·6	5·6	1·8	3·2	2·8	1·6	0·3	3·2	0·1	1·2	3·0	4·1
(b) All technicians	3·0	15·3	12·3	8·6	20·9	22·0	21·3	8·1	2·4	4·0	8·7	4·7	2·3	7·9	13·8
(i) Draughtsmen	0·7	1·8	3·7	5·5	11·0	16·2	9·4	1·5	0·1	0·5	4·1	3·1	0·4	2·6	6·0
(ii) Other technicians	2·3	13·5	8·6	3·1	9·9	5·8	11·9	6·6	2·3	3·5	4·5	1·7	2·2	5·4	7·7
3. Clerks	53·1	43·5	49·3	56·5	46·6	31·6	48·3	47·2	60·0	55·5	51·3	60·2	60·3	49·1	49·5
4. Other white-collar workers	24·0	18·0	13·9	15·2	15·3	13·6	13·1	10·4	12·6	17·3	15·4	12·9	23·8	22·2	16·5
5. All white-collar workers	100·0	100·0	100·0	100·0	100·0	100·0	100·0	100·0	100·0	100·0	100·0	100·0	100·0	100·0	100·0

TABLE 2.8

The Female White-Collar Labour Force as a Percentage of the Total White-Collar Labour Force in Manufacturing Industries in Great Britain, 1964

Occupational group	Food, drink, tobacco	Chemical	Metal manuf.	Metal N.E.S.	Eng. elect.	Ship. M.E.	Vehicles	Textiles	Leather, fur	Clothing, footwear	Bricks, etc.	Timber, furn., etc.	Paper, print, pub.	Other manuf.	All manuf.
1. Foremen	19·1	9·0	1·4	8·4	6·4	0·2	1·3	12·8	16·5	55·0	7·0	3·9	16·5	13·4	10·6
2. All scientists, technologists, technicians	16·4	10·6	3·5	3·2	2·5	2·3	2·2	18·4	5·4	35·4	4·7	6·3	7·1	8·4	5·0
(a) Scientists, technologists	11·9	7·0	2·8	5·0	2·2	0·0	1·1	8·3	6·7	35·0	5·6	0·0	5·8	2·4	4·1
(b) All technicians	19·0	13·0	2·1	2·8	2·6	2·6	2·4	21·9	4·5	35·5	4·3	6·4	7·7	10·6	5·3
(i) Draughtsmen	0·0	0·3	0·9	1·3	2·0	2·5	1·4	0·6	0·0	35·5	1·3	2·1	4·1	1·1	1·8
(ii) Other technicians	25·0	14·7	4·9	1·7	3·3	2·8	3·2	26·6	4·8	35·5	7·1	14·5	8·4	15·2	7·9
3. Clerks	68·5	68·5	53·2	67·6	61·9	44·0	48·6	66·1	83·9	82·6	59·7	68·1	63·7	67·6	62·8
4. Other white-collar workers	13·4	14·6	16·9	24·5	20·2	26·4	19·1	25·8	3·4	46·4	16·1	12·8	15·0	21·5	19·1
5. All white-collar workers	43·8	36·3	29·4	43·8	33·3	18·1	26·7	39·9	54·9	68·0	35·2	43·8	44·3	41·3	36·8

Scientists, technologists, and technicians are of much greater importance in engineering, chemicals, vehicles, and shipbuilding than in the other industries; foremen are of greater importance in textiles and shipbuilding than elsewhere.

Sex composition

As in the economy as a whole, women form a significant proportion of the white-collar labour force in manufacturing, but here they are largely restricted to one occupational group—clerks. In 1964, 36·8 per cent of all white-collar employees in manufacturing were female (see Table 2.8) and over 84 per cent of these were engaged in clerical work.[1] Women are relatively unimportant in the scientific, technical, and supervisory occupations, except in clothing and footwear, and, to a lesser extent, in textiles, where there are a high proportion of females in all the white-collar occupations.

CONCLUSIONS

The number of white-collar workers in Britain is rapidly increasing. Already almost four out of ten workers are white-collar employees. There is every likelihood that this trend will continue and that the labour force will soon be dominated by white-collar workers. The American economy has already reached a point where the white-collar employees outnumber the manual, and, if present occupational trends continue in Britain, this point will be reached here during the 1980s.[2] If the trade union movement is to continue as a dynamic and effective force in British society, it must recruit these white-collar workers. The extent to which it has already done so is considered in the next chapter.

[1] The latter figure was calculated from Table 2A.4 in Appendix A.

[2] Automation is unlikely to reverse or even greatly slow this trend. At most, it will probably simply change the composition of the white-collar labour force: more technologists, fewer clerks. See *infra*, pp. 70–1 for a discussion of the effect of automation on the demand for white-collar workers.

III

THE PATTERN OF WHITE-COLLAR UNIONISM

VIEWED over the long run the growth of British trade unionism is most impressive. Although total union membership has fluctuated widely with changes in the social and economic environment, the long-run trend has been steadily upwards (see Table 3.1). Between 1892 and 1964 trade union membership increased from 1·5 million to slightly over 10 million while the number of employees increased from 14·1 million to 23·6 million. Union membership therefore increased by 539 per cent while potential union membership increased by only 67 per cent. As a result, the over-all density of unionization increased from a little over 11 per cent to almost 43 per cent.

Viewed over the immediate short run the growth of British trade unionism is much less impressive. Lately many signs have appeared which suggest that an era of stabilization is following upon the last great upsurge of union growth which began around 1933. During the fifteen years between 1933 and 1948, actual union membership increased by 113 per cent while potential union membership increased by only 6·5 per cent. But during the sixteen years between 1948 and 1964 union membership increased by only 8 per cent while potential union membership increased by 14 per cent.

These disparate increases in actual and potential union membership are reflected by changes in the density of unionization. Although union density figures are not continuously available prior to 1948, Table 3.1 makes it fairly clear that union density increased steadily from 1933 to 1946–7 when it reached a peak of 45–7 per cent. Since that time there has been a gradual but certain decline in union density. For density to increase, actual union membership must grow faster than potential union membership. This condition only existed in five of the sixteen years from 1948 to 1964, and, for the period as a whole, potential union membership increased almost twice as

---

[1] Although some reference will be made throughout this chapter to the development of British union membership in general, the main emphasis will be placed on the growth of white-collar union membership. For a more general analysis of membership growth see: Keith Hindell, *Trade Union Membership* (London: Political and Economic Planning, 1962); B. C. Roberts, 'The Trends of Union Membership', *Trade Union Government and Administration in Great Britain* (London: Bell, 1956), Appendix 1; and Guy Routh, 'Future Trade Union Membership', *Industrial Relations: Contemporary Problems and Perspectives*, B. C. Roberts, editor (London: Methuen, 1962), pp. 62–82.

much as actual union membership. Consequently, the over-all density of unionization declined from 45·1 per cent in 1948 to 42·6 per cent in 1964.[1]

TABLE 3.1

Total Union Membership in the United Kingdom, 1892–1964

Year	Labour force (000s)	Annual % change in labour force	Total union membership (000s)	Annual % change in union membership	Density of union membership (%)
1892	14,126	..	1,576	..	11·2
1901	15,795	..	2,025	..	12·8
1911	17,555	..	3,139	..	17·9
1921	17,618	..	6,633	..	37·6
1931	19,328	..	4,624	..	23·9
1933	19,498	..	4,392	..	22·5
1938	20,258	..	6,053	..	29·9
1948	20,767	..	9,362	..	45·1
1949	20,818	+0·2	9,318	−0·5	44·8
1950	21,096	+1·3	9,289	−0·3	44·0
1951	21,222	+0·6	9,535	+2·6	44·9
1952	21,322	+0·5	9,588	+0·6	45·0
1953	21,401	+0·4	9,527	−0·6	44·5
1954	21,718	+1·5	9,566	+0·4	44·0
1955	21,990	+1·3	9,738	+1·8	44·3
1956	22,230	+1·1	9,776	+0·4	44·0
1957	22,382	+0·7	9,827	+0·5	43·9
1958	22,346	−0·2	9,636	−1·9	43·1
1959	22,404	+0·3	9,621	−0·2	42·9
1960	22,764	+1·6	9,832	+2·2	43·2
1961	23,037	+1·2	9,893	+0·6	42·9
1962	23,354	+1·4	9,883	−0·1	42·3
1963	23,470	+0·5	9,928	+0·5	42·3
1964	23,616	+0·6	10,065	+1·4	42·6

There are two major reasons for the decline in the growth-rate of unionism and in over-all union density. The first is the changing pattern of employment which was described in Chapter II and is further illustrated by Table 3.2. This table shows that there has been a shrinkage of employment in a number of basic industries which have a long tradition of union activity and the highest density of membership—railways, coal-mining, national government, cotton, and manual employment in general.[2] At the same time there has been a steady expansion of employment in those areas which have proved

---

[1] Not only has there been a decline in the density of total union membership, but also in the density of that section of the total which is affiliated to the TUC. In spite of a number of new affiliations and an increase of 834,000 in its membership between 1948 and 1964, the density of TUC membership declined from 38·2 per cent to 37·1 per cent.

[2] The fact that employment has declined in these industries does not necessarily mean that union density has also declined. In spite of a decline in employment in cotton, agriculture, coal-mining, and national government, the density of unionization in these industries has increased.

most difficult to organize and have a relatively low density of unionization—professional and business services; insurance, banking, and finance; distribution; chemicals; food, drink, and tobacco; and white-collar occupations in all industries. But not all the industrial redistribution of employment has worked against the unions. Employment in agriculture, a low-density industry,

TABLE 3.2

Changing Employment and Density of Union Membership by Industry in the United Kingdom, 1948–64

Industry	Employees (000s)			Density (%)	
	1948	1964	% change 1948–64	1960	% change 1948–60
1. Education	521	1,094	+110	50	−11
2. Professional and business services	806	1,268	+57	24	−5
3. Insurance, banking, and finance	432	637	+48	31	+10
4. Distribution	2,093	3,026	+45	15	−2
5. Paper, printing, and publishing	472	632	+34	57	+2
6. Gas, electricity, and water	329	413	+26	51	−9
7. Building	1,375	1,708	+24	37	−6
8. Metals and engineering	3,739	4,537	+21	54	−1
9. Chemicals and allied	447	515	+15	20	+1
10. Food, drink, and tobacco	731	842	+15	11	−5
11. Other transport and communications	1,221	1,320	+8	75	+2
12. Local government	720	776	+8	84	+16
13. Theatres, cinemas, sport, etc.	238	251	+6	39	+4
14. Furniture, timber, etc.	294	296	+1	37	−4
15. Footwear	116	116	0	63	−1
16. Clothing	498	453	−9	30	−3
17. Textiles other than cotton	708	613	−13	21	−3
18. Cotton	293	228	−22	75	+2
19. National government	717	550	−23	83	+19
20. Coal-mining	803	596	−26	89	+10
21. Railways	576	396	−31	84	−5
22. Agriculture, forestry, and fishing	868	551	−37	27	+5

declined while employment in metals and engineering and in paper, printing, and publishing expanded, although a large proportion of this increase was composed of white-collar employees. Nevertheless, Table 3.2 does demonstrate that on balance the industrial tide has been running against the trade union movement. In the ten areas where employment expanded most rapidly between 1948 and 1964, density of unionization was in every case less than 60 per cent and in three of these areas it was 20 per cent or less. In the ten industries where employment expanded the least or declined, density of unionization was in every case over 20 per cent and in five of these areas it was over 60 per cent. Clearly, union density is highest in the declining industries and lowest in the expanding industries, and this is causing the over-all density of unionization to fall.

The second factor explaining the diminishing growth-rate of unionism and the decrease in over-all density is that the unions are not recruiting members quickly enough among the expanding areas of employment, in particular among the white-collar occupations, to offset the decline in the traditional industries and among manual workers generally. As can be seen from Table 3.2, density of unionization declined in eight of the fourteen expanding industries between 1948 and 1960. Moreover, in spite of the increase in trade unionism among white-collar employees during the period 1948–64 being over thirty times greater than the increase among manual workers,[1] this growth was not sufficient to increase or even maintain the over-all density of unionization. In order to maintain, let alone extend, its numerical strength, the trade union movement must increase even further its rate of growth among white-collar employees.

THE GROWTH OF WHITE-COLLAR UNIONISM, 1948–1964

The growth of white-collar unionism in the economy as a whole

To assess the growth and extent of white-collar unionism in Britain is a most difficult task. The membership figures of each of almost 600 unions must be classified into manual and white-collar categories. Moreover, more than 20 per cent of total white-collar union membership belongs to partially white-collar unions,[2] and they do not always compile separate figures for their white-collar membership. In a sense, almost every manual union in Britain is a partially white-collar union because most of them take foremen into membership. Unfortunately, very few of these unions keep separate membership figures for this occupational category. In spite of all these difficulties some conclusions can be drawn regarding the growth and extent of white-collar unionism.

Of the 591 unions operating in the United Kingdom in 1964, there were approximately 280 purely white-collar unions and at least 19 partially white-collar unions.[3] Forty-three of the purely white-collar unions and all the partially white-collar unions were affiliated to the TUC. Total white-collar union membership in 1964 was 2,623,000 and close to 1,711,000 of this total

---

[1] *Infra*, Table 3.3.

[2] A partially white-collar union caters for both manual and white-collar employees while a purely white-collar union caters solely for white-collar employees. See Appendix A, Table 3A.1, for a complete list of all the purely and partially white-collar unions affiliated to the TUC.

[3] Only those partially white-collar unions which could estimate their white-collar membership are included in this figure.

was affiliated to the TUC (see Table 3.3); this represented almost 20 per cent of total TUC membership. In short, approximately one in four trade unionists were white-collar employees and slightly more than 65 per cent of them were affiliated to the TUC.

TABLE 3.3

The Growth of Total White-Collar and Manual Unionism in the United Kingdom, 1948–64

Type of union membership	1948 (000s)	1964 (000s)	% change 1948–64
1. Total white-collar unionism	1,964	2,623	+33·6
(a) Adjusted membership of TUC white-collar unions	1,257	1,711	+36·2
(b) Adjusted membership of non-TUC white-collar unions	707	912	+29·0
2. Total manual unionism	7,398	7,442	+0·6

The growth of white-collar unionism has been an extremely important factor in the post-war development of the TUC. In fact, almost the entire expansion of the TUC since the war has been due to the increase in its affiliated white-collar membership. Between 1948 and 1964 the affiliated membership of the TUC expanded by 11 per cent. This average over-all expansion resulted from an increase of 79 per cent in the affiliated membership of purely white-collar unions, and an increase of only 4 per cent in the affiliated membership of manual and partially white-collar unions.[1] To look at it another way, if there had been no purely white-collar unions affiliated to the TUC between 1948 and 1964, then instead of expanding by 11 per cent the TUC would have expanded by only 4 per cent. If it were possible to segregate the white-collar membership of the partially white-collar unions prior to 1964, then the importance of white-collar membership to the TUC would be even more striking. If it is assumed that the white-collar

[1] White-collar membership figures prior to 1964 could not be obtained for all the partially white-collar unions. Consequently, the white-collar membership of these unions had to be grouped with the manual membership.

The increase in the membership of unions affiliated to the TUC in the post-war period is composed of three elements. First, the increase in size between 1948 and 1964 of those unions which were affiliated to the TUC prior to 1948. Second, the initial affiliating membership of those unions which affiliated to the TUC between 1948 and 1964. Third, the increase in the size of these unions between the time they affiliated and 1964. Since seven purely white-collar unions affiliated to the TUC between 1948 and 1964, the growth-rate of the TUC's purely white-collar unions is considerably inflated by the initial increase in membership occurring at the time of affiliation. If the membership of post-1948 affiliated unions is included even for the years they were not affiliated, and the membership of all unions which left or were expelled during the period are excluded (except for the Electrical Trades Union) for the whole period, then the growth-rate of the purely white-collar unions becomes 36 per cent rather than 79 per cent. Membership figures obtained in this way are referred to as 'adjusted' membership. For all calculations see Appendix A, Table 3A.1.

membership of the partially white-collar unions expanded at the same rate as the purely white-collar unions[1] and that none of this had been affiliated to the TUC between 1948 and 1964, then the TUC would have expanded by only 2·5 per cent, and during the latter half of this period, 1955 to 1964, it would actually have shrunk in size by 0·6 per cent.

Although the above TUC figures exaggerate the actual growth of white-collar unionism, it has nevertheless increased substantially in total amount since 1948. Table 3.3 demonstrates that between 1948 and 1964, the 'adjusted' white-collar membership affiliated to the TUC expanded by 36·2 per cent while that portion of the total which remained unaffiliated grew by 29 per cent. Total white-collar unionism increased by 33·6 per cent as opposed to an increase in total manual unionism of only 0·6 per cent.

Taken by themselves these white-collar growth figures are most impressive. To determine their real significance, however, changes in the white-collar labour force must also be taken into account. Although the government does not publish figures of the number of white-collar employees in the economy as a whole, some rough estimates can be obtained by performing a few arithmetical manipulations.[2] During the period 1948–64 total white-collar union membership increased by 33·6 per cent while the white-collar labour force increased by 32·4 per cent. During this same period manual union membership increased by 0·6 per cent while the manual labour force increased by 4·6 per cent. In other words, the over-all density of white-collar unionism increased only very slightly while the over-all density of manual unionism fell slightly.

In fact, as Table 3.4 shows, the density of total white-collar unionism only increased from 28·8 per cent to 29 per cent between 1948 and 1964, while the density of manual unionism declined from 53·1 per cent to 51 per cent. Table 3.4 also reveals a significant difference in the density of unionism between men and women. Density of unionization among both manual and white-collar female workers is considerably less than among male workers. Moreover, the density of unionization among female white-collar workers has remained more or less constant since 1948.

Because of lack of detail in the systems of classifying both labour force and union membership figures, only rough estimates of the real growth of

---

[1] The 'adjusted' growth-rate of 36 per cent was used. If anything, this figure understates the growth of the partially white-collar unions. Appendix A, Table 3A.1, indicates that the white-collar membership of most of these unions grew by amounts substantially in excess of 36 per cent.

[2] The total number of white-collar persons gainfully occupied in Great Britain in 1951 and 1961 as a percentage of the total gainfully occupied (excluding employers, but including self-employed and the armed forces) was 32·5 per cent and 37·7 per cent respectively (see Table 2.1). The total number of employees in the United Kingdom in 1948 and 1964 (see Table 3.1) were distributed on the same basis as the gainfully occupied population in 1951 and 1961 respectively. This gave 6,749,000 white-collar and 14,018,000 manual employees in 1948 and 8,903,000 white-collar and 14,713,000 manual employees in 1964.

white-collar unionism could be obtained. Nevertheless, the relative changes in the size of white-collar union membership and the white-collar labour force are so nearly equal that, even granted an error of a few percentage points, at the very most the density of white-collar unionism in the economy as a whole could have increased only very slightly.

TABLE 3.4

The Density of Total White-Collar and Manual Unionism in the United Kingdom, 1948–64

Type of union membership	1948			1964		
	Male	Female	Total	Male	Female	Total
1. Total white-collar unionism	33·6	22·8	28·8	34·9	22·6	29·0
(a) Adjusted membership of TUC white-collar unions	22·4	13·5	18·4	23·1	14·4	18·9
(b) Adjusted membership of non-TUC white-collar unions	11·3	9·3	10·4	11·9	8·2	10·1
2. Total manual unionism	63·9	25·3	53·1	60·3	28·0	51·0

The growth of union membership in the post-war period will hardly excite or reassure a realistic supporter of trade unionism. The trade union movement must do much better than simply keep up with changes in the labour force. Even if both white-collar and manual membership had increased sufficiently to maintain their respective densities, the density of total union membership would still have declined because the high-density manual sector of the labour force was contracting while the low-density white-collar sector was expanding. Thus the trade union movement is at present faced with the paradoxical situation that in order simply to mark time, it must advance.

The growth of white-collar unionism in various industrial sectors

It is extremely difficult to assess accurately the density of unionization in particular industries or occupations. The membership of most British unions conforms neither to an industrial nor to an occupational pattern but sprawls across a wide variety of industries and occupations. Many unions do not classify their membership figures, and, even if they do, it is generally by negotiating group rather than by the official systems of classifying occupations and industries.[1] Even if someone undertook the formidable task of rationalizing union membership figures with the official systems of classification, it would still be difficult to calculate white-collar membership densities throughout

---

[1] Central Statistical Office, *Standard Industrial Classification* (revised edition; London: HMSO, 1958); General Register Office, *Classification of Occupations, 1960* (London: HMSO, 1960).

every industrial sector because the government's manpower figures give the number of white-collar employees only in manufacturing industries. Nevertheless, enough published data exist to give some idea of the extent of white-collar unionism in various industries.

A very rough estimate of the extent of white-collar unionism in various sectors can be acquired by looking at the total union density figures of those industries in which white-collar workers predominate. Table 3.5 gives the total union density figures for such industries and also for manufacturing for which a special survey was undertaken.[1]

TABLE 3.5

The Density of White-Collar Unionism by Industrial Sector in the United Kingdom, 1960

Industry	Total union density 1960 (%)	Change in union density 1948–60 (%)
1. Local government	84	+16
2. National government	83	+19
3. Education	50	−11[a]
4. Theatres, cinemas, sport, etc.	39	+4
5. Insurance, banking, and finance	31[b]	+10
6. Distribution	15	−2
7. Manufacturing industries	12[c]	..

[a] The density of unionism among teaching staff has not decreased but the number of non-teaching ancillary staff such as secretaries and caterers, who are not generally unionized as yet, has greatly increased and this has caused an over-all decline in the density of unionization in the education sector.

[b] The density of unionization among bank clerks is much higher than this figure would suggest. As of 1 January 1962 the density of unionization among bank clerks was 76 per cent. Even excluding the staff associations, the density of the National Union of Bank Employees was 31 per cent. See R. M. Blackburn, *Union Character and Social Class* (London: Batsford, 1967), Appendix A.

[c] This figure is for 1963 and only covers Great Britain. Moreover, the labour-force figure used to calculate the density excludes the unemployed. Consequently, this figure is slightly inflated relative to the other figures in the table.

Although, with the exception of manufacturing, the figures are little more than estimates within a wide margin of error, at least two conclusions emerge clearly from this table. First, there is obviously a strong relationship between density of unionization and whether the industry is publicly or privately owned. National and local government not only have a very high density of unionization, but they have also increased their density substantially in the post-war period. This relationship between public ownership and high union density is also apparent in industries in which manual workers predominate.

[1] For the details of this survey see the notes to Table 3.8 in Appendix A.

In 1960 in the nationalized coal-mining industry, union density was 89 per cent and in the nationalized railways 84 per cent, while in paper, printing, and publishing and in the engineering and metal industries, density of unionization was respectively only 57 per cent and 54 per cent in spite of the power and maturity of the unions in these areas.[1] Second, although the approximate nature of the statistics does not permit a detailed ranking of the various industries in terms of the degree of white-collar unionization, the differences in density are so vast that it is safe to conclude that with the possible exception of the distributive trades, manufacturing industries have the lowest density of white-collar unionism.

THE GROWTH OF WHITE-COLLAR UNIONISM IN MANUFACTURING INDUSTRIES, 1948-1964

The union pattern

There were eight major unions catering for the various categories of white-collar employees in manufacturing industries between 1948 and 1964. Like most British unions their membership was generally not confined to one occupation or industry. The names of these unions and some of the pertinent details regarding the occupational and industrial distribution of their membership are given in Table 3.6.[2] The Clerical and Administrative Workers' Union (CAWU), the Draughtsmen's and Allied Technicians' Association (DATA), and the National Union of Journalists (NUJ) are purely white-collar unions, as were the Association of Scientific Workers (AScW) and the Association of Supervisory Staffs, Executives and Technicians (ASSET).[3] The British Iron, Steel and Kindred Trades Association (BISAKTA)[4] and the Transport and General Workers' Union (TGWU)[5] are partially white-collar unions, as was the National Society of Operative Printers and Assistants (NATSOPA).[6] Except for the two industrial unions, BISAKTA and NATSOPA, all the unions had membership in both the manufacturing and non-manufacturing sectors of the economy. In each of these unions, however,

[1] See Table 3.2.

[2] The exact occupational and industrial distribution of each of these unions' membership is known. For fairly obvious reasons, however, most of the unions requested that their exact strength within any one occupation or industry should not be published. Consequently, in Table 3.6 only the strength of each union in all manufacturing industries is given and the individual industries in which it has membership are merely listed in order of importance. The exact industrial and occupational distribution of total white-collar unionism in manufacturing is given in Table 3.8 but in such a way that it is not possible to determine the industrial or occupational strength of most of the individual unions.

[3] The AScW and ASSET merged in 1968 to form the Association of Scientific, Technical and Managerial Staffs (ASTMS).

[4] This union is also known as the Iron and Steel Trades Confederation (ISTC).

[5] The white-collar section of the TGWU is known as the National Association of Clerical and Supervisory Staffs (NACSS).

[6] NATSOPA merged during 1966 with the National Union of Printing, Bookbinding and Paper Workers to form the Society of Graphical and Allied Trades (SOGAT).

TABLE 3.6

Characteristics of the Major Unions Catering for White-Collar Workers in Manufacturing Industries in Great Britain, 1963–4

Unions	Total membership	Total W-C membership	W-C membership as percentage of total membership	Total W-C membership in manufacturing industries	W-C membership in manufacturing as a percentage of total W-C membership	Occupational composition of W-C membership	Major industries in which manufacturing W-C membership was concentrated (listed in order of importance)	Major industries in which non-manufacturing W-C membership was concentrated (listed in order of importance)
AScW	19,098	19,098	100	9,127	48	Roughly 25% composed of qualified scientists, engineers, and technologists. The remainder was made up of laboratory technicians	1. Engineering and electrical goods 2. Chemicals	1. National Health Services 2. Universities and Technical Colleges
ASSET	29,939	29,939	100	24,251	81	Roughly 50% composed of foremen; the other half was made up of technicians other than draughtsmen and laboratory assistants	1. Engineering and electrical goods 2. Vehicles 3. Metal manufacture 4. Rubber and plastics	1. Civil air transport
CAWU	74,529	74,529	100	51,043	69	Entirely composed of clerical and administrative employees	1. Engineering and electrical goods 2. Vehicles 3. Metal manufacture 4. Food and drink	1. Coal-mining 2. Co-operatives 3. Trade union staffs 4. Electricity supply
DATA	61,446	61,446	100	58,715	96	Composed of draughtsmen, tracers, and other technicians allied to design	1. Engineering and electrical goods 2. Vehicles 3. Shipbuilding and marine engineering 4. Metal manufacture	1. Construction
BISAKTA	107,205	7,520	7	7,520	100	Roughly 63% were clerks, 19% were technicians, 16% were foremen, and 2% were in other grades	1. Entirely metal manufacture	
NATSOPA	45,832	11,308	25	11,308	100	Composed almost entirely of clerical and administrative grades	1. Entirely paper, printing, and publishing	

						Industries
NUJ	17,826	17,826	100	16,063	90	Composed entirely of journalists, press photographers, and publicists	1. Printing and publishing	1. Freelance-journalists 2. Radio and T.V. 3. Public relations
TGWU	1,412,603	51,337	4	28,236	55	Composed almost entirely of clerical and supervisory grades. Almost all the supervisors were employed in non-manufacturing industries	1. Vehicles 2. Engineering and electrical goods 3. Metal manufacture 4. Food and drink 5. Rubber and plastics 6. Textiles 7. Chemicals	1. Road and water transport

their white-collar membership in manufacturing made up roughly half or more of their total white-collar membership in 1964, ranging from a low of 48 per cent for the AScW to a high of 96 per cent for DATA. Manufacturing therefore provided the membership base for all these unions. Occupationally, the unions are difficult to classify except that in very general terms DATA is predominantly a technicians' union, as were the AScW and ASSET;[1] the CAWU, BISAKTA, and the TGWU (Nacss) are predominantly clerks' unions, as was NATSOPA; and the NUJ is a journalists' union.

In addition to these eight major unions, there were a number of other unions with a small white-collar membership in manufacturing in 1964. Almost every manual workers' union in manufacturing has some white-collar membership by virtue of having foremen and supervisors among its members. Of these unions, however, only the Electrical Trades Union (2,200)[2] and the Amalgamated Engineering Union (700) kept separate membership records for foremen in 1964. In the textile industry there are a number of unions catering strictly for overlookers, foremen, and supervisors: the General Union of Associations of Loom Overlookers (4,700), the Yorkshire Association of Power Loom Overlookers (1,800), the Managers' and Overlookers' Society (1,800), the Textile Officials' Association (700), and the National Federation of Scribbling Overlookers (130).[3] The National Union of General and Municipal Workers had approximately 12,000 white-collar members, mostly among clerks in the gas- and electricity-supply industries, but a few of them were employed in engineering, rubber, chemicals, and food. The British Association of Chemists had 1,800 qualified chemists in the chemical industry, while the Institute of Journalists with 2,400 members competed with the NUJ in the printing and publishing industry. There were also approximately 2,000 circulation representatives in this industry in membership of the National Union of Printing, Bookbinding and Paperworkers.[4]

The growth of manufacturing white-collar unionism

The growth of white-collar union membership in manufacturing industries between 1948 and 1964 was more than twice as great as that in the economy

[1] Historically, ASSET was a foreman's union. But after 1942 it began to concentrate much more on recruiting technicians. In 1964 approximately half of its membership was composed of technicians.

[2] The figures in brackets give the size of the total white-collar membership of the various unions in 1964. Besides the unions given here there are several others with a little white-collar membership. They are too numerous to list here, but they are included in Table 3.8 and are listed in the notes to this table in Appendix A.

[3] Strictly speaking, only spinning overlookers are white-collar workers. Weaving overlookers are simply highly skilled craftsmen who are responsible for the maintenance of the looms, and unlike the spinning overlookers few, if any, are expected to perform a supervisory function. However, both spinning and weaving overlooker union memberships have been included in this survey in order to make the union membership figures comparable to the *Census of Population* 'foremen' figures.   [4] *Supra*, p. 29 n. 6.

as a whole. Table 3.7 shows that during this period the major white-collar unions operating in manufacturing industries increased their membership by 77 per cent[1] while the increase in white-collar unionism for the economy as a whole was only 34 per cent. Not only did total white-collar unionism in manufacturing industries increase, but in addition each of the individual unions catering for white-collar workers in manufacturing increased their membership by substantial amounts ranging from 34·1 per cent for the AScW to 107·1 per cent for ASSET.

White-collar union density in manufacturing has also increased, but not as impressively as white-collar union membership. During the period 1948–64 white-collar union membership in manufacturing increased by 77 per cent while the white-collar union potential increased by 58 per cent.[2] Thus the density of white-collar unionism in manufacturing probably did not rise by more than 2–3 per cent between 1948 and 1964.

The industrial and occupational pattern of manufacturing white-collar unionism

In 1964 approximately 225,000 out of the potential of 1,900,000 white-collar employees in manufacturing industries, or 12 per cent of the potential, were unionized. This average figure covers a number of significant industrial and occupational variations, however, as Table 3.8 demonstrates. This table presents the dependent variable of the study—the density of white-collar unionism in manufacturing industries by occupation and by industry. Since the remainder of the study will largely be an attempt to explain the variations in the density of manufacturing white-collar unionism, this central set of statistics should be carefully studied and its limitations fully understood.[3]

In very general terms, Table 3.8 can be quickly summarized. Industrially, the most striking aspect of the table is the low level of white-collar union density in all the manufacturing industries relative to other areas of the economy. Even the degree of white-collar unionism in the best-organized manufacturing industry—23 per cent in paper, printing, and publishing—is much lower than that prevailing in most other industrial sectors.[4] Relative to each other the various manufacturing industries can be classified into three categories in terms of their density of white-collar unionism. First, there are the relatively high-density industries which fall into two groups: the paper,

---

[1] As was shown in Table 3.6, some of the white-collar membership of these unions is outside manufacturing industries. However, on average, the great majority of their total white-collar membership—75 per cent in 1964—is in these industries. It is assumed here that the non-manufacturing white-collar unionism in these totals does not significantly affect the rate of growth of the totals.

[2] The actual figures for the white-collar labour force in manufacturing industries in Great Britain from which the white-collar labour force growth-rate was calculated are given in Appendix A, Table 2A.2.

[3] For a discussion of the methods used in compiling this table see the notes to Table 3.8 in Appendix A.

[4] Cf. Table 3.5.

827209X   D

TABLE 3.7

The Growth of the Major Unions Catering for White-Collar Workers in Manufacturing Industries in the United Kingdom, 1948–64

Union	1948	1950	1955	1960	1964	% increase 1948–64	Ranking by % increase 1948–64	% increase 1955–64	Ranking by % increase 1955–64
AScW	15,521	13,264	11,911	12,645	20,809	+34·1	8	+74·7	2
ASSET	15,709	12,630	16,010	21,776	32,540	+107·1	1	+103·2	1
CAWU	38,493	33,150	55,921	59,545	79,177	+105·7	2	+41·6	5
DATA	45,049	45,039	51,806	60,740	62,048	+37·7	7	+19·8	7
BISAKTA	4,774	4,797	6,306	7,167	9,039	+89·3	4	+43·3	4
NATSOPA	6,846	7,879	10,462	10,800	12,250	+78·9	5	+17·1	8
NUJ	10,684	11,684	13,364	15,780	18,526	+73·4	6	+38·6	6
TGWU (Nacss)	27,620	29,133	36,525	44,491	56,541	+104·7	3	+54·8	3
Total	164,696	157,576	202,305	232,944	290,930	+76·6		+43·8	
Growth index (1948 = 100)	100	96	123	141	177				
Growth index (1955 = 100)			100	115	144				

TABLE 3.8

The Density of White-Collar Unionism in Manufacturing Industries in Great Britain by Industry and by Occupation, 1964

Occupational group	Food, drink, tobacco	Chemical manuf.	Metal manuf.	Metal N.E.S.	Eng. elect.	Ship. M.E.	Vehicles	Textiles	Leather, fur	Clothing, footwear	Bricks, etc.	Timber, furn., etc.	Paper, print, pub.	Other manuf.	All manuf.
1. Foremen	—[a]	1·6	8·3	3·2	13·6	2·9	10·8	28·2	1·1	—	2·0	3·8	n/a[b]	4·7	8·8
2. All scientists, technologists, technicians	1·7	9·6	26·4	2·6	28·2	53·5	38·0	2·6	0·5	0·9	8·3	12·6	0·4	14·1	24·0
(a) Scientists, technologists	1·2	12·5	3·0	—	3·9	13·5	2·3	1·7	—	3·0	4·4	—	0·3	3·3	5·3
(b) All technicians	2·0	7·7	34·3	3·1	34·7	56·8	43·6	3·0	0·9	0·8	9·8	12·8	0·5	18·1	29·6
(i) Draughtsmen	—	5·8	50·3	—	50·2	67·1	80·0	—	1·0	—	—	—	—	12·1	48·7
(ii) Other technicians	2·7	7·9	27·4	8·5	17·4	27·9	14·7	3·6	1·0	0·9	18·8	36·8	0·6	21·0	14·7
3. Clerks	5·4	2·3	21·3	2·4	12·3	5·6	22·3	3·4	—	0·6	5·2	0·4	15·2	10·2	10·5
4. Other white-collar workers	—	—	1·5	—	1·8	3·7	2·9	—	—	—	—	—	59·5[c]	0·1	7·1
5. All white-collar workers	3·0	3·7	16·8	2·2	15·0	15·9	22·0	10·8	0·3	0·3	4·1	1·7	23·4	7·4	12·1

[a] The symbol (—) is used where density is less than 0·1 per cent.

[b] The symbol 'n/a' means 'not available'. Unfortunately, none of the unions in this industry keep their membership figures in such a way that it is possible to determine the number of foremen in membership. It is generally known, however, that a relatively large number of employees in this industry retain their membership in a union when promoted to supervisory positions.

[c] A large proportion of the labour force in this category is composed of journalists and almost all the union membership is among the journalists. A very small amount of the total membership is found among circulation representatives.

printing, and publishing group (23·4 per cent), and the metal group of industries—vehicles (22 per cent), metal manufacture (16·8 per cent), ship-building and marine engineering (15·9 per cent), and engineering and electrical goods (15 per cent). Then there are the medium-density industries: textiles (10 per cent) and other manufacturing (7·4 per cent), mainly rubber and plastics. All the remaining industries fall into the low-density category with densities ranging from a high of 4 per cent in bricks, pottery, glass, cement, etc., to a low of 0·3 per cent in leather and fur, and clothing and footwear.

Occupationally, the most striking aspect of Table 3.8 is the very high density of unionization among draughtsmen (48·7 per cent) and journalists (90 per cent),[1] and the very low levels of density among all the other occupational groups. Here also there are significant differences between industries. Draughtsmen are over 80 per cent unionized in vehicles, but only 5·8 per cent organized in chemicals; clerks are over 22 per cent organized in vehicles but have a negligible degree of unionization in leather and fur, timber and furniture, and clothing and footwear; foremen are over 28 per cent unionized in textiles but are relatively poorly organized in most of the other industries.

In order to obtain comparable manpower statistics, union membership figures had to be arranged according to the official systems of industrial and occupational classification.[2] These systems of classification may be useful for classifying over-all social and economic organization, but they are not always useful for classifying trade union membership. In some cases the real significance of white-collar unionization in a particular area is obscured because an area of high density is combined with an area of low density to give an average figure.

In paper, printing, and publishing, for example, over 90 per cent of the clerical membership of NATSOPA was concentrated among the clerks of the major national dailies in Fleet Street. The number of clerks employed in Fleet Street is not known exactly, but union officials and employers estimated that union density among these workers is well over 90 per cent as opposed to the average of 15·2 per cent for the industry as a whole. In the same industry journalists are grouped under the heading 'other white-collar workers' for which the average density figure is 59·5 per cent. The density of unionization among journalists alone, however, is over 90 per cent and in Fleet Street it is very close to 100 per cent.[2] In metal manufacture most of the white-collar membership is concentrated in the heavy-steel trade. The government does

---

[1] The total membership of the NUJ and the Institute of Journalists in 1964 was approximately 21,000. The NUJ estimated that the potential number of journalists, photographers, etc., eligible for recruitment in 1964 was 22,000. Even allowing for dual membership between the two organizations, this makes the density of unionization over 90 per cent. See George Viner, *Basic Statistics on Journalism in the British Isles* (London: The NUJ, 1965), p. 2. (Mimeographed.)

[2] *Supra*, p. 27 n. 1.

not publish separate manpower figures for this section of the industry, but the density figures for the heavy-steel trade would certainly be higher than those given for metal manufacture generally. A large proportion of clerical membership in the food, drink, and tobacco industry is concentrated in the chocolate trade, and density of unionization here would be substantially above the 5·4 per cent for clerks in the industry as a whole. Finally, the manufacture of rubber and plastic goods is grouped with a number of other industries under the heading 'other manufacturing' to give an over-all density of white-collar unionism of 7·4 per cent. If it were possible to segregate the manpower figures of these two industries from the rest, their densities would be much more significant. If some of the other industry groups could be broken down into smaller units, no doubt additional variations would emerge.

The geographical pattern

Although there are no statistics available on the geographical distribution of membership in Britain, it is commonly believed that there are considerable regional variations in the membership pattern. As can be seen from Table 3.9, the geographical distribution of white-collar union membership in manufacturing tends to support this belief. Unfortunately, a great deal of the regional variation in the density of manufacturing white-collar unionism is hidden by the over-all averages which result from the government's very broad geographical groupings, the lack of separate white-collar labour force figures for the major conurbations, and the lack of a reliable occupational breakdown.[1] About the only conclusion which can be drawn from Table 3.9 is that the density of white-collar unionism tends to be highest in Wales and to a lesser extent in the northern and north-western areas of the country and lowest around London and the eastern and southern areas.[2]

CONCLUSIONS

The degree of unionization among white-collar employees is considerably less than that found among manual workers. In Britain only three out of ten white-collar workers belong to a union whereas five out of ten manual workers are members.

Since 1948 the absolute amount of white-collar unionism has increased greatly. This has prompted many people to speak of a boom in white-collar unionism. Such people are suffering from a growth illusion which results from considering changes in union membership in isolation from changes in the labour force. In real terms this membership boom is non-existent. In spite of the phenomenal growth of some white-collar unions, white-collar unionism in general has done little more than keep abreast of the increasing white-collar

[1] For a comment on the system of classification see notes to Table 3.9 in Appendix A.
[2] Trade unionism among bank clerks also tends to be stronger in Wales and in the northern areas than in the south. See Blackburn, op. cit., pp. 116–20.

TABLE 3.9

The Density of White-Collar Unionism in Manufacturing Industries in Great Britain by Industry and by Region, 1964

Region[a]	Food, drink, tobacco	Chemical	Metal manuf.	Metal N.E.S.	Eng. elect.	Ship M.E.	Vehicles	Textiles	Leather, fur	Clothing, footwear	Bricks, etc.	Timber, furn., etc.	Paper, print, pub.	Other manuf.	All manuf.
Scotland	1·2	3·0	14·3	1·2	20·9	32·7	27·8	2·3	1·8	—	4·0	0·6	15·6	9·3	13·3
Northern	1·7	3·5	40·2	7·8	24·4	24·2	8·3	8·3	—	—	—	1·7	35·1	9·2	16·6
North-west	1·3	4·1	19·8	1·9	22·0	15·1	25·8	21·6	—	0·2	6·7	1·0	19·7	8·4	14·3
East and West Ridings of Yorkshire and east and west Midlands	6·7	3·7	10·6	1·1	16·8	26·8	21·9	8·8	0·6	0·4	2·3	0·6	13·4	10·1	11·4
Wales	1·5	2·5	38·6	10·6	24·2	n/a	51·4	11·6	—	4·1	4·4	2·0	24·4	11·1	22·9
Eastern and southern	2·1	1·3	6·4	9·2	11·1	15·2	19·9	0·1	—	—	3·3	0·8	10·7	5·8	9·5
London and south-east	2·2	4·2	3·4	0·6	8·6	4·0	13·8	0·7	—	0·3	2·5	1·3	29·3	2·2	9·1
South-western	4·6	6·8	0·8	—	12·9	2·4	26·2	8·3	—	—	17·7	0·5	10·7	19·8	13·3
ALL REGIONS[b]	3·1	3·6	16·8	2·0	14·7	20·7	21·7	10·7	0·2	0·3	3·7	1·5	21·8	7·5	11·8

[a] For definitions of the various regions see notes to this table in Appendix A.

[b] These figures are slightly different from the ones given in Table 3.8 as the manpower figures are from a different source and include managers but not foremen. The difference in percentage terms is not great for most industries. For a more complete discussion of the source of these statistics see Appendix A.

labour force, and the density of white-collar unionism has not increased significantly during the post-war period. Of even greater importance, the growth of trade unionism among white-collar employees has not been sufficient to offset a decline in the density of manual unionism or to prevent a decline in the density of total unionism. Thus despite all the recruiting activity of white-collar unions during the post-war period, the real membership strength of white-collar unions in general is roughly the same today as it was in 1948, while the real membership strength of manual unionism and the trade union movement as a whole has actually decreased.

But of greater interest than the over-all level and growth-rate of white-collar unionism, are the occupational and industrial variations in the degree of white-collar unionism. The density of white-collar unionism in the public sector of the economy is over 80 per cent while in the private sector it is just slightly over 10 per cent. Even within the private sector there are great variations in the degree of white-collar unionism: printing and the metal group of industries are relatively highly unionized, the rest are not; journalists and draughtsmen have joined unions in large numbers, other white-collar groups have not. Even within the same occupational group there is considerable variation in the degree of unionization from one industry to another: draughtsmen are 80 per cent unionized in vehicles, but only 50 per cent in engineering and less than 6 per cent in chemicals. Clearly, there are great variations in the density of white-collar unionism, and, as Lockwood has remarked, 'it cannot be assumed that these variations are purely random'.[1] What then is their explanation? This is the question which the remainder of this study attempts to answer.

[1] David Lockwood, *The Blackcoated Worker* (London: Allen & Unwin, 1958), p. 138.

IV

SOCIO-DEMOGRAPHIC CHARACTERISTICS

P ERHAPS the most obvious place to begin looking for an explanation of the pattern of white-collar unionism is at the white-collar workers themselves—at their sex, social origins, age, and status in the community. Social scientists have demonstrated that these personal characteristics determine many aspects of the individuals' outlook and behaviour; they may also determine their response to trade unionism.

SEX

Women make up a large proportion of the white-collar labour force. Approximately 45 per cent of all white-collar employees are female, and, in such white-collar groups as lower professionals, shop assistants, and clerks, women outnumber men.[1] The major characteristics of female employment are well known: most women do not participate continuously in the labour market because of marriage and family responsibilities, and they generally are supplementary earners in the sense that their pay is not the family's main source of income but merely supplements the earnings of their husbands. It is often suggested that these characteristics tend to reduce women's commitment to work thereby increasing their indifference to trade unionism,[2] and that the large proportion of women among white-collar workers therefore helps to account for their generally low degree of unionization.

This view has been challenged by Lockwood. He found that the proportion of women in most of the major clerical unions is 'roughly equal to their representation in the field of employment which the unions seek to organise' and this led him to conclude that 'differences in the degree of unionization are therefore to be attributed to something other than differences in the sex ratio'.[3] Lockwood's findings are sufficient to indicate the inadequacy of generalizations about women having a dampening effect on the level of unionization, but they are not sufficient to discount this argument completely.

It is common knowledge that the density of unionization is much less among women than among men. Density of unionization among manual workers is approximately 60 per cent for males as opposed to 28 per cent for females,

---

[1] See Table 2.3.
[2] See, for example, R. M. Blackburn, *Union Character and Social Class* (London: Batsford, 1967), p. 56.
[3] *The Blackcoated Worker* (London: Allen & Unwin, 1958), p. 151.

while that among white-collar workers is 35 per cent for males as compared
to 23 per cent for females.[1] Obviously, the unions Lockwood examined are
not representative of trade unionism in general. Moreover, it is also noticeable
from comparing Tables 2.8 and 3.8 that there is some relationship between
the density of unionization and the proportion of women among white-collar
workers in manufacturing industries. Industries which have a large proportion
of women, such as textiles, leather and fur, clothing and footwear, and timber
and furniture, also have a low degree of white-collar unionism while those
which have a small proportion of women, such as metal manufacture, engineering and electrical goods, shipbuilding and marine engineering, and
vehicles, also have a relatively high degree of white-collar unionism. Similarly, clerical occupations have a large proportion of women and are poorly
organized while technical occupations have a small proportion of women
and are quite highly unionized. A regression analysis of Tables 2.8 and 3.8
confirms that the density of unionization and the proportion of women among
white-collar workers in manufacturing industries are correlated, although
not quite significantly at the 5 per cent level.[2]

But although Lockwood does not provide sufficient evidence to substantiate his conclusion that differences in the degree of unionization are to be
attributed to something other than differences in the sex ratio, it is nevertheless largely correct. The fact that a low degree of unionization is associated
with a high proportion of women and that women generally are not as
highly unionized as men can be accounted for by differences in the way males
and females are distributed across firms. Chapter VI will demonstrate that density of unionization is higher in areas where the average size of establishments
is large and employment concentrated than in areas where the average size
of establishments is small and employment diffused.[3] That the distribution of
female employment is skewed in the direction of small establishments is
obvious from Table 4.1. The proportion of women is highest in the smaller
establishments and lowest in the larger establishments. In fact, only 25 per
cent of the women employed in manufacturing industries work in establishments with 1,000 or more employees compared with 39 per cent of males
while 43 per cent of the women work in establishments with less than 250
employees as compared with 33 per cent of males.[4]

The close association between female employment and establishment size is
also indicated by the data presented in Tables 2.8 and 6.1 on the proportion

[1] See Table 3.4.
[2] Regressing density of unionization on proportion of women and allowing for the level
of the equation to shift with occupation produces a $\bar{R}^2$ of 0·109 and a t value for the proportion of women coefficient of $-1·79$.
[3] See *infra*, pp. 72–81 and also p. 42 n. 2.
[4] If establishments with less than eleven employees could be included in this table, it
would be seen that the distribution of female employment is even more skewed in the
direction of small establishments. See Viola Klein, *Britain's Married Women Workers*
(London: Routledge & Kegan Paul, 1965), pp. 94–5.

of women and the degree of employment concentration among white-collar workers in manufacturing industries. Even a superficial glance at these tables demonstrates that industries which have a high degree of employment concentration, such as engineering and electrical goods, shipbuilding and marine engineering, metal manufacture, and vehicles, also have a low proportion of women while those which have a low degree of employment concentration, such as textiles, leather and fur, clothing and footwear, and timber and furniture, also have a high proportion of women. A regression analysis of Tables 2.8 and 6.1 confirms that the proportion of women and the degree of employment concentration among white-collar workers in manufacturing industries are very highly correlated.[1]

TABLE 4.1

Employment in Manufacturing Industries in Great Britain by Size of Establishment

Size of establishment (no. of employees)	Males as a percentage of total males	Females as a percentage of total females	Females as a percentage of total employment
11–24	2·6	2·9	34·6
25–49	5·9	7·2	36·5
50–99	10·0	12·9	38·1
100–249	14·7	19·7	38·7
250–499	13·8	17·0	36·9
500–999	13·8	14·9	33·7
1,000–1,999	13·8	11·7	28·7
2,000–4,999	14·6	8·3	21·4
5,000 or more	10·4	4·9	18·2
Totals	100·0	100·0	32·1

The very high correlation between proportion of women and employment concentration suggests that the former will exert little influence upon density of unionization independently of the latter. This is, in fact, the case. Chapter VI will demonstrate that density of unionization and the degree of employment concentration among white-collar workers in manufacturing industries are correlated very highly.[2] This chapter has already shown that the density

[1] Regressing employment concentration on proportion of women and allowing for the level of the equation to shift with occupation produces a $\bar{R}^2$ of 0·392. Regressing proportion of women on employment concentration and allowing for the level of the equation to shift with occupation produces a $\bar{R}^2$ of 0·835. Both $\bar{R}^2$s are significant at the 5 per cent level.

[2] Regressing density of unionization on employment concentration and allowing for the level of the equation to shift with occupation produces a $\bar{R}^2$ of 0·177 and a t value for the employment concentration coefficient of 2·96. Allowing for the slope of the equation to shift with occupation produces a $\bar{R}^2$ of 0·641 and a t value for the employment concentration coefficient of 2·14. Allowing for both the level and the slope of the equation to shift with occupation produces a $\bar{R}^2$ of 0·669 and a t value for the employment concentration coefficient of 2·28. These are all significant at the 5 per cent level. See *infra*, pp. 72–81.

of unionization and the proportion of women among white-collar workers in manufacturing industries are correlated, although not quite significantly at the 5 per cent level.[1] But if density of unionization is regressed simultaneously on both employment concentration and proportion of women, then employment concentration remains very significantly associated with density of unionization but proportion of women does not.[2] This suggests that density of unionization is influenced by proportion of women mainly because it is correlated with employment concentration. Once the effect of employment concentration upon proportion of women has been allowed for, proportion of women as such exerts little influence on density of unionization. To put it another way, density of unionization and proportion of women have no significant connection with each other except through their separate relationships to a third variable, the degree of employment concentration.

The conclusion to be drawn from this rather technical discussion is a simple one. Female employees appear to have no inherent characteristics which make them more difficult to unionize than men, or, at least if they have, unions have been able to overcome them. 'Where men are well organised in a particular plant', as the TUC has noted, 'generally women are too. The fact that the proportion of women in employment who belong to trade unions is only about half that of men is mainly to be accounted for by differences in their industrial and occupational distribution.'[3] In short, the proportion of women has not been in itself a significant determinant of the pattern of manual or white-collar unionism in Britain.

SOCIAL ORIGINS

Sociologists have argued that the social origins of workers determine many aspects of their behaviour. In particular, they have hypothesized that those who come from the homes of manual or unionized workers are more likely to join trade unions than those who come from the homes of white-collar or non-unionized workers. The suggested explanation for this is that white-collar or non-unionized parents are likely to possess anti-union attitudes while manual or unionized parents are likely to possess pro-union attitudes, and these attitudes are transmitted to their children.[4]

This is a difficult hypothesis to test because of lack of adequate data.

[1] See *supra*, p. 41 n. 2.

[2] Allowing for the level of the equation to shift with occupation produces a $\bar{R}^2$ of 0·174 and a t value for the employment concentration coefficient of 2·46 and for the proportion of women coefficient of $-0·859$.

[3] *Selected Written Evidence Submitted to the Royal Commission* (London: HMSO, 1968), p. 185.

[4] See, for example, Seymour M. Lipset and Joan Gordon, 'Mobility and Trade Union Membership', *Class, Status and Power*, Reinhard Bendix and Seymour M. Lipset, editors (London: Routledge & Kegan Paul, 1954), pp. 491–500.

Although a considerable amount of information has been collected on the social origins of various white-collar groups,[1] the various sets of data are not comparable with each other because of differences in sample size, reliability, and date, nor are they comparable with the data on union membership which has been collected for this study. But several social surveys have generated comparable data on union membership and social origins, and scholars have used it to test the above hypothesis.

Lipset and Gordon analysed data from a 1949 sample of 953 Californian manual workers and found that workers whose fathers had non-manual occupations were the least likely to belong to trade unions.[2] Kornhauser analysed the data generated by a national public opinion survey in 1952 and also by a survey of labour mobility in six major American cities in 1951 and found no relationship between the social origins of manual workers and union membership in either sample.[3] But Lipset also analysed the data provided by the six-city sample and found that clerical workers and shop assistants who came from manual homes were much more likely to be union members than those who did not.[4] Goldstein and Indik could find no significant correlation between social origins and union membership among the 705 professional engineers they surveyed, but did find that union members were significantly more likely to have had fathers who were also union members.[5] In his sample of 6,115 professional engineers and 596 technicians, Kleingartner found that union members were not significantly more likely than non-members to have had fathers who belonged to a trade union.[6]

In Britain Blackburn found that among his sample of thirty-five male bank clerks there was a tendency for those from higher-status homes to be in the staff associations or nothing, while the lower the status of their background, the more likely they were to be in NUBE.[7] But this relationship did not hold among his sample of sixty-six female bank clerks. Nor did it hold for either males or females among his second sample of fifty-eight bank clerks. Many

[1] See David Glass (ed.), *Social Mobility in Britain* (London: Routledge & Kegan Paul, 1954); for clerical workers, see Lockwood, op. cit., pp. 106–16 and J. R. Dale, *The Clerk in Industry* (Liverpool: Liverpool University Press, 1962), p. 33; for draughtsmen, see Guy Routh, 'The Social Co-ordinates of Design Technicians', *The Draughtsman* (September 1961), p. 7; for engineers, see J. E. Gerstl and S. P. Hutton, *Engineers: The Anatomy of a Profession* (London: Tavistock Publications, 1966), chap. 3; and for civil servants, see R. K. Kelsall, *Higher Civil Servants in Britain* (London: Routledge & Kegan Paul, 1955), chap. 7.

[2] Op. cit., p. 492, table 1.

[3] Ruth Kornhauser, 'Some Social Determinants and Consequences of Union Membership', *Labor History*, ii (Winter 1961), p. 43.

[4] Seymour M. Lipset, 'The Future of Non-Manual Unionism' (an unpublished paper, Institute of Industrial Relations, University of California, Berkeley, 1961), pp. 21–2.

[5] Bernard Goldstein and Bernard P. Indik, 'Unionism as a Social Choice: The Engineers' Case', *Monthly Labor Review*, lxxxvi (April 1963), pp. 366–7.

[6] A. Kleingartner, 'The Organization of White-Collar Workers', *British Journal of Industrial Relations*, vi (March 1968), pp. 85–6.

[7] Op. cit., pp. 197–8.

draughtsmen come from manual homes and many of them start their working lives as manual workers.[1] Phillipson analysed the data provided by his sample of 182 white-collar workers and found that draughtsmen who had manual fathers were more likely to be union members than those who did not. But he could find no relationship between fathers' union membership and union membership among draughtsmen, nor could he find any connection between fathers' occupation or union membership and union membership among clerical and administrative workers.[2]

It is difficult to draw any firm conclusions from these studies, not only because of their contradictory findings, but also because of their methodology. The American samples were large and random, but the British ones were small and something less than random.[3] More serious, none of the studies controlled for all the other factors which might influence workers to join unions. For example, none of the studies controlled for size of firm or for the way in which the firm was administered, and none but Blackburn's even controlled for industry. It may be that many of the non-unionists were working in small paternalistically-administered firms in which they had close interpersonal relations with their employers, and that this rather than their social origins explains their reluctance to join trade unions.[4]

About all that can be said until such time as there are better empirical studies is that there is not generally a connection between social origins and union membership. This conclusion is reinforced by the data on union membership which has been collected for this study. The variations in the density of white-collar unionism reflected by Table 3.8 would seem to be too large to be explained by variations in social origins. The density of unionism among draughtsmen is 80 per cent in vehicles, 50 per cent in engineering and electrical goods, and less than 6 per cent in chemicals. It is extremely doubtful if the social origins of draughtsmen vary sufficiently from industry to industry to account for these variations in union density. Nor is it very likely that the high degree of clerical unionism in the public sector and the low degree in the private sector is accounted for by differences in social origins. Most foremen come from manual homes and almost all of them would have once had manual jobs, but they are one of the most poorly organized groups in private industry. It is very probable that the social origins of journalists are more middle class than those of clerks, yet the former are much more highly unionized than the latter. It is unnecessary to pursue this line of argument in order to conclude

[1] Routh found that in his sample of 941 DATA members, 63 per cent had come from manual homes and 43 per cent had entered the profession after serving a craft apprenticeship (op. cit., pp. 7–8).
[2] C. M. Phillipson, 'A Study of the Attitudes Towards and Participation in Trade Union Activities of Selected Groups of Non-Manual Workers' (unpublished M.A. thesis, University of Nottingham, 1964), pp. 279–80.
[3] The researchers themselves admit this. See ibid., pp. 164–70, and Blackburn, op. cit., pp. 64–5.
[4] Lipset and Gordon frankly admit this (op. cit., p. 705 n. 14).

that there is no clear connection between the density of unionization and social origins.[1]

AGE

The age distribution of an occupation seldom is mentioned as a factor which might affect the growth of trade unionism. But at least one scholar has claimed that younger workers are likely to show a greater propensity to unionize than older workers.[2] He advances several reasons in support of this proposition. Firstly, younger workers usually have shorter tenure of service with a firm and therefore feel less 'loyalty' towards it than older workers. Secondly, if victimized because of their union activity, younger workers stand to lose much less than older workers in terms of any company benefits which may exist, and, in addition, it is easier for them to find a job elsewhere and adjust themselves to it. Thirdly, younger workers are likely to be better educated than older ones, and therefore more resentful of arbitrary treatment by management and better able to give leadership at the rank and file level. Finally, younger workers have been nurtured in an era when unionism has become an integral part of the institutional framework and they look upon it, therefore, not as something new and exceptional, but as the 'natural' way of handling worker problems.

The empirical evidence is rather fragmentary, but what there is does not support this *a priori* reasoning. The percentage age distribution for selected white-collar occupations is given in Table 4.2. It is clear that laboratory

TABLE 4.2

Percentage Age Distribution for Selected White-Collar Occupational Groups, England and Wales, 1961

Occupational group	Total	15–19	20–4	25–9	30–4	35–44	45–54	55–9	60–4	65+
All gainfully occupied	100	10·8	10·3	9·1	9·4	21·1	21·4	9·0	5·9	3·2
Foremen	100	0·2	1·7	4·6	9·0	28·5	32·7	13·6	8·0	1·8
Clerks	100	18·8	15·6	10·1	8·8	18·2	15·8	6·4	4·2	2·0
All professionals and technicians	100	6·8	13·9	13·0	12·1	21·2	19·2	7·3	3·9	2·6
Authors and journalists	100	4·8	10·1	13·1	12·8	20·8	20·8	7·3	5·2	5·1
Draughtsmen	100	12·7	22·0	18·8	14·5	18·1	8·3	3·0	1·9	0·8
Laboratory assistants	100	23·4	24·1	13·4	9·6	14·2	9·0	3·5	2·1	0·6

[1] The amount and type of education which white-collar workers receive is another personal characteristic which might influence their propensity to unionize. It has not been analysed in this chapter because of lack of adequate data. But it is well known that the amount and type of education received by occupational groups is correlated very highly with their social origins (see Lockwood, op. cit., pp. 119–20, and Jean Floud, 'The Educational Experience of the Adult Population of England and Wales at July 1949', *Social Mobility in Britain*, op. cit., pp. 120–39). Hence the influence of education upon the propensity to unionize is probably much the same as the influence of social origins, namely— little, if any. Goldstein and Indik (op. cit., p. 366) could find no significant relationship between education and union membership among professional engineers.

[2] Joseph Shister, 'The Logic of Union Growth', *Journal of Political Economy*, lxi (October 1953), pp. 421–2.

technicians, draughtsmen, and clerks are among the younger occupations: the proportion under thirty-five years of age is 70·5 per cent for laboratory technicians, 68 per cent for draughtsmen, 53·4 per cent for clerks, 45·9 per cent for professionals and technicians as a group, 40·7 per cent for authors and journalists, 39·6 per cent for all the gainfully occupied, and 15·5 per cent for foremen. Yet the members of these young occupations have had widely differing responses to trade unionism: draughtsmen are highly unionized, laboratory technicians and clerks are not. Moreover, journalists are a relatively old occupation, yet almost all of them belong to a union.

The only white-collar group for which the age distribution is available on a detailed industrial basis is foremen, and this is given in Table 4.3.[1] A regression analysis of Tables 3.8 and 4.3 revealed that there was no significant connection between the age distribution of foremen and the degree to which they are unionized.[2]

TABLE 4.3

Percentage Age Distribution of Foremen in Manufacturing Industries in England and Wales, 1961

Industry	Total	15–19	20–4	25–9	30–4	35–44	45–54	55–9	60–4	65+
Food, drink, and tobacco	100	0·2	2·4	5·6	8·5	28·1	33·3	13·4	7·1	1·3
Chemical and allied	100	0·2	1·5	4·3	8·6	32·1	33·7	12·1	6·7	0·9
Metal manufacture	100	0·1	0·9	3·7	7·8	29·7	32·8	14·5	8·5	2·0
Metal goods N.E.S.	100	0·1	2·0	5·2	10·0	33·0	29·2	11·8	6·4	2·2
Engineering and electrical goods	100	0·1	1·7	5·1	11·3	35·3	28·2	10·8	6·1	1·5
Shipbuilding and marine engineering	100	0·0	0·3	1·5	6·5	26·1	29·8	20·1	12·7	3·1
Vehicles	100	0·1	0·4	3·1	8·5	33·5	32·1	13·0	7·9	1·3
Textiles	100	0·3	2·8	6·1	8·3	22·5	33·0	15·3	8·8	2·9
Leather, leather goods, and fur	100	0·5	2·0	3·0	8·0	27·4	30·3	14·9	8·5	5·5
Clothing and footwear	100	0·9	5·5	6·8	10·2	24·8	30·2	11·6	6·5	3·5
Bricks, pottery, glass, etc.	100	0·5	1·5	5·0	10·6	28·3	34·0	12·0	6·3	1·9
Timber, furniture, etc.	100	0·1	1·6	6·5	10·9	27·6	36·4	10·2	5·0	1·6
Paper, printing, and publishing	100	0·1	2·2	5·3	7·7	26·7	34·9	13·3	7·3	2·4
Other manufacturing	100	0·3	2·8	5·9	13·5	32·1	30·8	9·3	4·2	1·0
All manufacturing	100	0·2	1·9	4·9	9·5	30·4	31·5	12·6	7·1	1·8

[1] These figures are derived from Industry Table 13 of the 1961 *Census of Population*. For each Minimum List Heading only the 'principal occupations' (those with 500 or more males or females in the sample figure) are given. 'Foremen' is the only occupational group of interest to this study which exceeds this 'threshold' in every industry (Minimum List Heading) and hence the only group for which an industrial age distribution can be calculated with any accuracy.

[2] The first row (foremen) of Table 3.8 was regressed on each column of Table 4.3. Then each column of Table 4.3 was cumulated one at a time from left to right and then right to left, and the first row of Table 3.8 was regressed on each of the resulting columns (that is, on 15–19, 15–24, 15–29, etc., and on 65+, 60–5+, 55–65+, etc. All the resulting correlation coefficients were very much below the figure required for significance at the 5 per cent level. The highest correlation coefficient was 0·296. To be significant at the 5 per cent level with 12 degrees of freedom, the correlation coefficient must be at least 0·532. Of course, other combinations of the age distribution (for example, 20–34 or 35–64) could have been used, but this did not seem worth while in view of the unpromising results obtained above.

STATUS

The most common explanation for white-collar resistance to trade unionism is what various writers have referred to as 'false class consciousness', the 'psychology of prestige striving', or plain old-fashioned 'snobbishness'.[1] They argue that white-collar workers have possessed considerable social aspirations but have had limited means for achieving them. 'Unlike the members of the upper class they could not claim prestige as their birthright; nor could they, like the captains of industry, base it on power and authority.' Hence 'they sought it in the only way left open to them—by concentrating on social differences'. They claimed higher prestige on the basis of such factors as their social origins, manner of dress and speech, tastes, education, working conditions, and association with the 'managerial cadre'.

But 'prestige involves at least two persons: one to claim it and another to honor the claim'. In the case of white-collar workers, the community in general and employers in particular were prepared to honour the claims. Indeed, they even fostered them by encouraging white-collar workers 'to identify their interests with those of the employers and to regard themselves as having a personal relationship with them'. To emphasize this, white-collar workers were called staff, not hands; they were paid salaries, not wages; they received better terms and conditions of employment; and they were provided with their own entrances and had different starting and finishing times.[2] 'The separation of staff from workmen was built into the structures of industrial organizations as if the two represented different castes.'

The supposed result of all this is that white-collar workers 'formed an image of themselves which bore little resemblance to economic realities. They saw themselves as individuals, superior to manual workers and able to progress through society unaided and without protection.' Most of them felt that unions were only for those who did not have sufficient determination and merit to succeed on their own. Even those who did not feel this way were afraid to join unions for fear of identifying themselves with manual workers and thereby losing their middle-class status.

But fortunately for the supporters of trade unionism this argument has a happy ending. 'Every basis on which the prestige claims of the bulk of the white-collar employees have historically rested has been declining in firmness and stability.' Such trends as the spread of educational opportunity, the narrowing of the manual/white-collar pay differential and the granting of staff

---

[1] The major American exposition of this thesis is found in C. Wright Mills, *White Collar* (New York: Oxford University Press, 1956), chaps. 11 and 14. The major British exposition is found in V. L. Allen, 'White-Collar Revolt?', *The Listener*, lxvi (30 November 1961), pp. 895–7. The statement of the argument given below is paraphrased largely from these two sources.

[2] Many employers retain these distinctions today because they believe that such status symbols discourage white-collar workers from joining trade unions. See 'Status Has Its Compensations', *Personnel Magazine* (November 1965), p. 13.

status to manual workers, the concentration of white-collar employees in big work places and their resulting separation from management, the recruitment of white-collar employees from lower social strata, and the vast increase in the total numbers of white-collar people are all 'tearing away the foundations of the white-collar rejection of unions on the basis of prestige'. In short, the 'status proletarianization' of white-collar workers will reduce their traditional hostility towards trade unionism.

There can be little doubt that most white-collar workers generally think of themselves as being socially superior to manual workers, as belonging more with management and the middle class than with manual workers and the working class.[1] Nor can there be much doubt that the status of almost all white-collar groups has been declining over the course of the twentieth century.[2] But this does not necessarily mean that the first fact prevents white-collar workers from joining unions or that the second will encourage them to do so.

Lockwood has demonstrated the fundamental weakness with 'snobbishness' as an explanation of white-collar union growth, and it is worth while to quote him at some length:

Has snobbishness varied through time? If so, assuming that it has lessened, say between 1921 and 1951, why has the proportion of commercial and industrial clerks in unions hardly increased at all? If not, how is the fact to be explained that twice as many blackcoated workers are unionized nowadays as thirty years ago? Is snobbishness a factor which operates 'all along the line', something displayed by all clerks equally? If so, why are there very significant differences in the degree of clerical unionization from one field to another? Alternatively, is snobbishness connected with relative social status among blackcoats? If so, why have certain groups of clerks with high social status been highly unionized, and others with a relatively low social status poorly unionized? Most perplexing of all, why have two groups of clerical workers, both with a relatively low standing in the blackcoated world— railway clerks and industrial clerks—joined their respective unions to such radically different degrees? It is unnecessary to pursue this line of argument in order to conclude that no clear connection can be established between a factor such as 'snobbishness' and the empirical variations in clerical trade unionism. Whatever influence snobbishness has on the mutual relations of clerks and manual workers

---

[1] Studies in this and other countries support such a contention, although they indicate that among the lower level white-collar groups an increasing number see themselves as members of the working class. In general see Richard F. Hamilton, 'The Marginal Middle Class: A Reconsideration', *American Sociological Review*, xxxi (April 1966), pp. 192–9. For Britain see John Bonham, *The Middle Class Vote* (London: Faber, 1954), p. 60; F. M. Martin, 'Some Subjective Aspects of Status', *Social Mobility in Britain*, D. V. Glass, op. cit., p. 56; Lockwood, op. cit., p. 127; Dale, op. cit., pp. 28–9; and W. G. Runciman, *Relative Deprivation and Social Justice* (London: Routledge & Kegan Paul, 1966), p. 158, table 1. For America see Richard Centers, *The Psychology of Social Classes* (Princeton: Princeton University Press, 1949), p. 86. For France see Natalie Rogoff, 'Social Stratification in France and the United States', *Class, Status and Power*, op. cit., p. 585.

[2] If documentation is thought necessary see Runciman, op. cit., chap 5; Lockwood, op. cit., chap. 4; and Dale, op. cit., chap. 3.

it does not seem to have prevented the former from organising themselves in trade unions.[1]

While Lockwood argues his case only in respect of clerical trade unionism, it obviously applies to other types of trade unionism as well. Technicians and journalists enjoy a higher social standing in the community than clerical workers, and yet the former are more highly unionized than the latter. Craftsmen are obviously very status conscious, but this has not prevented them from organizing some of the strongest and most militant unions in the country.[2] Clearly, there is no general correlation between social status and the extent of trade unionism.

Even granting for the moment that the white-collar workers' concern for their middle-class status has prevented them from joining unions in the past, this does not necessarily mean that they will become more receptive to unionism as their status declines. Mills himself has suggested that as white-collar workers are increasingly proletarianized there may be a 'status panic' —a frantic drive to protect the remaining bases for separate consideration. The white-collar worker may 'seize upon minute distinctions as bases for status' and this may 'operate against any status solidarity among the mass of employees . . . lead to status estrangement from work associates, and to increased status competition'.[3] If this occurs, then by this argument's own logic white-collar unionism is unlikely to be the result.

CONCLUSIONS

In writings on white-collar unionism, much has been made of the personal characteristics of white-collar workers. Such features as their sex, social origins, and generally higher status in the community are supposed to produce a 'psychology' or 'mentality' which is unsympathetic to trade unionism. A review of the available evidence lends little support to this view. It suggests that white-collar workers do not possess any intrinsic qualities which make them less receptive to trade unionism than manual workers. At least the personal characteristics of white-collar workers do not account for variations in the density of white-collar unionism. If the white-collar workers' decision to join or not to join trade unions is not explained by the nature of their psyches, then perhaps it can be explained by such 'external' factors as their economic position or work situation. The influence of such factors is considered in the following chapters.

[1] Op. cit., pp. 150–1.
[2] See E. J. Hobsbawm, 'The Labour Aristocracy in Nineteenth-Century Britain', *Labouring Men* (London: Weidenfeld & Nicolson, 1964), pp. 272–315.
[3] Op. cit., p. 254.

V

THE ECONOMIC POSITION

THAT workers will join trade unions if they are dissatisfied with their terms and conditions of employment and the insecurity of their jobs, or refrain from joining if they are not, would seem to be common sense. But what appears to be common sense sometimes is revealed, on closer examination, to be little more than nonsense. Hence this chapter will systematically analyse the most important aspects of the white-collar workers' economic position in order to ascertain what influence it has, if any, on their decision to join or not to join trade unions.

EARNINGS

There always has been, and probably always will be, some overlap between the levels of white-collar and manual earnings. But, historically, white-collar workers have generally earned more than manual workers. This is still true of many white-collar workers today. Evidence to support these statements is presented in Table 5.1. The average annual earnings of all manual workers in 1922–4 were £149 for males and £93 for females; female industrial clerks were the only white-collar occupational group to earn less than these amounts. By 1960 the average annual earnings of all manual workers had increased to £663 for males and £343 for females; with the exception of male laboratory technicians and male clerks in the civil service, all the white-collar groups earned more than these amounts.

Not only have most white-collar workers generally earned more than manual workers as a whole, but many also have earned more than the best paid manual workers—the skilled. The only white-collar groups not to earn more than skilled manual workers in 1922–4 were male and female industrial clerks and male bank clerks. By 1960 all the male clerical groups were earning less than the skilled as were male laboratory technicians, but the rest of the white-collar groups were still better off.

The white-collar workers' economic position relative to that of manual workers is actually more favourable than these earnings figures suggest. Even leaving aside the question of fringe benefits,[1] there are a number of factors which tend to increase the economic disparity between the two groups of workers. In remissions from the Exchequer, which include both

---

[1] This is discussed *infra*, pp. 63–7.

TABLE 5.1

The Average Annual Earnings of Various White-Collar and Manual Occupational Groups in Great Britain, 1922/4–1960

(£ per annum)

Occupational group	Sex	1922–4	1935–6	1955–6	1960
1. All higher professionals	M	582	634	1,541	2,034
(a) Engineers	M	468	..	1,497	1,973
(b) Chemists	M	556	512	1,373	1,717
2. All lower professionals	M	320	308	610	847
and technicians	F	214	211	438	606
(a) Draughtsmen	M	250	253	679	905
(b) Laboratory technicians	M	201	186	420	536
3. Foremen	M	268	273	784	1,015
	F	154	156	477	602
4. All clerks	M	182	192	523	682
	F	106	99	317	427
(a) Railway clerks	M	221	224	559	751
(b) Industrial clerks	M	153	..	506	669
	F	87	..	305	412
(c) Bank clerks	M	174	223	627	746
	F	162	150	366	440
(d) Civil-service clerks	M	284	260	503	661
	F	171	155	360	520
5. All manual workers	M	149	159	527	663
	F	93	94	273	343
(a) Skilled manual workers	M	180	195	622	796
	F	87	86	317	395

deductible expenses and allowances for retirement schemes, white-collar workers gain much more than manual workers.[1] Professor Titmuss and others have shown that considerably higher state 'welfare' benefits can accrue to persons with higher incomes.[2] White-collar workers also generally have greater net worth and personal assets than manual workers. The Oxford Savings Survey of 1953 found that although the mean gross income of clerical and sales workers was lower than that of skilled manual workers—£403 as against £466—the former were better off by nearly a third both in terms of mean net worth—£394 as against £299—and of mean personal assets—£479 as against £368.[3] The same survey also demonstrated that the position of

[1] W. G. Runciman, *Relative Deprivation and Social Justice* (London: Routledge & Kegan Paul, 1966), p. 87.

[2] Titmuss gives an example based on the rates per annum for 1955–6 for child awards: a man earning £2,000 a year with two children under fifteen receives £97 while a man earning £400 receives £28. Over the lives of the two families, the first will receive a total of £1,455 while the second will receive a total of £422. See R. M. Titmuss, *Essays on 'The Welfare State'* (2nd ed.; London: Unwin University Books, 1958), p. 47.

[3] K. H. Straw, 'Consumers' Net Worth: The 1953 Savings Survey', *Bulletin of the Oxford University Institute of Statistics*, xviii (February 1956), pp. 12 and 14, tables 7 and 8, cited by Runciman, op. cit., p. 88.

white-collar workers was more favourable in terms of the ownership of stocks and shares. The mean among skilled manual workers was £4, with less than 1 per cent owning stocks and shares worth more than £100; the mean among clerical and sales workers was £50, with 2·6 per cent owning more than £100.[1] In respect of all these items, unskilled manual workers were even worse off while technical and managerial workers were even better off.

But although many, if not most, white-collar workers continue to receive larger incomes than manual workers, the relative pay of most white-collar groups has been reduced considerably over the past few decades. Table 5.2 shows that in spite of a slight increase in their relative earnings during the

TABLE 5.2

The Change in the Average Annual Earnings of Various White-Collar Occupational Groups Relative to the Change in the Average Annual Earnings of all Manual Workers in Great Britain, 1922/4–1960

(1922–4 = 100)

Occupational group	Sex	1922–4	1935–6	1955–6	1960
1. All higher professionals	M	100	102	75	78
(a) Engineers	M	100	..	90	95
(b) Chemists	M	100	86	70	69
2. All lower professionals	M	100	90	54	60
and technicians	F	100	98	70	77
(a) Draughtsmen	M	100	94	77	81
(b) Laboratory technicians	M	100	87	59	60
3. Foremen	M	100	95	83	85
	F	100	100	105	106
4. All clerks	M	100	98	81	84
	F	100	92	102	109
(a) Railway clerks	M	100	94	71	76
(b) Industrial clerks	M	100	..	94	98
	F	100	..	119	128
(c) Bank clerks	M	100	125	102	96
	F	100	92	77	74
(d) Civil-service clerks	M	100	86	50	52
	F	100	90	72	82

last few years, the average annual earnings of all the male white-collar groups relative to those of all male manual workers declined between 1922–4 and 1960 by amounts ranging from 2 per cent for industrial clerks to 48 per cent for civil-service clerks. During the same period, the earnings of fore-women, female industrial clerks, and female clerks as a whole relative to the earnings of all female manual workers increased by 6 per cent, 28 per cent,

[1] Ibid.

and 9 per cent respectively. But the relative earnings of female clerks in the civil service, female lower professionals and technicians, and female bank clerks declined by 18 per cent, 23 per cent, and 26 per cent respectively.

The narrowing of the white-collar manual earnings differential has been one of the most striking changes in pay structure during the twentieth century. Perhaps not surprisingly, therefore, many scholars,[1] as well as almost all the union and management officials interviewed during the course of this study, have claimed that this has been a major factor encouraging white-collar workers to join trade unions.

But the empirical evidence does not support this argument. White-collar workers whose earnings relative to those of manual workers have declined the most are not necessarily those who have been most ready to join trade unions. It is true that groups such as male and female civil-service clerks whose relative earnings have been reduced very greatly between 1922–4 and 1960 (see Table 5.2) are unionized very highly, and that other groups such as male and female industrial clerks whose relative earnings have deteriorated very little or even improved are unionized very poorly. But the reverse is equally true: the relative earnings of male laboratory technicians and chemists have been eroded very seriously and yet they are organized very poorly while the relative earnings of male bank clerks have been reduced very little and yet they are organized quite highly.

Nor does there appear to be any relationship between the absolute level of white-collar workers' earnings and the degree to which these workers are unionized. As can be seen from Table 5.1, draughtsmen are better paid than male clerks, yet the former are unionized much more highly than the latter. Male and female bank clerks, male railway clerks, and female civil-service clerks earn more than their opposite numbers in industry, yet industrial clerks are the most poorly organized clerical group. The lowest paid white-collar workers, like the lowest paid manual workers, are not generally among the most highly unionized.

Data on the earnings of white-collar workers are also available for the various manufacturing industries. The Ministry of Labour has been computing the average earnings of male and female weekly paid and monthly paid white-collar workers in manufacturing industries since 1959, and roughly comparable data can be obtained from Board of Trade sources from 1954 onwards. In addition, both the Ministry of Labour and the Board of Trade collect similar series on the earnings of manual workers. The figures are not given in sufficient detail to allow any conclusions to be drawn

---

[1] See, for example, G. D. H. Cole, 'Non-Manual Trade Unionism', *North American Review*, ccxv (January 1922), pp. 38–9; F. D. Klingender, *The Condition of Clerical Labour in Britain* (London: Martin Lawrence, 1935), *passim*; B. C. Roberts, *Trade Unions in a Free Society* (2nd ed.; London: Institute of Economic Affairs, 1962), p. 109; and E. M. Kassalow, 'White-Collar Unionism in Western Europe', *Monthly Labor Review*, lxxxvi (July 1963), p. 768.

regarding the absolute level of white-collar earnings prevailing in these industries.[1] But by employing the same methods as were used in the construction of Table 5.2, indices can be derived which give a fairly good idea of the change in white-collar earnings relative to the change in manual earnings in manufacturing industries between 1959–63 and 1954–63. These indices are given in Table 5.3.

As can be seen by comparing Tables 3.8 and 5.3, there is no obvious relationship between the degree to which white-collar workers in manufacturing industries have been unionized and the extent to which the differential between their earnings and those of manual workers has been narrowed. For example, the average annual earnings of all white-collar workers relative to the average annual earnings of all manual workers in other manufacturing industries; leather, leather goods, and fur; and clothing and footwear have increased between 1959 and 1963 and these are industries in which white-collar workers are very poorly unionized. But the relative earnings of all white-collar workers in metal manufacture and paper, printing, and publishing also have increased between 1959 and 1963 and these are industries in which the density of white-collar unionism is relatively high. Similarly, white-collar workers in shipbuilding and marine engineering are organized fairly well and their earnings have decreased relative to those of manual workers. But so have the earnings of white-collar workers in food, drink, and tobacco; timber and furniture; and chemicals; yet these workers are very poorly organized.

It is difficult, however, to discover the exact nature of the relationship between the pattern of unionization among white-collar workers in manufacturing industries and their pattern of relative earnings merely by a visual comparison of Tables 3.8 and 5.3. This can most easily be accomplished by undertaking a simple regression analysis. Consequently, each column of Table 3.8 was regressed on each row of Table 5.3.[2] The results of this regression analysis support the conclusion suggested by the visual assessment. The density of unionism among white-collar workers in manufacturing industries did not correlate significantly with the degree to which the differential between their earnings and those of manual workers had been reduced.[3]

[1] Since the proportion of white-collar employees in the various occupational and age-groups varies considerably by industry, the over-all averages given by the Ministry of Labour and the Board of Trade can not be used to compare the absolute level of earnings in one industry with another.

[2] Foremen were omitted from this analysis because the data presented in Table 5.3 excludes the earnings of all foremen except works foremen.

[3] Too many regressions were undertaken to give the results here in any detail. But well over 90 per cent of the correlation coefficients were very much below the figure required for significance at the 5 per cent level. Of those few which were significant, several possessed the wrong sign. That is, they had a positive sign, indicating that instead of the density of white-collar unionism being high where the white-collar/manual earnings differential had been narrowed the most, density was high where the differential had been narrowed the least. Scatter diagrams revealed that the remaining significant correlation coefficients were

TABLE 5.3

The Change in the Average Annual Earnings of White-Collar Workers Relative to the Change in the Average Annual Earnings of Manual Workers in Manufacturing Industries in the United Kingdom, 1959–63 (1959 = 100) and 1954–63 (1954 = 100)

Industry	1959–63							1954–63
	Males			Females			All	All
	Weekly paid	Monthly paid	Weekly and monthly paid	Weekly paid	Monthly paid	Weekly and monthly paid	Weekly and monthly paid	Weekly and monthly paid
Food, drink, and tobacco	93·5	89·9	95·8	96·5	93·5	100·3	96·8	89·2
Chemicals and allied	92·2	92·6	96·4	101·0	96·4	101·8	97·9	91·7
Metal manufacture	99·1	93·2	100·7	101·8	97·9	103·3	101·8	92·0
Metal N.E.S.	97·1	94·7	99·7	102·1	99·5	103·1	100·1	87·5
Engineering and electrical goods	98·1	96·6	102·3	104·0	102·7	105·9	104·5	100·8
Shipbuilding and marine engineering	95·6	85·9	96·0	91·8	89·8	92·2	95·6	97·9
Vehicles	98·8	98·0	103·4	99·6	89·9	100·4	103·9	94·5
Textiles	93·9	93·8	98·0	99·9	99·5	101·4	97·3	81·9
Leather, leather goods, and fur	102·0	96·5	103·7	102·7	96·5	102·8	101·9	86·5
Clothing and footwear	99·5	95·3	103·1	99·2	98·6	101·4	105·1	87·5
Bricks, pottery, glass, cement, etc.	90·9	90·8	95·8	98·4	98·3	101·6	96·7	86·9
Timber and furniture	93·1	95·8	99·4	99·3	94·4	99·2	97·1	83·0
Paper, printing, and publishing	99·8	95·1	103·3	101·9	98·1	104·6	104·2	85·9
Other manufacturing	97·0	97·3	99·7	96·4	100·4	98·4	101·4	87·5

Of course, the absence of significant correlation coefficients between the change in relative earnings of white-collar workers in manufacturing industries and the degree to which these workers are unionized does not necessarily 'prove' that a relationship between these two variables does not, in fact, exist. The above analysis contains too many statistical and methodological shortcomings to allow such a definite conclusion to be drawn.

The white-collar earnings statistics are of limited value. They are not exactly comparable with the union density figures for they exclude the earnings of all foremen except works foremen but include those of all managers and directors except those paid by fee only. This obviously causes the white-collar earnings to be higher than they otherwise would, and, more important, it may also affect the rate of change of these figures. In addition, these figures are averages for industries as a whole and give no information about the dispersion of earnings, earnings in particular occupations within each industry, or variations in earnings according to skill and age. While the figures are nevertheless of some use for the purpose at hand—to give a general indication of the change in white-collar earnings relative to the change in manual earnings—they would be even more useful and allow firmer conclusions to be drawn if they were given in greater detail.

Even if this analysis were free of these statistical difficulties, it would still be characterized by methodological shortcomings. Although there does not seem to be any relationship between the *change* in relative white-collar earnings and the *absolute* level of white-collar unionism, there might be a significant relationship between the *change* in relative white-collar earnings and the *change* in the level of white-collar unionism. Unfortunately, detailed figures on the density of white-collar unionism exist only for the year 1964, and it is thus impossible to calculate the change in union density in particular industries over time. It seems most improbable, however, that the trend of white-collar union density over the course of the twentieth century has followed faithfully that of relative white-collar earnings.

There is also the possibility that earnings and density of unionization may be mutually dependent variables. That is, not only may earnings influence the density of unionization, but the density of unionization may also influence earnings. If this is the case, then the nature of the relationship between them could be ascertained only by the construction of a simultaneous model.[1] In view of the limitations of the earnings data, the returns from building such a model probably would not justify the effort involved, and,

---

affected by one or two 'outliers'. That is, a very large proportion of the variance was caused by one or two points, and hence any regression line passing near them inevitably produces a very high correlation.

[1] That is, by simultaneously solving two equations: one in which the density of white-collar unionism is a function of the change in relative white-collar earnings and other variables, and another in which the change in relative white-collar earnings is a function of the density of white-collar unionism and other variables.

consequently, it has not been attempted. In any case, if there is some inter-dependence between these two variables, it would not seem to be very strong. The increase in white-collar earnings between 1948 and 1964 has been con-siderable; yet, as Chapter III demonstrated, the density of white-collar unionism held more or less constant during this period.

Thus the empirical evidence and analysis only suggest that there is no relationship between white-collar unionism and relative earnings; it does not prove this. But there are other reasons for believing that the narrowing of the white-collar/manual earnings differential has not been a major factor en-couraging white-collar workers to join trade unions.

To begin with, whether or not it can even be said that the earnings differ-ential has generally been narrowed depends upon the time period chosen. If the baseline is taken as 1922–4 or even 1935–6, it can be demonstrated (see Table 5.2) that the relative earnings of most white-collar groups have been reduced.[1] But if 1955 is taken as the baseline, it is obvious from Table 5.2 that the relative earnings of most white-collar groups have increased. Data from the Central Statistical Office confirms this trend. It indicates that between 1948 and 1963 the average annual earnings of all manual workers increased by 137 per cent while those of white-collar workers increased by only 118 per cent. But during the period 1955–63 white-collar earnings in-creased by 55 per cent while manual earnings increased by only 48 per cent.[2]

The reduction in the relative earnings of white-collar workers has 'not occurred gradually, as a result of a general tendency, but suddenly, within short periods and owing to an extraordinary conjuncture of circumstances'.[3] It was primarily during and immediately after the Second World War that the relative pay of white-collar workers was reduced; during the latter part of the post-war period, relative white-collar pay has tended to increase. Hence it is only by the standards of pre-war Britain that most white-collar workers can be said to have lost ground to manual workers. But 1938 is a long way off, and it is unlikely that most present-day white-collar workers know how their relative earnings of today compare with their relative earnings before the war, or, more exactly in view of the large proportion of white-collar workers who are now under thirty years of age,[4] how their relative earnings of today compare with those of the individuals who were filling their posts before the war. They are much more likely to know how their present

[1] The relative earnings of most white-collar workers probably were higher between 1922 and 1936 than at any other time during the period 1906–60. See Guy Routh, *Occupation and Pay in Great Britain 1906–60* (Cambridge: Cambridge University Press, 1965), chap. 2, especially table 48.

[2] Computed from unpublished data supplied by the Central Statistical Office. Ministry of Labour data is available for the period 1955–63 and agrees with that from the CSO. It indicates that white-collar earnings increased by 55·8 per cent while average weekly manual earnings increased by 48·9 per cent. See *Statistics on Incomes, Prices, Employment and Production*, No. 20 (March 1967), p. 8, table B.1.

[3] Routh, op. cit., p. x.   [4] See *supra*, pp. 46–7.

economic position compares with that of 1955 or later. If this is so, then the very phenomenon which so many people have relied upon to explain the growth of white-collar unionism in the post-war period—the narrowing of the white-collar/manual earnings differential—has, in fact, not even occurred.

Of course, while the relative earnings of most white-collar groups have increased over the past decade, those of some white-collar groups have not. But this does not mean that the relative earnings of all or even most of the individual workers within these groups also have fallen. Manual workers generally reach their final grade early in life, quickly rise to a peak of earnings within this grade, and then earn less towards retiring age.[1] White-collar workers, on the other hand, take much longer to reach their final grade,[2] and, even after they have reached it, their earnings are likely to increase right up to retirement because of the practice of awarding them annual increments based on age or length of service. Thus even when the relative earnings of a white-collar group are falling, those of individual white-collar workers within this group may be increasing because of promotion and age or length of service increments. For example, between 1947 and 1960 the average annual earnings of Civil Service Executive Officers as a class, as measured by the average of their pay scale, increased by only 97 per cent. But by 1960 the average annual earnings of an individual Civil Service Executive Officer who started working in 1947 at the age of eighteen would have increased by 362 per cent, even if he had not been promoted to a higher grade.[3] This is a rate of increase which few manual workers could match. Most white-collar workers, unlike their manual colleagues, are fortunate in possessing a number of escape routes from the 'tyranny of the "rate for the job"'.[4]

Although the number of white-collar workers whose earnings have been reduced relative to those of manual workers has been grossly exaggerated, there are no doubt some white-collar workers who have lost ground. There are probably also other white-collar workers who, whatever the realities of the situation, believe that their relative earnings have been reduced. But even granted this, it does not necessarily follow that these workers will respond by joining trade unions.

[1] For unskilled labourers the peak seems to be around age 30, and the drop in earnings from then to age 55–64 averages 15–20 per cent. For skilled men the peak is often around age 40 and the drop much smaller, around 10–15 per cent. See M. P. Fogarty, 'The White-Collar Pay Structure in Britain', *Economic Journal*, lxix (March 1959), p. 57. There are exceptions to this, notably in the steel industry, where a manual worker's earnings will increase markedly as a result of promotion within the range of manual work (Runciman, op. cit., p. 47).

[2] Male clerks, for example, seem most often to reach it about age 35–44 (Fogarty, loc. cit.).

[3] Computed from data provided in Guy Routh, 'Future Trade Union Membership', *Industrial Relations: Contemporary Problems and Perspectives*, B. C. Roberts, editor (London: Methuen, 1962), p. 67, table 2.

[4] Ibid., p. 65.

Those who have argued this have assumed that the more white-collar workers are proletarianized in terms of income, the more likely they are to follow the proletarian's example and join trade unions in order to improve or at least maintain their economic position. But an equally plausible assumption is that as white-collar workers become increasingly identified with manual workers in economic terms, they may react by emphasizing even more strongly those ways in which they are still different and upon which a claim to special prestige may be based.[1] One way of doing this is by refusing to join those organizations which have been reserved largely for manual workers—trade unions.

A similar point has been made by Runciman.[2] He has argued that workers may react to a relative deprivation of earnings primarily in one of two ways —'egoistically' or 'fraternalistically'. Egoists have no sense of common cause with others in a like situation; they want to 'better themselves', even at the expense of the group. Fraternalists, on the other hand, want to better their own situation by improving that of the group to which they belong. Runciman's research led him to conclude that the relative deprivation felt by most manual workers is likely to be 'fraternalistic' while that felt by most white-collar workers is likely to be 'egoistic'. If he is correct, then few white-collar workers are going to join trade unions simply because they have suffered a relative deprivation of earnings.

The response of white-collar workers to unions will also be influenced by whether they see management or unions as the cause of their relative disadvantage. Is management at fault for being insensitive to the needs and aspirations of white-collar employees and unappreciative of the contribution which they feel they make to the company's success? Or, are the unions at fault for forcing management to give part of the white-collar employee's share of the firm's earnings to manual workers? Those white-collar workers who adopt the latter interpretation of events may refuse to embrace those organizations which they see as being responsible for their predicament.

It must be remembered also that it is not at all certain that white-collar workers take manual workers as their comparative reference group on questions of earnings. At least those who have so claimed have offered little or no evidence in support of their contention. Besides, there is some evidence to the contrary. Runciman's research suggests that the reference group comparisons of most workers on economic matters have been and still are very much restricted: most manual workers compare themselves to other manual workers while most white-collar workers compare themselves to other white-collar workers.[3] If this is generally true, then most white-collar workers will not feel relatively deprived because their earnings have been

[1] See *supra*, p. 50.
[2] Op. cit., especially pp. 32–5 and 50.
[3] Ibid., chap. 4, and also pp. 192–208; see especially p. 196, table 20.

reduced relative to those of manual workers, and they are unlikely to join trade unions as a result.

If most white-collar workers do judge their earnings as satisfactory or unsatisfactory by comparison with those of other white-collar workers, it does not seem that those whose earnings compare least favourably are those who are most likely to join a union. Table 5.4 shows the change in earnings of white-collar workers in each manufacturing industry relative to the change in earnings of white-collar workers in the economy as a whole between 1959 and 1963. It is obvious that white-collar workers in almost every manufacturing industry have fared worse in terms of earnings than white-collar workers in most other sectors of the economy. Yet, as Chapter III made clear, white-collar workers in manufacturing industries are the most poorly unionized of all white-collar groups.

Nor does there appear to be any relationship within the manufacturing sector itself between the pattern of unionization of white-collar workers and the extent to which their earnings have been reduced relative to those of white-collar workers as a whole. A simple regression analysis, similar to that undertaken on Tables 3.8 and 5.3, was carried out on Tables 3.8 and 5.4. The result was much the same. The degree of unionism among white-collar workers in manufacturing industries generally was not significantly correlated with the extent to which the differential between their earnings and those of white-collar workers as a whole had been narrowed.[1]

The empirical evidence and analysis presented in the preceding pages suggests a twofold conclusion: white-collar workers have less reason to be dissatisfied with their salaries than is generally imagined, and even those who are unhappy will not necessarily respond by joining a trade union. The findings of several attitude surveys among white-collar workers support this conclusion.[2] Dale found that only 26 per cent of the 208 male industrial

[1] Once again, the overwhelming majority of the correlation coefficients were very much below the figure required for significance at the 5 per cent level. In fact, the only correlation coefficients which were significant at this level were those produced by regressing: (a) the density of unionization among draughtsmen on the change in the relative earnings of monthly paid, weekly paid, and monthly and weekly paid females, and (b) the density of unionization among other technicians on the change in the relative earnings of weekly paid males.

It is most surprising that there should be any relationship between female relative earnings and the degree of unionization among draughtsmen since less than 2 per cent of this occupational category are female, and it can only be assumed that the high correlation produced by (a) was the result of chance factors. The significant correlation coefficient produced by (b) cannot be dispensed with by such *a priori* considerations. But even if this correlation coefficient does indicate a significant relationship—and, in view of the statistical and methodological difficulties associated with the analysis, it would be unwise to draw such a firm conclusion—this particular case certainly does not provide the basis for a general argument that those white-collar workers whose earnings have been most seriously eroded relative to those of white-collar workers as a whole are those workers who are most likely to join trade unions.

[2] The findings of these surveys should be treated with caution not only because the

TABLE 5.4

The Change in the Average Annual Earnings of White-Collar Workers in Manufacturing Industries Relative to the Change in the Average Annual Earnings of White-Collar Workers in the Economy as a Whole in the United Kingdom, 1959–63 (1959 = 100)

Industry	Males			Females			All
	Weekly paid	Monthly paid	Weekly and monthly paid	Weekly paid	Monthly paid	Weekly and monthly paid	Weekly and monthly paid
Food, drink, and tobacco	96·4	92·7	98·8	94·4	91·4	98·1	98·1
Chemicals and allied	94·6	95·0	98·9	97·4	93·0	98·2	99·3
Metal manufacture	94·3	88·7	95·9	93·6	90·1	95·1	96·4
Metal N.E.S.	94·6	92·2	97·1	95·9	93·5	96·9	97·7
Engineering and electrical goods	94·6	93·1	98·6	94·8	93·6	96·6	98·8
Shipbuilding and marine engineering	93·8	84·3	94·2	88·9	86·9	89·3	93·4
Vehicles	95·8	95·0	100·2	93·9	84·8	94·8	100·2
Textiles	93·8	93·6	97·8	95·2	94·8	96·6	96·4
Leather, leather goods, and fur	100·0	94·7	101·7	97·1	91·2	97·2	98·4
Clothing and footwear	97·4	93·3	100·9	94·5	93·9	96·5	99·0
Bricks, pottery, glass, cement, etc.	92·5	92·5	97·6	95·6	95·4	98·6	98·4
Timber and furniture	92·4	95·1	98·7	97·2	92·4	97·1	96·6
Paper, printing, and publishing	96·7	92·1	100·1	95·4	91·8	97·9	100·2
Other manufacturing	96·4	96·8	99·1	92·7	96·6	94·7	100·2

clerks he interviewed considered the salary they received was not a 'fair' one.[1] Prandy found that only 30 per cent of his sample of 44 engineers and 40 per cent of his sample of 49 AScW members expressed any dissatisfaction with their salaries.[2] He also found that only 17 per cent of his sample of 286 metallurgists were dissatisfied with their salaries by comparison with those of other groups, and that the figure fell to 11 per cent when they compared their salaries with those of other metallurgists.[3] When Phillipson asked the 112 union members in his sample of clerks and technicians their reasons for membership, only 13 per cent of the answers he received specifically concerned salaries.[4] Similarly, when Prandy asked his sample of 49 AScW members their reasons for joining the union, none specifically mentioned dissatisfaction with salaries or other terms and conditions of employment.[5] In short, neither macro- nor micro-analysis reveals any significant connection between white-collar unionization and salaries.

OTHER TERMS AND CONDITIONS
OF EMPLOYMENT

Not only have white-collar workers generally earned more than manual workers, but they have also enjoyed a privileged position with respect to other terms and conditions of employment. Writing in 1916, the editor of *The Clerk* noted that 'although by reason of their unorganized state, clerks suffer many economic disabilities, yet they have a great many economic advantages not enjoyed by manual workers'. Among them he cited 'permanency of employment, periodical increases of salary, payment of salary during sickness and holidays, comparatively reasonable hours of work, and in certain sections superannuation'.[6] Writing in 1965, a journalist was still able to report that most 'office staff get longer holidays, better pensions and better sickness pay, work shorter hours and have longer notice than their fellows in the factories'. He also observed that the 'two groups come to work through different gates, park their cars in separate places, eat in separate places and excrete in separate places'.[7]

samples are small and something less than random, but also because they fail to control for other variables which might influence white-collar workers' attitudes towards trade unions. See *supra*, p. 45.

[1] J. R. Dale, *The Clerk in Industry* (Liverpool: Liverpool University Press, 1962), pp. 23–4, table 13.

[2] K. Prandy, *Professional Employees: A Study of Scientists and Engineers* (London: Faber, 1965), p. 115, table 3, and p. 164.

[3] Ibid., p. 97, table 5.

[4] C. M. Phillipson, 'A Study of the Attitudes Towards and Participation in Trade Union Activities of Selected Groups of Non-Manual Workers' (unpublished M.A. thesis, University of Nottingham, 1964), pp. 223–4, table 18.

[5] Op. cit., p. 160, table 2.

[6] Cited by David Lockwood, *The Blackcoated Worker* (London: Allen & Unwin, 1958), p. 40.

[7] Jeremy Bugler, 'Shopfloor Struggle for Status', *New Society* (25 November 1965), p. 19.

Manual workers may have been able to narrow the differential between their earnings and those of white-collar workers and, in some cases, even reverse it in their own favour, but they have been obliged to work a longer day and a longer year in order to do so. Although the hours worked by manual workers have declined, they were still averaging over 44 hours a week in 1966[1] compared with roughly 37½ for white-collar workers.[2] White-collar workers had grown accustomed to holidays with pay, mostly of a fortnight, long before the First World War,[3] but holidays with pay for manual workers, usually of a week's duration, were only generally introduced towards the end of the inter-war period.[4] Since then, holiday entitlement has increased for both groups of employees, but manual workers still tend to lag behind. A study undertaken in the early 1960s found that manual workers were the 'least favoured group' in 67 per cent of the firms studied and that the maximum holiday granted to any manual worker was still only two weeks in over 46 per cent of the firms. In contrast, a maximum of two weeks for white-collar workers was found in only 13 per cent of the firms.[5] It is also unusual for manual workers to be paid for any time off for domestic reasons. A survey in 1965 by the Industrial Society of 180 of its member-firms indicated that only 27 per cent of them granted paid leave of absence for reasons other than sickness to manual workers, but 65 per cent extended this facility to white-collar employees.[6]

Another way in which white-collar and manual workers traditionally have differed is in terms of method of payment. Manual workers have generally

[1] *Statistics on Incomes, Prices, Employment and Production*, No. 20 (March 1967), p. 66, table D.1.

[2] *Status and Benefits in Industry* (London: Industrial Society, 1966), p. 41, and Philip Marsh, 'Recent Developments in Office Staff Practices', *Office Management* (Spring 1966), p. 40.

[3] For example, an inquiry among typists in 1906 found that holidays were a grievance 'as only a fortnight is normally allowed and paid for'. See B. L. Hutchins, 'An Enquiry Into the Salaries and Hours of Work of Typists and Shorthand Writers', *Economic Journal*, xvi (September 1906), p. 449.

[4] G. L. Cameron, 'The Growth of Holidays with Pay in Britain', *Fringe Benefits, Labour Costs and Social Security*, G. L. Reid and D. J. Robertson, editors (London: Allen & Unwin, 1965), pp. 273–85.

[5] *Holidays: Current Practice and Trends* (London: Industrial Welfare Society, 1963), pp. 18, 4, and 6.

[6] *Status and Benefits in Industry*, op. cit., p. 44. This study is one of the few comprehensive and up-to-date sources of information on both manual and white-collar 'fringe benefits'. It is thus extremely useful. But its findings should be treated with some caution as the sample is almost certainly biased towards the practice in 'better' firms. For instance, 84 per cent of manual employees covered by the sample firms were included in a pension scheme, compared with 45 per cent of all manual workers as shown by the Government Actuary's 1965 inquiry (*infra*, p. 66). There was also a higher coverage of manual workers by sickpay schemes among the sample firms than shown in the Ministry of Labour's inquiry of 1961 (*infra*, pp. 66–7). A great deal of information on the pay and conditions of manual and white-collar workers in engineering is contained in the National Board for Prices and Incomes' Report No. 49 and its supplement. See Cmnd. 3495 and 3495–I.

been paid a fluctuating wage at weekly intervals which is based at least partly on the number of hours worked. White-collar workers, on the other hand, have generally received a fixed salary at monthly intervals. Related to this, manual workers have been required to record the number of hours worked by clocking in and out, have been paid for overtime, and have generally received one week's notice, while white-collar workers have not been required to clock in and out, have not been paid overtime, and have generally received one month's notice.

Recently, however, there has been a tendency to reduce the differences between the two groups of workers in some of these respects. The Industrial Society found that although most of the firms in its sample still pay their manual employees a fluctuating wage based on payment-by-results systems, a considerable proportion (30 per cent) now pay them a standard salary.[1] A weekly pay interval is now the usual practice for both groups of employees, with all the sample firms following this practice for manual workers and 81 per cent following it for white-collar workers.[2] An example of the levelling-up process working in reverse is given by practice in respect of payment for overtime: 72 per cent of the firms in the Industrial Society's sample now pay their white-collar employees for overtime (as compared with 99 per cent for manuals) while the remainder give them time off in lieu.[3] In spite of the passing of the Contracts of Employment Act in 1963, white-collar workers still appear to be better provided for than manual workers. As a result of the Act, both groups of workers can now claim one, two, or four weeks' notice depending solely upon the number of years of continuous service with their employer. But the Industrial Society found that while notice of termination for manual workers was limited to the provisions of the Act in 76 per cent of the sample firms, this was true for white-collar employees in only 54 per cent of the firms.[4] In regard to clocking, the traditional pattern has been maintained. Only 33 per cent of the Industrial Society's sample firms used this method for recording the attendances of white-collar employees, but 93 per cent still used it for manual employees. Moreover, in 96 per cent of the firms manual employees forfeit payment when late while in only 11 per cent of the firms do white-collar employees do likewise.[5]

[1] Ibid., pp. 41–2. Only 2 of the 180 companies paid their white-collar employees a fluctuating wage.

[2] Ibid., p. 42. A survey by the Institute of Office Management in 1965 of 485 firms employing 108,380 office workers also found that roughly 80 per cent of the establishments paid their clerical employees by the week (Marsh, op. cit., p. 38).

[3] Loc. cit.   [4] Op. cit., p. 43.

[5] Ibid., pp. 42–3. Of course, many of the firms used other methods for recording the attendances of white-collar employees. While only 33 per cent used clocking, 16 per cent used signature books and 11 per cent used recording by officials. But in 46 per cent of the firms there was no recording at all for staff employees. The Institute of Office Management survey (Marsh, op. cit., p. 44) supports this: only 50 per cent of the firms in its sample maintained time-keeping records for staff employees in 1965 (as compared with 76 per cent in 1952).

White-collar workers have been, and continue to be, better placed for retirement than manual workers, although the latter are catching up in this respect. The surveys by the Government Actuary, some of the results of which are presented in Table 5.5, show that although pension coverage for manual workers is increasing more quickly than for white-collar workers, the gap remains wide. Not only are manual workers at a quantitative disadvantage in terms of pensions, they are also at a qualitative disadvantage. The Industrial Society survey shows that in only 37 per cent of the firms in which pension schemes were provided for both manual and white-collar workers were the provisions the same for both groups, with a strong presumption that they were less favourable for manual workers.[1] In addition, Carr-Saunders and his colleagues have noted that whereas many pension schemes for white-collar workers are based on a capital payment and a pension tied to peak earnings, arrangements for manual workers are generally based on length of service only.[2]

TABLE 5.5

Proportion of Employees in Private Industry in the United Kingdom Covered by Occupational Pension Schemes, 1956 and 1963

	1956	1963
White-collar employees		
Male	71	80
Female	34	40
Manual employees		
Male	38	55
Female	23	15[a]

[a] The proportion of women manual workers covered by occupational pension schemes has fallen, presumably as a result of the introduction of the National Insurance Graduated Pension Scheme.

In line with general trends, an increasing number of sick-pay schemes are being made available to manual workers, not only by individual employers but also by the state.[3] But manual workers are still at a disadvantage in this respect compared with white-collar workers. A survey by the Ministry of Labour in 1961 revealed that 86 per cent of white-collar workers in private industry were covered by sick-pay schemes compared with 33 per cent of manual workers.[4] There was also data which showed that the amount of pay and the length of time for which it was made available for manual workers are less than for white-collar workers. This is supported by data from the

[1] Op. cit., p. 43.

[2] A. M. Carr-Saunders *et al.*, *A Survey of Social Conditions in England and Wales as Illustrated by Statistics* (Oxford: Oxford University Press, 1958), p. 198.

[3] A state earnings-related sick-pay scheme came into effect in October 1966 and applies equally to both manual and white-collar workers.

[4] *Sick Pay Schemes: A Report* (London: HMSO, 1964), p. 5, table A. See also G. L. Reid, 'Sick Pay', *Fringe Benefits, Labour Costs and Social Security*, op. cit., pp. 218–22.

Industrial Society's survey. Although 69 per cent of the sample firms provided sick-pay schemes for their manual employees, the benefits provided were the same as those for white-collar employees in only 21 per cent of these firms.[1]

Differences between white-collar and manual workers are also being reduced in respect of so-called 'company welfare benefits'—canteens, playing-fields, social clubs, and the like. Ninety-four per cent of the firms in the Industrial Society's sample provided canteen facilities for both manual and white-collar employees, and in the majority of these firms (60 per cent) facilities were the same for both groups. Similarly, 83 per cent of the firms provided recreational facilities, and in every case manual and white-collar workers shared the same facilities.[2]

Two conclusions emerge fairly clearly from the information which has been presented on white-collar fringe benefits. First, white-collar workers have, and continue to enjoy, a privileged position compared with manual workers. Second, the white-collar workers' relative advantage has dwindled somewhat during the post-war period. There is every likelihood that their relative advantage will be reduced even further, as the social trend in industry is against the maintenance of these differentials. What impact this has had and is likely to have in the future on white-collar unionism, it is difficult to say with any exactness. But for similar reasons to those advanced in respect of earnings,[3] it is very doubtful if either the absolute or relative level of white-collar fringe benefits is an important factor in explaining the pattern of white-collar unionism in this country. This conclusion is strengthened when it is remembered that fringe benefits, unlike earnings, tend to be very similar for most white-collar occupations within a given industry. They are, therefore, unlikely to explain a phenomenon such as white-collar unionism which shows considerable occupational variation even within a particular industry.

EMPLOYMENT SECURITY

Lockwood has argued that security of employment 'was perhaps the most significant difference between manual and non-manual work, for, although it fell short of the full independence which comes with property, job-security did constitute a partial alternative to ownership, conferring on the clerk a relative immunity from those hazards of the labour market which were the lot of the working classes'.[4] Most people would agree with him. Indeed, the security of white-collar employment was its major attraction in the eyes of manual workers. 'If,' commented the Pilgrim Trust investigators in 1938, 'working men and women seem to be unduly anxious to make their sons and

[1] Loc. cit.
[2] Ibid., p. 44. See also A. G. P. Elliott, 'Company Welfare Benefits', *Fringe Benefits, Labour Costs and Social Security*, op. cit., pp. 300–12.
[3] See *supra*, pp. 58–63.   [4] Op. cit., p. 204.

daughters into clerks, the anxiety behind it is not for more money but for greater security.'[1]

Prior to the First World War most white-collar workers could safely assume that they would be 'permanently employed, provided they were efficient and their character good'.[2] Even during the decades of the twenties and thirties when being out of work was the normal situation for a large proportion of the population, white-collar workers were less affected by unemployment than manual workers. Those on the railways as well as those in public service and banking[3] hardly suffered from unemployment at all. Those in private industry suffered somewhat, but even they were affected less seriously by unemployment than manual workers. Using data provided by the 1931 Census, Colin Clark has calculated that unemployment among male unskilled manual workers was 30·5 per cent and among skilled and semi-skilled manual workers 14·4 per cent, while that among shop assistants was 7·9 per cent, clerks and typists 5·5 per cent, professionals 5·5 per cent, and higher office workers 5·1 per cent.[4] Generally speaking, those higher in occupational status suffered less than those lower down.

While unemployment during the twenties and thirties was less among white-collar than among manual workers, it was nevertheless sufficiently high 'to destroy the traditional association of security and blackcoat employment'.[5] The General Secretary of the National Federation of Professional Workers estimated the total number of white-collar unemployed in 1934 at between 300 and 400 thousand.[6] Older and more senior white-collar workers were particularly hard hit. They often fell outside the National Insurance limit and were therefore ineligible for unemployment relief payments.[7] Older men also found it hardest to obtain another job and thus their period of unemployment was often of considerable duration. Even when they found another job, it was usually at work very much below their previous status and remuneration.[8] In short, although white-collar workers were not affected as badly by the depression as manual workers 'in bare quantitative terms', to quote Lockwood once again, 'they suffered as acutely as almost any other group due to the lack of communal provision for their plight and the conventional expectations of their position'.[9]

[1] Pilgrim Trust, *Men Without Work* (Cambridge: Cambridge University Press, 1938), p. 144.

[2] Memorandum submitted to the Royal Commission on Unemployment Insurance by Herbert Elvin, General Secretary of the CAWU, *The Clerk* (October 1931), p. 46, cited by Lockwood, op. cit., p. 56.

[3] Lockwood (ibid., p. 55) cites the *Bank Officer* (June 1932), p. 7, to the effect that in 1932 there were only twelve or fourteen bank clerks unemployed out of a total membership of 21,000.

[4] Colin Clark, *National Income and Outlay* (London: Macmillan, 1938), p. 46, table 19.

[5] Lockwood, op. cit., p. 57.

[6] Letter in *Manchester Guardian*, 25 April 1934, cited by Klingender, op. cit., p. 92.

[7] *Report of the Unemployment Insurance Statutory Committee on the Remuneration Limit for Insurance on Non-Manual Workers*, 1936.

[8] Klingender, op. cit., pp. 91–9, and Lockwood, op. cit., pp. 56–7.   [9] Ibid., p. 57.

What role the experiences of the twenties and thirties play in determining the behaviour of present-day white-collar workers, it is difficult to say. But it is probably small.[1] To have been affected by the unemployment of the thirties, never mind that of the twenties, a present-day worker would have to be over forty-five years of age, and few white-collar employees are. Only 28 per cent of clerks, 14 per cent of draughtsmen, and 15 per cent of laboratory technicians were over this age in 1961.[2] Most of today's white-collar workers were born during and after the Second World War, and they, like younger manual workers, do not share the fear of unemployment which overshadowed their parents.[3] Nor is there any reason why they should. For while the average annual unemployment rate between 1921 and 1939 was 13·9 per cent, that between 1946 and 1963 was only 1·9 per cent.[4] And most of this unemployment has been confined to manual workers.[5]

Given the relatively full employment conditions of the post-war period, white-collar workers can find new jobs fairly quickly even after a large-scale and geographically concentrated redundancy. Dorothy Wedderburn found that almost 50 per cent of the 1,000 white-collar workers made redundant by an aviation company in 1962 had secured other jobs even before their period of notice expired. Within two weeks of leaving, 70 per cent were working again, and 90 per cent had new jobs within six weeks of leaving.[6] The redundancy caused some hardship: the earnings of almost all the dismissed employees were lower in their new jobs, and many lost 'fringe benefits' such as pension rights. But the impact of the redundancy was softened by a system of *ex gratia* payments which averaged $3\frac{1}{2}$ to $4\frac{1}{2}$ weeks' pay for weekly staff and $3\frac{1}{2}$ to $4\frac{1}{2}$ months' pay for monthly staff. While it would be unwise to generalize too widely on the basis of a single case study, it at least indicates that the duration of white-collar unemployment may not always be as long and the hardship resulting from it may not be as great as is commonly believed.

[1] For a contrary view see W. D. Wood, 'An Analysis of Office Unionism in Canadian Manufacturing Industries' (unpublished Ph.D. thesis, Princeton University, 1959), p. 196.

[2] See *supra*, p. 46, table 4.2.

[3] For manual workers see N. Dennis, F. Henriques, and E. Slaughter, *Coal Is Our Life* (London: Eyre & Spottiswoode, 1956). For white-collar workers see Dale, op. cit., p. 20, table 10, and p. 84.

[4] *The British Economy: Key Statistics 1900–1966* (London: London & Cambridge Economic Service, 1967), p. 8, table E.

[5] Between September 1961, when the Ministry of Labour first began to segregate white-collar workers in the quarterly unemployment figures, and December 1963 the number of white-collar workers unemployed averaged only 19 per cent of total employment, although they composed roughly 36 per cent of the insured population. To look at it another way, the white-collar unemployment rate was roughly half the manual. See, for example, 'Occupational Analysis: Wholly Unemployed Adults and Unfilled Vacancies for Adults, December 1963', *Ministry of Labour Gazette*, lxxii (February 1964), pp. 66–7. The following occupational groups were counted as white-collar: clerical workers; shop assistants; and administrative, professional, and technical workers.

[6] Dorothy Wedderburn, *White-Collar Redundancy: A Case Study* (Cambridge: Cambridge University Press, 1964).

It has been suggested that white-collar workers are likely to be more affected by unemployment in the future than they have been in the past as a result of office automation, and that this will encourage them to seek job security through trade union membership.[1] But current research indicates that very few employees are discharged as a result of a computer installation. The most comprehensive survey of office automation undertaken in this country found that only 13 out of 331 organizations which had installed a computer discharged any staff as a result. In each case the employees discharged were few in number—averaging less than ten per installation—and were mostly married and part-time women workers.[2] This finding is supported by almost every detailed case study undertaken in this and several other industrialized countries.[3]

Nor is office automation likely to reduce greatly the over-all demand for office workers in the foreseeable future. The Ministry of Labour estimates that the net effect of office automation up to 1 January 1965 has been to reduce the total number of office jobs which otherwise would have been available by about three-quarters of 1 per cent. It goes on to predict that even by 1975 the number of additional office jobs being created will still outnumber those being eliminated, and concludes that the most probable effect of computers over the next decade will be to 'offer some relief to a growing shortage of office workers'.[4]

It might be argued that whatever the realities of the situation, white-collar workers will nevertheless fear that automation will make them redundant and join trade unions as a result. Unfortunately, the evidence available on white-collar workers' attitudes to automation is rather inconclusive. Some researchers report a considerable degree of anxiety and unrest while others are impressed by the equanimity with which office workers contemplate the change.[5]

[1] See, for example, the sources cited in *Effects of Mechanisation and Automation in Offices* (Geneva: ILO, 1959), p. 106; J. C. McDonald, *Impact and Implications of Office Automation* (Ottawa: Department of Labour, Economic and Research Branch, 1964), chap. 8; and G. M. Smith, *Office Automation and White-Collar Employment* (New Brunswick, N.J.: Rutgers University, Institute of Management and Labor Relations, Bulletin No. 6, 1959), pp. 19–20.

[2] Ministry of Labour, *Computers in Offices* (London: HMSO, 1965), p. 18.

[3] The literature on office automation is vast, but for a sample of the studies supporting this point see the following: R. B. Thomas, *Computers in Business* (Wednesbury: Staffordshire College of Commerce, 1964); Enid Mumford and Olive Banks, *The Computer and the Clerk* (London: Routledge & Kegan Paul, 1967); W. H. Scott, *Office Automation and the Non-Manual Worker* (Paris: OECD, 1962); Roy B. Helfgott, 'EDP and the Office Work Force', *Industrial and Labor Relations Review*, xix (July 1966), pp. 503–16; Ida R. Hoos, *Automation in the Office* (Washington: Public Affairs Press, 1961); Ida R. Hoos and B. L. Jones, 'Office Automation in Japan', *International Labour Review*, lxxxvii (June 1963), pp. 3–24; *Automation and Non-Manual Workers* (Geneva: ILO, 1967), pp. 99–100.

[4] Op. cit., pp. 7 and 42.

[5] See, for example, Thomas, op. cit., p. 36; Mumford and Banks, op. cit., pp. 196–9; and F. C. Mann and L. K. Williams, 'Some Effects of the Changing Work Environment in the Office', *Journal of Social Issues*, xviii (July 1962), pp. 90–101.

In any case, the purpose here is not to predict the future, but to explain the present. It may be uncertain whether office automation will cause unemployment and insecurity among white-collar employees in the future,[1] but it is clear that since the Second World War unemployment or insecurity among white-collar workers from this or any other cause has been negligible. Therefore, unemployment and the fear of unemployment cannot be considered important determinants of the existing pattern of white-collar unionism.

CONCLUSIONS

As white-collar workers have become more plentiful, they have played an increasingly important role in the social, political, and economic life of the nation. But, paradoxically, at the same time they have also become worth less in economic terms; their economic position relative to that of manual workers has become less favourable. White-collar workers have lost something, but only in the sense that the terms and conditions of employment to which they previously had an exclusive right are now being shared by other workers.

If this has left white-collar workers unhappy, it does not seem to have encouraged them to unionize. At least, it is not possible to demonstrate any connection between the economic position of various white-collar groups and the degree to which they are unionized. This does not mean that white-collar workers who join unions are not interested in higher salaries, better fringe benefits, and greater security. They obviously are. But then, so is almost everyone else including those white-collar workers who do not join trade unions. In fact, it may be just because these objectives are so widely appreciated and pursued, that the workers' economic position is not a differentiating factor with respect to their propensity to unionize. Whatever the reason, economic factors do not seem to offer an explanation for the occupational and industrial variations in the density of white-collar unionism in Britain. For this, attention must be directed to another aspect of the white-collar workers' environment—their work situation.

---

[1] The impact of office automation upon work techniques and conditions and the effect this might have on white-collar unionism is considered *infra*, pp. 82–4.

VI

THE WORK SITUATION

IN spite of the increased amount of leisure which has become available in modern society, for the majority of people work remains the most important aspect of adult life. Some sociologists have gone so far as to claim that 'work is not a part of life, it is literally life itself', and its impact 'is found in almost every aspect of living and even in the world of dreams and unconscious fantasies'.[1] Other sociologists have been more moderate in their statements, but nevertheless have seen experience at work as a pervasive influence on a person's life. In Lockwood's view, 'the most important social conditions shaping the psychology of the individual are those arising out of the organization of production, administration and distribution. In other words, the "work situation".'[2] Even economists have noted the importance of this factor. Alfred Marshall wrote that 'the business by which a person earns his livelihood generally fills his thoughts during by far the greater part of those hours in which his mind is at its best' and that 'during them his character is being formed by the way in which he uses his faculties in his work, by the thoughts and the feelings which it suggests, and by his relations to his associates in work, his employers or his employees'.[3]

Perhaps not surprisingly, therefore, social scientists have relied heavily upon this factor in analysing white-collar unionism. In explaining its growth they have isolated four aspects of the work situation as being particularly significant: the degree of employment concentration, opportunities for promotion, the degree of mechanization and automation, and proximity to unionized manual workers. Hence the following analysis will concentrate upon them.

EMPLOYMENT CONCENTRATION

There are several reasons why density of unionization is likely to be higher among larger rather than smaller groups of employees. To begin with, the larger the number of employees in a group the more necessary it becomes to administer them in a 'bureaucratic' fashion. In the present context the essential feature of bureaucratic administration 'is its emphasis on the office

---

[1] D. C. Miller and W. H. Form, *Industrial Sociology: An Introduction to the Sociology of Work Relations* (New York: Harper, 1951), p. 115.

[2] David Lockwood, *The Blackcoated Worker* (London: Allen & Unwin, 1958), p. 205.

[3] *Principles of Economics* (8th ed.; London: Macmillan, 1920), p. 1.

rather than upon the individual office-holder'.[1] This means that employees are treated not as individuals but as members of categories or groups. Their terms and conditions of employment as well as their promotion prospects are determined not by the personal considerations and sentiments of their managers but by formal rules which apply impersonally to all members of the group to which they belong. The result is that the group's working conditions tend to become standardized.[2]

'Bureaucratization' is the administrative answer to the problem of governing large numbers of employees. It makes for administrative efficiency in a business. But it is also likely to assist the growth of unionism. For, as Dubin has argued, making the rule for the work group rather than for the individual worker is likely to affect him in the following ways:

He becomes aware of his personal inability to make an individual 'deal' for himself outside the company rules and procedures, except under the circumstances of a 'lucky break'. He tends also to view himself as part of a group of similarly situated fellow-employees who are defined by the rules as being like each other. In addition, uniform rule-making and administration of the rules make unionism easier and, in a sense, inevitable. It should be reasonably clear that collective bargaining is joint rule-making. It is no great step to the joint determination by union and management of rules governing employment from the determination of them by management alone. Both proceed from the basic assumption that generally applicable rules are necessary to govern the relations between men in the plant. Once a worker accepts the need for general rules covering his own conduct, he is equally likely to consider the possibility of modifying the existing ones in his favor rather than to seek their total abolishment.[3]

Since the rules apply to him as a member of a group rather than as an individual, the most effective way of modifying them in his favour is by collective rather than individual bargaining.

But the greater degree of bureaucratization associated with larger groups of employees is not the only reason they are likely to be more highly unionized. Another reason is that trade unions tend to concentrate their recruiting efforts on such groups.[4] It is fairly obvious why they should do this. Larger groups of employees are probably more favourably disposed towards trade

---

[1] R. M. Blackburn and K. Prandy, 'White-Collar Unionization: A Conceptual Framework', *British Journal of Sociology*, xvi (June 1965), p. 117.

[2] The terms 'bureaucratic administration' and 'bureaucratization' have acquired a number of meanings in sociological writings. For a discussion of these see Richard H. Hall, 'The Concept of Bureaucracy: An Empirical Assessment', *American Journal of Sociology*, lxix (July 1963), pp. 32–40, and C. R. Hinings, *et al.*, 'An Approach to the Study of Bureaucracy', *Sociology*, i (January 1967), pp. 61–72. It is important to note that these terms are used in a very restricted sense throughout this study to refer simply to a method of administering the labour force.

[3] Robert Dubin, 'Decision-Making by Management in Industrial Relations', *Reader in Bureaucracy*, Robert K. Merton, *et al.*, editors (Glencoe, Ill.: The Free Press, 1952), p. 234.

[4] See *infra*, pp. 90–100 for a discussion of the policies followed by unions in recruiting members.

unionism because of the bureaucratic manner in which they are governed on the job, and they are therefore likely to be easier to recruit. They are also likely to be less expensive to recruit. Trade union recruiting is characterized by economies of scale: in general, the larger the group recruited the lower the *per capita* costs. Similarly, larger groups of members are less expensive for unions to administer: the larger the group the greater the probability that one or two of its members will possess the qualities required for leadership at the rank and file level, and the easier it is to police the collective agreement and ensure that its provisions are observed.[1] Moreover, collective agreements covering large groups of employees have a greater impact on the general level of salaries and conditions than a whole series of agreements covering small groups. Finally, the more members a union recruits the more power it is able to wield in negotiations with employers as well as within the labour movement.

This *a priori* reasoning tends to be supported by empirical evidence. In the United States, studies by the Bureau of Labor Statistics,[2] Cleland,[3] Meyers,[4] and Steele and McIntyre[5] have found a strong positive relationship between the size of establishments and the extent to which they are unionized. Studies in Norway,[6] Sweden,[7] Austria,[8] and Japan[9] indicate that the level of unionism is higher in larger than in smaller offices. In reviewing the extent and nature of white-collar unionism in eight countries, Sturmthal finds that its density is generally higher in the public than in the private sector of the economy, and concludes that this is primarily because public employees tend to be concentrated in large groups which are administered in a bureaucratic fashion.[10]

The argument is also supported by a wealth of evidence which Lockwood

---

[1] For example, when the Wages Council system was established, it was expected that it would promote the growth of voluntary collective bargaining. But this expectation has not been fulfilled largely because 'neither employers nor workers want to lose the services of the wages inspectorate in enforcing wage rates' in industries characterized by a large number of small firms. See Ministry of Labour, *Written Evidence*, p. 117.

[2] 'Extent of Collective Agreements in 17 Labor Markets, 1953–54', *Monthly Labor Review*, lxxviii (January 1955), p. 67.

[3] Sherrill Cleland, *The Influence of Plant Size on Industrial Relations* (Princeton, N.J.: Industrial Relations Section, Princeton University, 1955), pp. 14–21.

[4] Frederic Meyers, 'The Growth of Collective Bargaining in Texas—A Newly Industrialized Area', *Proceedings of the Industrial Relations Research Association*, ix (December 1956), p. 286.

[5] H. Ellsworth Steele and Sherwood C. McIntyre, 'Company Structure and Unionization', *The Journal of the Alabama Academy of Science* (January 1959), p. 38.

[6] Egil Fivelsdal, 'White-Collar Unions and the Norwegian Labor Movement', *Industrial Relations*, v (October 1965), p. 85 n. 7.

[7] Arne H. Nilstein, 'White-Collar Unionism in Sweden', *White-Collar Trade Unions*, Adolf Sturmthal, editor (Urbana: University of Illinois Press, 1966), pp. 275–6.

[8] Ernst Lakenbacker, 'White-Collar Unions in Austria', ibid., p. 53.

[9] Solomon B. Levine, 'Unionization of White-Collar Employees in Japan' ibid., pp. 222–3.

[10] Ibid., pp. 379–80.

has collected for Great Britain. He demonstrates that in the civil service, especially after the reorganization of 1920, 'a clear-cut classification of functions, qualifications, remuneration and criteria of advancement permitted a high degree of standardization of conditions throughout government departments . . . [and] . . . the resulting isolation of a clerical class, common to the service and made up of individuals whose chances of promotion were relatively small, provided the basis for the Civil Service Clerical Association'.[1] Similarly, he shows that in local government 'the growth of NALGO . . . has gone hand in hand with the subordination of local particularism in working conditions to a set of national standards common to the service'.[2] Conversely, he argues that the 'relatively small size of the office, the internal social fragmentation of the office staff through occupational, departmental and informal status distinctions, and the absence of any institutionalized blockage of mobility' characteristic of the private sector largely accounts for its low degree of clerical unionization.[3] He also establishes that the administration of banking is neither as bureaucratic as that of the public sector nor as paternalistic as that of private industry, and suggests that this explains why banking has an intermediate degree of clerical unionization. Other researchers have found that even the extent to which individual banks are unionized is partly accounted for by the extent to which their size forces them to administer their employees in a bureaucratic manner.[4]

If this line of reasoning is generally valid, then it should also help to account for the pattern of white-collar unionism in manufacturing industries in Britain. Fortunately, sufficient data is available to determine whether or not it does. Table 6.1 gives the average number of employees per establishment in each white-collar group for each manufacturing industry. These figures are the only readily available index of white-collar employment concentration in manufacturing industries, and hence they are extremely useful. But certain objections might be raised against using them to assess the validity of the argument being advanced here.

The degree of employment concentration would seem to be an accurate enough measure of the economies of scale characteristic of trade union recruitment and administration, but it might not adequately reflect the degree of bureaucratization which actually exists. An establishment may have relatively few white-collar employees yet administer them in a bureaucratic fashion, for it may be part of a much larger company with a centralized personnel policy. If this is the case, then regardless of how few employees there may be at a single establishment, they will probably be subject to company-wide grading schemes and salary structures, and, in general, their terms and conditions of employment will be determined by formal rules

[1] Op. cit., pp. 142–3.   [2] Ibid., p. 145.   [3] Ibid., p. 207.
[4] Blackburn and Prandy, op. cit., p. 118 n. 17.

TABLE 6.1

The Average Number of White-Collar Employees per Establishment in Great Britain by Industry and by Occupation

Occupational group	Food, drink, tobacco	Chemical	Metal manuf.	Metal N.E.S.	Eng. elect.	Ship. M.E.	Vehicles	Textiles	Leather, fur	Clothing, footwear	Bricks, etc.	Timber, furn., etc.	Paper, print, pub.	Other manuf.	All manuf.
1. Foremen	3·12	6·27	8·48	1·68	4·52	7·80	12·86	4·02	1·12	1·39	2·29	1·01	1·77	3·65	3·25
2. All scientists, technologists, technicians	0·81	12·06	6·82	0·95	10·45	5·98	22·62	1·38	0·19	0·26	1·26	0·22	0·49	2·24	3·57
(a) Scientists, technologists	0·30	4·79	1·72	0·15	2·21	0·45	3·05	0·35	0·07	0·02	0·34	0·01	0·16	0·61	0·82
(b) All technicians	0·51	7·27	5·10	0·80	8·23	5·53	19·57	1·02	0·11	0·24	0·92	0·21	0·33	1·63	2·76
(i) Draughtsmen	0·12	0·84	1·54	0·51	4·34	4·07	8·65	0·18	0·01	0·03	0·44	0·14	0·05	0·53	1·21
(ii) Other technicians	0·39	6·42	3·56	0·28	3·89	1·45	10·91	0·83	0·10	0·21	0·48	0·07	0·27	1·10	1·55
3. Clerks	9·13	20·75	20·52	5·27	18·34	7·97	44·46	6·00	2·87	3·39	5·47	2·77	8·63	10·11	9·92
4. Other white-collar workers	4·13	8·56	5·78	1·41	6·03	3·43	12·08	1·32	0·60	1·08	1·64	0·59	3·40	4·56	3·31
5. All white-collar workers	17·21	47·66	41·61	9·33	23·61	25·20	92·04	12·73	4·78	6·12	10·68	4·60	14·32	20·59	20·07

which apply impersonally throughout the company. But although these employment concentration figures may therefore understate the degree of bureaucratization, there is no evidence to suggest that the extent to which they do so varies significantly from one manufacturing industry to another. Thus this limitation of the figures does not greatly reduce their usefulness for the purposes of the following analysis.

Rather than understating the degree of bureaucratization, the employment concentration figures may actually overstate it. Blackburn and Prandy have suggested that private employers generally try to resist the pressures towards greater bureaucratization because of an 'ideological need' for loyalty from their employees. Bureaucratic administration is often tempered with a measure of 'administrative particularism' whereby each employee is treated as much as possible as an individual and not just as one of a group.[1] But the more workers a firm employs the more difficult it becomes to administer them in a 'particularistic' manner. For as Ingham has argued:

> In the absence of bureaucratic rules, effective coordination and control within an industrial organization requires a body of norms which are shared by both management and men . . . . small organizations, with a high degree of vertical inter-action, favour the development of these norms . . . large organizations inhibit such vertical interaction and therefore favour the use of bureaucratic rules in the problem of the administration of the labour force and its work. Such rules are, in this case, important in the 'remote control' of the organization which, by virtue of its size, is difficult to deal with in any other way.[2]

Thus although employers may be able to slow down the trend towards bureaucratization, the problems posed by governing large numbers of employees nevertheless tend to lead to bureaucratization. Hence it does not seem unreasonable to take the degree of employment concentration as a measure of bureaucratization.

Even granted this, the employment concentration figures still possess at least one other major limitation: they are expressed as averages and give no information about the dispersion of employment. Different occupational groups are likely to be distributed in different ways across the administrative hierarchy of a firm as well as across the various firms within an industry. For example, draughtsmen are generally concentrated in one or two departments within a firm, while clerks are usually dispersed among a number of different departments. Similarly, clerks are likely to be more evenly distributed across the various firms within an industry than are draughtsmen. Virtually all firms require at least a few clerks, but not all firms require draughtsmen. Thus the distribution of draughtsmen is probably skewed in the direction of larger work groups and larger firms, while that of clerks is

[1] Blackburn and Prandy, op. cit., pp. 117–18.
[2] Geoffrey K. Ingham, 'Organizational Size, Orientation to Work and Industrial Behaviour', *Sociology*, i (September 1967), pp. 243–4.

probably skewed in the direction of smaller work groups and smaller firms. But simply because the techniques of production dictate that in all industries clerks are more numerous than draughtsmen, the average number of clerks per firm is generally larger than the average number of draughtsmen. It would be wrong, however, to conclude that the employment of clerks is therefore more concentrated than that of draughtsmen. The reverse is undoubtedly true.

Fortunately, this limitation of the data can be overcome. If Table 6.1 is used for inter-industry as opposed to intra-industry or occupational comparisons, then the problem of different occupational dispersions does not arise. That is, it cannot be concluded that because the average number of clerks per establishment is greater than the average number of draughtsmen in, say, the vehicles industry, the employment of clerks in this industry is more concentrated than that of draughtsmen. But it does not seem unreasonable to conclude that because the average number of clerks per establishment is higher in vehicles than in metal manufacture, the employment of clerks is more concentrated in the former industry than in the latter.[1] Nor does it seem unreasonable, given the above argument, to expect to find for each white-collar group some relationship between the degree of employment concentration and the degree of white-collar unionism.

That there is at least some connection between employment concentration and the density of white-collar unionism in manufacturing industries can be seen simply by comparing each row of Table 3.8 with each row of Table 6.1. Many of the industries in which white-collar employment is most highly concentrated—vehicles, metal manufacture, shipbuilding and marine engineering, and engineering and electrical goods—are also those which have the highest density of white-collar unionism, while many of the industries in which white-collar employment is most diffused—timber and furniture, leather and fur, clothing and footwear, metal goods n.e.s., and bricks, pottery, glass, cement, etc.—are those with the lowest degree of white-collar unionism.[2]

It is also noticeable that the two most highly organized white-collar

[1] This assumes that for each occupational group the distribution of employment is roughly the same in each industry. This assumption is later relaxed. See *infra*, p. 80.

[2] Two exceptions to this generalization are chemicals which ranks second in terms of employment concentration but ninth in terms of membership density, and paper, printing, and publishing which ranks eighth in terms of employment concentration but first in terms of membership density. Low membership density in chemicals, in spite of high employment concentration, is explained by employer policies which are perhaps more unfavourable to the growth of white-collar unionism here than in any other manufacturing industry. (See Chapter VIII for a discussion of the importance of this factor.) In a sense paper, printing, and publishing is not really an exception for almost all the white-collar unionism in this area is in newspaper publishing which has a relatively high degree of employment concentration. It is also noticeable that employer policies towards the growth of white-collar unionism have been more favourable over a longer period in newspaper publishing than in any other manufacturing industry.

occupational groups in private industry—draughtsmen and journalists—are those whose employment is most highly concentrated. Draughtsmen are employed primarily in the engineering and shipbuilding industries, and, in addition, as the official historian of the draughtsmen's union has pointed out:

A particularly important factor for trade unionism among draughtsmen is that many drawing office workers in engineering and shipbuilding are employees of fairly large firms, and are brought together in relatively large offices. They work in circumstances where collective bargaining provides the only satisfactory method for determining certain common conditions of employment.[1]

Journalists are even more highly concentrated than draughtsmen. Although they tend to work in small groups, almost all of them are employed within one industry, and a large proportion of them are employees of the large national dailies, most of which are located on one London street.[2]

The conclusion suggested by these impressionistic observations was confirmed by regressing each row of Table 3.8 on each row of Table 6.1. With the exception of other technicians and other white-collar workers,[3] the association between density of unionization and the degree of employment concentration is quite strong for all the occupational groups. The correlation coefficients for draughtsmen; all technicians; clerks; all scientists, technologists, and technicians; foremen; and all white-collar workers are all significant at the 5 per cent level, while that for scientists and technologists is just below this level of significance.[4]

Scatter diagrams revealed that these correlation coefficients generally reflected quite accurately the strength of the relationship between employment concentration and union density. But, given the small number of industry observations, it is possible that in some cases the correlation

---

[1] J. E. Mortimer, *A History of the Association of Engineering and Shipbuilding Draughtsmen* (London: The Association, 1960), p. 417.

[2] Approximately 90 per cent of all journalists in the United Kingdom are employed in publishing (the remainder are employed in radio and television and public relations) and roughly 25 per cent of these are employed by the national dailies and Sundays. See George Viner, 'Basic Statistics on Journalism in the British Isles' (London: The NUJ, 1965), p. 2. (Mimeographed.)

[3] No explanation readily suggests itself for the very low correlation coefficient for other technicians, but, in the case of other white-collar workers, the low correlation coefficient probably is explained by the almost complete absence of unionism from this heterogeneous category except among journalists in printing and publishing.

[4] The correlation coefficient was 0·597 for foremen; 0·639 for all scientists, technologists, and technicians; 0·518 for scientists and technologists; 0·689 for all technicians; 0·911 for draughtsmen; 0·111 for other technicians; 0·756 for clerks; −0·065 for other white-collar workers; and 0·567 for all white-collar workers.

The textile observation was omitted for foremen because of classification difficulties which give it a greatly exaggerated density figure (see *supra*, p. 32 n. 3). Consequently, the equation for foremen has only 11 degrees of freedom, while those for all the other occupational groups have 12 degrees of freedom. With 11 degrees of freedom the correlation coefficient must exceed 0·553 and with 12 degrees of freedom it must exceed 0·532 to be significant at the 5 per cent level.

coefficients were unduly influenced by one or two outliers.[1] Consequently, the observations for foremen, scientists and technicians, draughtsmen, other technicians, and clerks were pooled and a further regression analysis was undertaken on these seventy observations. To overcome the difficulty of different occupational employment dispersions referred to above,[2] the same regression technique as was employed in Chapter IV was used here: explicit occupational variables were introduced into the density-employment concentration equation which allow for the fact that the level as well as the slope of the equation may shift with the type of occupation.[3] When the effect of occupation on the distribution of employment was allowed for in this way, employment concentration was found to be very significantly associated with the density of white-collar unionism.[4]

The above analysis has assumed that for each occupational group the distribution of employment is roughly the same in each industry. But this may not be the case. For example, it is conceivable that clerks are distributed both within and across firms in a different way in metal manufacture than in vehicles and that, therefore, averages do not adequately reflect differences in the actual degree of employment concentration between industries. Consequently, using the procedure adopted above in respect of different occupational dispersions, different industrial dispersions were allowed for and a further regression analysis was undertaken. But the results were not significant at the 5 per cent level,[5] and this suggests it is reasonable to assume that for each occupational group the distribution of employment is roughly the same in each industry.

Inasmuch as bureaucratization, as opposed to trade union recruitment and administration, is the reason why the density of unionization is higher among larger groups of employees, there is at least one major objection which might be raised against the above analysis. Several writers have suggested that bureaucratization and unionization are 'mutually cumulative' in their

---

[1] That is, a very large proportion of the variance is caused by one or two points, and hence any regression line which can pass near them will have a very high correlation.

[2] *Supra*, pp. 77–8.

[3] This is a standard econometric procedure and is explained fully in Appendix B.

[4] Allowing simply for the level of the equation to shift with occupation, the employment concentration coefficient had a t value of 2·96 and produced a $\bar{R}^2$ of 0·177. Allowing simply for the slope of the equation to shift with occupation, the employment concentration coefficient had a t value of 2·14 and produced a $\bar{R}^2$ of 0·641. Allowing for both the level and the slope of the equation to shift with occupation, the employment concentration coefficient had a t value of 2·28 and produced a $\bar{R}^2$ of 0·669. All of these are significant at the 5 per cent level.

[5] Allowing simply for the level of the equation to shift with industry, the employment concentration coefficient had a t value of $-0·493$ and produced a $\bar{R}^2$ of 0·139. Allowing simply for the slope of the equation to shift with industry, the employment concentration coefficient had a t value of 0·003 and produced a $\bar{R}^2$ of $-0·106$. Allowing for both the level and the slope of the equation to shift with industry, the employment concentration coefficient had a t value of $-0·094$ and produced a $\bar{R}^2$ of $-0·053$. None of these are significant at the 5 per cent level.

effects.[1] That is, the two variables are interdependent: not only does bureaucratization encourage the growth of trade unions, but trade unions, by demanding the standardization of working conditions, further bureaucratization. But at least in British manufacturing industries the degree of interdependence between these two variables would seem to be slight. The over-all degree of white-collar unionism in this area is so low, roughly 12 per cent, that it is unlikely to have greatly furthered the process of bureaucratization. In any case, the unions catering for white-collar employees in these industries bargain minimum not maximum terms and conditions of employment, and, in addition, they generally do not prevent employers from administering large doses of 'administrative particularism' to their employees in, for example, the form of merit pay.[2] Even assuming that unionization has somewhat furthered the process of bureaucratization, there can be little doubt that the latter preceded the former.

OPPORTUNITIES FOR PROMOTION

Several researchers have found that blockage of promotion opportunities is favourable to the development of trade unionism among white-collar workers. C. Wright Mills claims to have found 'a close association between the feeling that one *cannot* get ahead, regardless of the reason, and a pro-union attitude' among a group of 128 white-collar workers in the United States.[3] British researchers have noticed that the process of bureaucratization in teaching and the civil service 'has been accompanied by a policy of recruitment from outside at two or more levels, with little or no opportunity for those recruited at low level to surmount the internal barriers blocking their promotion'. They claim that as a result:

'Elementary' school teachers, and civil servants without a university training who entered the clerical or executive classes, have had such poor chances of upward job and social mobility that their efforts to improve their lot have inevitably taken the form of creating powerful interest groups restricted to those whose promotion was virtually barred in this way. As the lower salariat often attracted socially aspiring individuals for whom the blockage of their upward mobility was especially frustrating, they often became the leading spirits in the formation and running of such organisations.[4]

Sykes interviewed ninety-six, or one-third, of the male clerks in the sales office of a Scottish steel company and found that almost all of them wanted promotion and felt they had a reasonable chance of obtaining it, but only

[1] See, for example, Lockwood, op. cit., p. 142, and Blackburn and Prandy, op. cit., p. 117.

[2] On this point see the author's *Trade Union Growth and Recognition* (London: HMSO, Royal Commission on Trade Unions and Employers' Associations, Research Paper No. 6, 1967).

[3] C. Wright Mills, *White Collar* (New York: Oxford University Press, 1956), p. 307.

[4] R. K. Kelsall, D. Lockwood, and A. Tropp, 'The New Middle Class in the Power Structure of Great Britain', *Transactions of the Third World Congress of Sociology*, iii (1956), p. 322.

four approved of trade unionism for clerks. Later, most of these clerks joined a trade union. Sykes then interviewed them again and found that as a result of the company introducing a management trainee scheme many of the clerks no longer felt that promotion to management level was a real possibility. He has suggested that the changed attitude of these clerks towards their promotion prospects explained their changed attitude towards trade unionism.[1]

These studies are too limited in scope to allow any firm conclusions to be drawn regarding the effect of restricted promotion opportunities on union growth.[2] But blockage of promotion opportunities is very often associated with bureaucratization,[3] and it is highly probable that the effects of the latter upon unionization are reinforced by the effects of the former. The fewer opportunities the members of a work group have to rise out of it the more likely they are to become aware of their common situation. But although this awareness may be reinforced by blocked promotion channels, it is, as Lockwood has argued, 'first and foremost a product of standard working conditions' produced by bureaucratization.[4]

While blockage of promotion opportunities may be favourable to the development of white-collar unionism, it is clear that this is not a necessary condition for its growth. Promotion prospects were not blocked in banking, but a considerable degree of unionization was nevertheless possible simply on the basis of large-scale bureaucratic organization.[5] Draughtsmen are a highly unionized occupational group, yet their promotion prospects are quite good and highly valued.[6] While there is no quantitative evidence available, it is also fairly obvious that another very highly unionized group in private industry, the journalists, have considerably better promotion prospects than poorly organized groups such as clerks.

MECHANIZATION AND AUTOMATION

The office is being increasingly mechanized.[7] Several authorities claim that this is altering both the techniques by which the work is performed and the

---

[1] A. J. M. Sykes, 'Some Differences in the Attitudes of Clerical and of Manual Workers', *Sociological Review*, xiii (November 1965), especially tables i and iv and pp. 307–10.

[2] Such as Sykes's that 'there is evidence for an association between opportunities for promotion and trade unionism among clerical workers generally' (ibid., pp. 308–9).

[3] The reasons why this may happen are given by Lockwood (op. cit., p. 142). First, with the bureaucratic emphasis on technical competency and formal qualifications, there may be direct recruiting to managerial positions from outside the organization. Second, the economies of administrative rationalization may lead to a reduction in the ratio of managerial to clerical functions.

[4] Ibid., p. 149.   [5] Ibid., pp. 149–50.

[6] A survey of 941 draughtsmen in 1960 showed that 'prospects of advancement' was the third most frequent advantage of the occupation (with 350 mentions), compared with 188 giving 'poor prospects of promotion' as a disadvantage. See Guy Routh, 'The Social Coordinates of Design Technicians', *The Draughtsman* (September 1961), p. 9.

[7] For a detailed account and history of office mechanization see A. A. Murdoch and J. R. Dale, *The Clerical Function* (London: Pitman, 1961), and *Effects of Mechanisation and Automation in Offices* (Geneva: ILO, 1959), chaps. 2 and 3.

conditions in which it is performed in such a way as to encourage office workers to unionize.[1] They argue that office mechanization reduces the average level of skill, increases the danger of 'dead-end' specialization thereby decreasing promotion prospects, facilitates 'assembly line' work flows, requires shift work, demands a faster work pace and more continuous attention to work, makes possible the introduction of work study and piecework methods thereby emphasizing the size rather than the quality of output, obliterates any inherent interest or pride of work in the job, and generally lowers the status of office work by erasing the line of distinction between the techniques of manual and non-manual work and creating a factory-like atmosphere in the office. The ostensible result is greater anxiety and nervous tension, increased physical and mental fatigue, and reduced morale and job satisfaction, all of which supposedly encourage white-collar workers to unionize.

The advocates of this argument have tended to exaggerate both the extent and the effects of office mechanization and automation. Their main impact has been on the jobs of clerical workers, and even relatively few of these have been affected. Less than 20 per cent of female clerks and 13 per cent of total clerks in manufacturing industries were engaged as typists or office-machine operators in 1951.[2] The electronic computer was first used for office work in Britain towards the end of 1953.[3] But their rate of introduction did not gather much momentum until around 1959, and by mid 1963 there were only about 300 computers operating in Britain. The majority of these were employed in sectors of the economy other than manufacturing. Even in those organizations which have introduced computers, only about 20 per cent of the office workers have been affected by them. The size of the office and the nature of office work itself have set fairly narrow limits to the application of technology. There is 'a vast amount of office business which must be conducted personally—salesmanship, the discussion of business, the writing and typing of individual letters, secretarial work—and these as far as can be foreseen at present are unlikely to become amenable to automatic methods to any great extent'.[4]

Even those office workers who have felt the impact of mechanization and automation have not been affected as adversely as is commonly imagined. It is difficult to generalize because the impact which mechanization and

[1] For example, see the sources cited in ibid., p. 106; *Automation and Non-Manual Workers* (Geneva: ILO, 1967), pp. 36–8; and by Albert A. Blum, *Management and the White-Collar Union* (New York: American Management Association, 1964), pp. 59–62; as well as F. D. Klingender, *The Condition of Clerical Labour in Britain* (London: Martin Lawrence, 1935), pp. 61–4.

[2] *Census of Population 1951*, England and Wales, Industry Table 7. The figures for the economy as a whole were 14·5 per cent for female clerks and 8·8 per cent for total clerks. The 1961 Census did not distinguish office-machine operators separately.

[3] All the information regarding computers in this paragraph is from *Computers in Offices* (London: HMSO, 1965).   [4] Ibid., p. 6.

automation have upon office workers depends upon such factors as the nature of the functions taken over by the machine and the demographic characteristics of the clerks involved. But there has been a large quantity of research in this area, and, while there is not room here to report the findings in any detail, it is clear that so far office mechanization and automation have not had the dire results which some people have predicted.[1]

It is still probably too early to evaluate the effects of technical change upon white-collar workers with any certainty. But even if mechanization and automation should have an unfavourable impact upon white-collar workers in the future, it does not follow that this will necessarily encourage them to join trade unions. It has not been the least-skilled manual workers who have been most ready to join trade unions, but the most skilled. Similarly, it has not been those white-collar workers such as clerks and office-machine operators who have the most routine and monotonous work who are the most highly unionized, but those such as draughtsmen and journalists who have the more creative and interesting work.

This does not mean that office mechanization and automation will not have any effect on white-collar unionism in the future. The capacity of machines for handling large quantities of routine clerical work and facilitating managerial decision-making, as well as the economic necessity for keeping them fully occupied, will probably encourage the centralization of administrative functions within enterprises. If this occurs to any extent it will further the process of bureaucratization.[2] Hence by promoting bureaucratization, mechanization and automation may indirectly foster white-collar unionism. But this is mere speculation. The only thing which can now be stated with certainty is that office mechanization and automation are not yet sufficiently advanced to have had any appreciable impact on the pattern of white-collar unionism in Britain.

PROXIMITY TO UNIONIZED MANUAL WORKERS

Some writers[3] have argued that white-collar employees are more likely to join trade unions if they work in close proximity to unionized manual workers

---

[1] In particular, see the summary of the literature given in *Automation and Non-Manual Workers*, op. cit., chap. 1. See also *Computers in Offices*, op. cit., *passim*, and Enid Mumford and Olive Banks, *The Computer and the Clerk* (London: Routledge & Kegan Paul, 1967), especially pp. 183–94.

[2] This has already occurred to some extent. See *Effects of Mechanisation and Automation in Offices*, op. cit., pp. 31–4, and *Computers in Offices*, op. cit., p. 36.

[3] See, for example, Lipset, op. cit., pp. 19c–24; *Non-Manual Workers and Collective Bargaining* (Geneva: ILO, 1956), pp. 31–4; C. Wright Mills, op. cit., p. 306; and Joseph Shister, 'The Logic of Union Growth', *Journal of Political Economy*, lxi (October 1953), pp. 422–4. Lockwood's position on this point is somewhat vague. He claims that the degree of contact with manual workers and their unions 'is one of those factors which affect the distribution of membership within clerical unions, but are not generally decisive in determining the differences in the degree of concerted action between one union and another' (op. cit., p. 154). It is difficult to see how a factor can affect the industrial distribution of membership

or have trade unionists among their friends or relatives.[1] Two reasons are advanced in support of this argument. First, there are the so-called 'demonstration' and 'learning' effects. It is alleged that white-collar employees who work in close physical proximity to unionized manual workers are provided with a demonstration of the benefits of trade unionism while those who have trade unionists among their friends are given an opportunity to learn about these benefits, and this makes them anxious to obtain some of these for themselves. Second, it is suggested that the organization of white-collar workers may be stimulated by manual unions directly recruiting white-collar workers into their ranks or at least lending white-collar unions moral, financial, and strategic support in their organizing drives.[2]

There is some empirical evidence which can be used to support this argument. Draughtsmen are one of the most highly unionized groups in private industry and their work brings them into close contact with skilled manual workers.[3] Several of the union organizers interviewed for this study claimed that works clerks were easier to recruit than office clerks, and that clerks in offices attached to production plants were easier to recruit than those in the downtown head offices of the same companies. Some of the most successful white-collar unionism has arisen in those industries where manual workers are represented by strong unions; railways, printing, coal-mining, and, to a lesser extent, the metal industries provide examples in both this and other countries. Research studies have indicated that white-collar workers who have union-member friends are more likely to be trade unionists themselves than those without such friends.[4]

within a union without at the same time affecting the density of union membership within an industry.

[1] That part of the argument which concerns relatives has already been considered *supra*, pp. 43–6 and will not be further analysed here.

[2] This aspect of the argument will be considered more fully in the following chapter.

[3] Routh (op. cit., p. 8) found that 43 per cent of his sample of 941 DATA members entered the profession by serving a craft apprenticeship. Even those who enter the profession directly by serving a drawing-office apprenticeship generally spend two to three years of it in the workshop learning such manual skills as fitting, turning, and machining. According to the official historian of the draughtsmen's union (Mortimer, op. cit., pp. 415–16):

> Many draughtsmen remain fairly closely associated with the workshops throughout their career, long after they have finished their apprenticeship. This is particularly true of jig and tool draughtsmen, whose work usually brings them into close contact with toolmakers, foremen and machine setters in the workshops. Many draughtsmen on other kinds of work also often find it necessary to visit the workshops to consult foremen and other workpeople. These experiences help to familiarise draughtsmen with workshop life and with the issues which confront the shop workers.

[4] See C. M. Phillipson, 'A Study of the Attitudes Towards and Participation in Trade Union Activities of Selected Groups of Non-Manual Workers' (unpublished M.A. thesis, University of Nottingham, 1964), pp. 283–4. In America a study by the Opinion Research Corporation indicated that 44 per cent of those who said they had union-member friends or relatives favoured unions for white-collar workers, as contrasted with 21 per cent in favour among those who did not have such acquaintances or relatives (cited by Blum, op. cit., p. 66).

But much of the force of this argument is dispelled by a closer examination of the reasoning and the evidence by which it is supported. It is true that white-collar workers are highly unionized in industries where manual workers are also highly unionized. But the opposite is equally true. Manual workers are relatively highly unionized in the footwear and cotton industries, but white-collar workers are not. Moreover, those areas in which the degree of white-collar unionism is highest—national and local government, education, and banking—are those in which there is the least contact between white-collar and manual workers, while the area in which white-collar workers are most poorly organized—manufacturing industries—is that in which there is the closest proximity between the two groups.

Even in those areas where manual and white-collar unionism are both strong, it does not necessarily follow that the latter results from the former. It is at least equally plausible that both result from factors common to both groups of workers within the given area such as the size of the firm and the attitude of the employer towards trade unionism. Nor does it necessarily follow that because white-collar unionists have a higher proportion of union members among their friends than non-unionists, these friends persuaded them to join trade unions. It may simply indicate that white-collar workers, like most other people, choose friends with similar attitudes and values to their own.

Social and physical proximity to unionized manual workers is obviously not a necessary condition for the growth of white-collar unionism, although in some instances it may be a favourable condition. But in other instances it may be unfavourable. White-collar workers who are in close proximity to unionized manual workers may learn not only of the advantages of trade unionism but also of what may appear to them as its disadvantages—strikes, lack of democratic procedures, and so on. Proximity and familiarity may breed contempt as easily as they breed understanding and support.

CONCLUSIONS

This chapter has shown that some but not all of the variation in the pattern of white-collar unionism in Britain can be accounted for by variations in the degree of employment concentration. The greater the degree of employment concentration the greater the density of white-collar unionism. The explanation for this would seem to be that employees are more likely to realize the need for trade unionism and trade unions are more likely to be interested in recruiting them, the more concentrated their employment.

But needs do not inevitably create ways of meeting them; many social needs often persist without being met. Even if white-collar employees feel the need for trade unionism and trade unions are interested in recruiting them, there are at least two reasons why they may still not be organized. First, trade unions may have poorly designed structures and use inappropriate techniques for recruiting white-collar employees. Second, employers may be opposed to their 'staff' joining trade unions and pursue policies designed to discourage them from doing so. Hence it is also necessary to look at the trade unions which recruit white-collar workers and the employers of these workers to obtain a complete picture of the factors which may promote or hinder the growth of white-collar unionism.

VII

THE TRADE UNIONS

IN an attempt to isolate the factors which influence the growth of trade unionism among white-collar workers this study has so far examined their socio-demographic characteristics, economic position, and work situation. Many people have claimed that the trade unions themselves must also be taken into account. The public image of the trade union movement as well as the recruitment policies and structures of unions have all been alleged to affect profoundly their growth among white-collar workers.[1] The purpose of this chapter is to determine whether this is, in fact, the case.

THE PUBLIC IMAGE OF THE TRADE UNION MOVEMENT

'Image' is a greatly overworked term. But the public image presented by the trade union movement may nevertheless be of considerable importance in determining its growth. At least one American writer has been willing 'to crawl out on a limb and assert that the most basic thing affecting the possibility of unionization in new fields is . . . the general community attitude towards unions'.[2] A British writer feels that the prominence given by the mass-communication media to such things as unofficial strikes, demarcation disputes, undemocratic procedures, restrictive practices, charges of Communist infiltration, and internal union squabbles between 'left' and 'right' may have caused many people who would otherwise have joined unions not to do so.[3] Many of the employers interviewed for this study argued that the 'inability of the trade union movement to bring itself up to date and to present a better image of itself' was a major factor hindering its expansion among white-collar workers.

Unfortunately, the evidence necessary to test this argument is rather thin. But it is probably correct to suggest that during the first half of the twentieth

---

[1] Writers such as Shister have also claimed that the leadership of unions affects their growth. Union leadership as such is not analysed in this chapter. But this does not mean that its possible impact upon union growth is not considered. If leaders do have any effect upon union growth, it is, as Shister himself has pointed out, primarily by devising better recruiting policies and structures. The impact of these factors upon union growth is considered here and hence indirectly so is the influence of union leadership. See Joseph Shister, 'The Logic Of Union Growth', *Journal of Political Economy*, lxi (October 1953), pp. 429–30.

[2] S. M. Miller, 'Discussion of "The Occupational Frontiers of Union Growth"', *Proceedings of the Industrial Relations Research Association*, xiii (December 1961), pp. 214–15.

[3] Keith Hindell, *Trade Union Membership* (London: Political and Economic Planning, 1962), p. 183.

century the public attitude towards trade unions was least favourable just before the First World War and just after the General Strike of 1926 and most favourable during and immediately after both world wars.[1] Since 1950 the public attitude towards trade unions can be traced more systematically as a result of information provided by successive Gallup Polls. The question— 'Generally speaking, and thinking of Britain as a whole, do you think trade unions are a good thing or a bad thing?'—has been put to a national sample of the population at fairly regular intervals. The proportion of the sample which thought that trade unions were a 'good thing' is given for the period 1952–64 by Fig. 7.1.

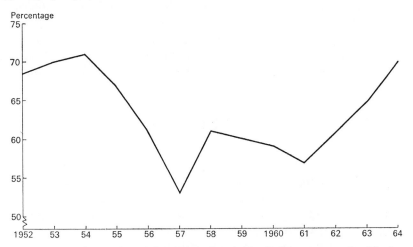

FIG. 7.1. Public standing of the trade unions, 1952–64. Percentage saying 'Trade Unions are a good thing for Britain'.

The major weakness of this argument is that the public image of the trade union movement is a general factor. It cannot, therefore, explain the occupational and industrial variations in the density of unionism which are of primary interest in this study. At best, it could only help to account for the country's over-all level of trade unionism. But it is doubtful if it even does this, for at least since 1950 the trends in over-all union membership have not followed very closely the trends in the public's attitude towards trade unions. Public opinion has been very fickle: the percentage of people who thought that trade unions were generally a 'good thing' has varied from a high of roughly 70 per cent in 1954 and 1964 to a low of 53 per cent in 1957. Yet, as Chapter III demonstrated, total union membership has remained on a gently rising plateau over the post-war period while its density has fairly steadily

[1] See W. G. Runciman, *Relative Deprivation and Social Justice* (London: Routledge & Kegan Paul, 1966), chap. 6, for references to the union movement's public image during the first half of the twentieth century.

declined. At the same time, white-collar union membership has increased very markedly while its density has remained more or less constant.

Prior to 1950 the periods in which the public attitude towards trade unions was most favourable—during and immediately after the two world wars—were also the periods of their greatest growth. But, as Chapter IX will demonstrate, the unions' membership increased primarily because government policies necessitated by war made it easier for them to obtain recognition from employers and their associations. The improvement in the unions' public image helped in this regard by making it harder for employers to deny unions recognition without at the same time damaging their own public image. But this improvement was itself largely a result of government policies which involved the unions in the administration of government and industry in order to help ensure maximum and uninterrupted production throughout the wars. Hence while the improvement in the unions' public image during the two world wars obviously assisted their growth, it was very much a secondary factor.

UNION RECRUITMENT POLICIES[1]

Recruitment strategy

The concept 'strategy' is generally applied to military affairs, but it may also be used to analyse trade union behaviour. Unions, like armies, are faced with solving the problem of strategic priorities. Just as armies must determine which fronts should get primary attention, so unions must decide, consciously or unconsciously, whether or not to concentrate their recruiting in certain geographical regions, occupations, industries, or firms.

White-collar unions in private industry generally do not focus their recruiting geographically, except inasmuch as certain industries tend to be concentrated in particular regions. Of course, the officials in charge of a particular region of a union may from time to time decide to concentrate on certain towns or cities within it, but these campaigns are generally very *ad hoc* and very short-run. Nor is there very much concentration of recruitment by occupation. Although most white-collar unions restrict their membership to fairly clearly defined occupational groups or 'crafts', this is more a reflection of craft consciousness, the Bridlington rules,[2] and union structures, than of occupational recruitment priorities. In other words, within the limits set

---

[1] Much of the information contained in the rest of this chapter was obtained from interviews with union officials. During 1965–6, the author interviewed sixty of the full-time officials of the major white-collar unions in private industry. The officials agreed to cooperate on the understanding that their replies would not be attributed to them as individuals. Consequently, material obtained from interviews has been cited in such a manner that it is not possible to identify the individual concerned.

[2] These were established at the 1939 TUC and place certain restrictions on inter-union competition for membership.

by the unions themselves and by external agreements, there is very little emphasis on occupational recruitment priorities.

The question of industrial recruitment priorities does not really arise for some white-collar unions. By virtue of its industrial structure, BISAKTA has tended to restrict its activities to the iron and steel industry. Similarly, NATSOPA tended to restrict itself to the printing and publishing industry. Given that the NUJ and DATA are relatively 'closed' unions in the sense that the former has tended to restrict its membership to journalists and the latter to technicians 'whose functions are related to design', it follows that they have generally confined their recruiting to those industries in which these two groups of workers are almost exclusively located, printing and publishing, and engineering and shipbuilding, respectively.

But all the other unions which cater for white-collar workers in private industry have a fairly 'open' structure, and they therefore must decide whether or not their recruiting should be concentrated industrially. Most of them have decided that at least to some extent it should be. In general, they have tended to concentrate on those industries in which their potential membership is greatest and in which they are generally recognized by employers. Thus the AScW concentrated on engineering,[1] chemicals, the National Health Service, and universities and technical colleges, and ASSET focused on engineering, civil air transport, and, to a lesser extent, chemicals and rubber. The NACSS has concentrated on engineering and road and water transport as well as those industries such as chemicals, rubber, and brewing in which their parent organization, the TGWU, is well established among manual workers. Since 1950 the CAWU has increasingly been concentrating its recruiting in the engineering industry, although to some extent the dispersed nature of clerical employment has forced it to recruit clerks wherever most of them were not already members of other unions.

Some unions have refined their recruitment priorities to the extent that they concentrate on certain types of firms. The NACSS has concentrated on those firms in which the TGWU is particularly well established among the manual workers. Within the engineering industry, the CAWU has tended to concentrate on the largest companies. ASSET went even further in this respect. After 1949 it increasingly concentrated its recruiting and collective bargaining on combines or large multi-plant firms and industries with a large proportion of such firms. ASSET believed that by concentrating on the pattern setters of British industry it would build up its financial and membership strength more rapidly and efficiently and have a greater impact on national salary and employment policies. In 1958 this strategy was formalized as a 'combines policy' and a directive was issued to all the union's full-time officers instructing them to:

[1] In this context the engineering industry is defined to include those areas covered by the Engineering Employers' Federation. See *infra*, p. 126 n. 3.

. . . above all else, develop mass membership in the largest manufacturing enter-prises. This means a concentration of activity in the engineering, transport and chemicals industries. In all these sectors there is an unmistakable trend towards fusion or alliance and the growth of larger and larger units. It is, therefore, essential that planned organising and bargaining work should be undertaken as a *first* priority in these dominating firms in the selected industries.[1]

The union's executive then drew up a list of approximately eighteen key companies—including such firms as Associated Electrical Industries, the British Aircraft Corporation, Standard Telephone and Cables, International Computers and Tabulators, Hawker Siddeley, Plessey, and Rolls Royce—and allocated responsibility firm-by-firm to the union's staff.

Recruitment tactics

Whatever the nature of union recruitment strategies, they have generally not been pursued with much tactical aggressiveness. The recruitment process tends to be more passive than active in the sense that potential members gener-ally have to contact a union before there is much attempt to recruit them. The comment of one AScW official is typical: 'Generally we wait for people to approach us before we try to recruit them. You might say that organization occurs by accident.' Even ASSET with its sophisticated recruitment strategy generally waited for individuals to contact it before trying to recruit them. But if the individuals happened to be from a combine, then they received special attention. As one ASSET official put it, 'I will drop everything to get them in. If they weren't from a combine I might not do this unless it was an extremely large group or I wasn't very busy.' But inasmuch as the union normally depended upon the initiative of potential members, its approach to recruitment was still more passive than active.

Reasons for this passivity are not hard to find. None of the unions recruiting white-collar workers in private industry are particularly wealthy organizations and all of them are understaffed relative to the size of the recruitment task they face. In 1964 the major unions catering for white-collar workers in private industry had a total of approximately 282,000 white-collar members and 98 full-time officers recruiting and servicing them, roughly 1 officer to every 3,000 members.[2] This relatively high ratio of members to officers[3] means that most officers spend the bulk of their time servicing

[1] Appendix to Organization Committee Minutes, 8 March 1958.

[2] The unions which were used to compute these figures include all those listed in Table 3.7 except BISAKTA. The TGWU has a few officers who handle manual as well as white-collar affairs. Each of them was counted as a half in deriving the figure for the total number of officers.

[3] This is relatively high by the standards of other countries. See S. M. Lipset, 'Trade Unions and Social Structure', *Industrial Relations*, i (February 1962), p. 93. But Lipset's calculation in this article of the ratio of members to full-time officers in Britain is incorrect. A survey in 1959 found that there were approximately 3,000 full-time trade union officers servicing a membership of approximately 9,600,000 roughly one to every 3,300 members. See H. A. Clegg, A. J. Killick, and Rex Adams, *Trade Union Officers* (Oxford: Blackwell, 1961), pp. 39 and 94.

existing members rather than recruiting new members. Only 3 of the 60 union officials interviewed for this study claimed they spent more than 10 per cent of their time recruiting.[1] Even unions such as the CAWU which have experimented with specialist recruitment officers in one or two regions have found that these officers eventually got drawn into servicing the members they recruited and increasingly had less time available for recruiting new members. 'It is very difficult', as one of these officers pointed out, 'for an official to do nothing but recruit. When people join a union they bring problems with them and it is only natural that the official who has been dealing with them up to the time they joined should continue to do so.'

Even if trade union officers were not so busy servicing existing members, the recruitment process probably would not become much less passive. For almost all of them believe, as one of them put it, that 'organizing in a vacuum is a waste of time and energy'. Most of the union officials who were interviewed had participated at one time or another in special recruitment campaigns complete with such techniques as blanket leafletting, loudspeaker vans, and open meetings advertised in the press, but none had found that these ever produced a significant number of new members. The following experiences are fairly typical. In 1964 an AScW official sent general recruiting literature to the laboratories of sixty companies and got no response whatsoever. In the early 1960s ASSET conducted a special recruitment drive along the Great West Road in London where several major companies have plants and offices, but, according to the official in charge of the campaign, it did not produce a single member. Almost every official who was interviewed spoke of several occasions on which he had advertised an open meeting for the staffs of a particular company and not one person had turned up. In view of these experiences it is not surprising that most union officials are convinced that 'a contact is an absolute prerequisite for successful recruiting' and refuse to engage in speculative recruiting unless they are 'desperate'.

But the recruitment process is not completely passive. Once a person approaches a union with a view to becoming a member, a number of steps are taken to ensure that he and, even more important, his colleagues actually do join. To begin with, an official usually writes to the contact enclosing some general recruiting literature and suggesting an informal meeting at his home or some other convenient location. When they meet, the official tries to get the facts regarding the company concerned and the employees' grievances, encourages the contact to try and get as many of his colleagues as possible to join the union, and suggests a time and place for a meeting of all interested employees. At this meeting the official generally gives an opening talk covering such topics as the union's history, structure, and policies, as well as the

---

[1] The 1959 survey also revealed that on average full-time officers felt that the recruitment of new members was only their fifth most important function in terms of the amount of time they spent on it. See ibid., p. 44.

case for trade unionism in general and his union in particular, and then discusses a variety of questions raised from the floor. Assuming a sufficient
number of people are interested in joining the union, a committee is elected,
and the employer is eventually approached to concede recognition.

The recruitment process is not entirely passive even prior to a contact
being obtained. Although unions generally do not attempt to recruit until
they have a contact, most of them take steps to increase the number of such
contacts or at least to ensure that they come to their union rather than
another. All the unions catering for white-collar workers in private industry
lay great stress upon recruitment in their journals.[1] By such means as com-
petitions, prizes, and just sheer exhortation they try to encourage existing
members and lay officials to 'go out and talk unionism, and our union in
particular, in community associations, churches, clubs, and pubs'; to distribute recruiting literature at their place of work and at day release classes; to
pass their copy of the union journal which often contains recruitment propa-
ganda and membership application forms to non-members; to convince
their friends and relatives to join; to put their local officer in touch with any
contacts they may have among groups of potential members; and, if transferred
to a non-union area, to try on their own initiative to spark off organization
there. Union officials sometimes make a tour of the trade councils in their
regions and ask them to help in supplying recruiting contacts. They also
approach manual unions for the same purpose. Officials of manual unions
which also recruit white-collar workers are very favourably placed in this
regard and often find that their manual members can put them in touch with
friends or relatives on the white-collar side of a firm.

Some unions go much further than this and use the mass media to advertise their services. The AScW advertised on buses which followed routes
servicing plants in which it had a special interest, as well as in certain technical and scientific journals.[2] The CAWU has also advertised on buses as well
as on hoardings and the Waterloo and City underground railway which
carries thousands of clerks into the City everyday. Although the NACSS
has not used the mass media to advertise itself, its parent organization, the
TGWU, has advertised on hoardings and buses, and, in addition, has experimented with give-away booklets of matches, drip mats, and car stickers.[3]
Individual branches in most of these unions also advertise themselves in the
local press from time to time.

The union which made the most extensive use of the mass media to
publicize itself was ASSET. In fact this was the main way in which the union
tried to implement its recruitment strategy. In words of one ASSET official,

---

[1] See, for example, 'Notes on Recruiting', *AScW Journal* (October 1949), pp. 13–15;
'A Call to Every Member', *AScW Journal* (January 1954), p. 3; and 'Organise! In Union
There Is Strength', *TGWU Record* (December 1963), pp. 32–4.

[2] *Report of Executive Committee*, 1957, p. 16.

[3] See 'Union Publicity', *TGWU Record* (June 1964), pp. 28–32.

'Our major tactic is to get lots of publicity, to make employees aware of us so that when they have a grievance they know where to come to get it resolved.' The union advertised on buses, on hoardings, in the local press, in football league programmes, and even on commercial television.[1] But it placed even greater emphasis on getting news coverage of its activities and successes. It took every opportunity to issue press releases, and to have its officials, in particular its general secretary, write articles for newspapers and magazines, speak on the radio, and appear on television.[2]

Recruitment appeals[3]

Although the message which unions try to put across to potential members by such means as the mass media, leaflets, broadsheets, and speeches tends to vary from one union to another and from one situation to another, there are certain common elements. The basis of the appeals of all the white-collar unions in private industry is economic—improved salaries and conditions, greater job security, plus attractive services and benefits.

The theme 'you can get it too' is central to all the appeals. The recruitment literature is filled with examples of the improvements in salaries and conditions which the unions claim to have gained for their members and suggests that these are 'typical of the progress which can be made where staff workers join and support' trade unions. BISAKTA notes that 'the manual worker, through his trade union, has achieved higher wages, shorter working hours, better working conditions, holidays with pay and many other improvements' and points out that 'if staff workers would join a Trade Union they would enjoy the same protection as the manual workers'. In a special broadsheet addressed to white-collar workers the NACSS announces that it has launched 'a big campaign to stop the drift of staff earnings to well below those of many manual workers'. In one AScW leaflet a scientific worker asks the question— 'Why should I be organised in a Union?'—to which the answer is:

All kinds of professional people like doctors, teachers, civil servants, have associations registered as Trade Unions. These represent them and act as pressure groups for them. In this day and age the isolated individual cannot hope

[1] The union became convinced that the results from advertising on television did not justify the cost. Several white-collar unions have tried to get the TUC to underwrite an advertising campaign in the national press and on television, but it has argued that the cost of using such media make this impossible. See TUC's Non-Manual Workers' Advisory Committee, *Proceedings* of the Annual Conference for 1956, pp. 11–12; 1957, p. 6; and 1961, pp. 20–6; as well as the *Report* to the Annual Conference for 1957, pp. 7–9 and for 1961, pp. 6–9.

[2] See Hindell, op. cit., pp. 174–82, and R. M. Blackburn, *Union Character and Social Class* (London: Batsford, 1967), pp. 91–3, for a discussion of the recruitment methods used by other unions.

[3] Except where otherwise noted, all the quotations in the following section are taken from recruiting literature published by the major white-collar unions in private industry. The various pamphlets, leaflets, and broadsheets have not been specifically cited because in most cases they do not have a title and it is therefore difficult to identify them uniquely.

successfully to press his interests and claims by himself. If salaries of scientific workers are inadequate today this is a consequence of their lack of organization.

A DATA leaflet argues that 'in recent years there has been a steady decline in the position of design technicians relative to other sections of the community' and declares 'this is a process that D.A.T.A. is determined to reverse'. The CAWU lists a number of advantages which a clerk obtains by joining the union including 'above all the opportunity of working with your fellow clerks to improve your salaries and conditions of service'.

Job security is also emphasized. The NACSS observes that 'as firms (and offices) grow bigger, and take-overs and technical changes threaten the security of staff employment, more and more staff workers are realizing that they, too, need a strong Union behind them, to protect them and raise their incomes—so they join the N.A.C.S.S.'. The CAWU claims that electronic computers are having a greater and greater impact upon office work causing 'many thousands of office workers to wonder whether their future is in jeopardy' and adds that 'trade union membership is an insurance against the uncertainty of the future'. A piece of general recruiting literature published by the TUC's Non-Manual Workers' Advisory Committee warns that 'more mechanisation means new worries for staff—fear of losing a job or the chance of promotion' but suggests that 'the individual's anxieties are not nearly so great when there is a union to tackle the problems of redundancy, compensation for loss of employment, proper provision for those who are to retire early and retraining for those who seek another post'.

But improved salaries and greater security are not the only wares the unions offer to potential members. All the white-collar unions in private industry provide most of the usual 'friendly' benefits—accident pay, educational grants and facilities, funeral benefits, convalescent facilities, superannuation benefits, free legal advice, unemployment benefits, and benevolent grants—and stress them in their recruiting literature. In addition DATA offers, as did ASSET and the AScW, a discount trading scheme covering a wide range of goods and services including most types of insurance; ASSET and the AScW gave free advice on income tax and house purchase; DATA provides a continental holiday scheme, technical publications, and a technical circulating library; the CAWU gives actuarial advice on superannuation schemes; and the NACSS has access to the TGWU's Advice and Service Bureau which helps members with individual problems.

The purely white-collar unions embellish this general economic appeal by claiming that they cater exclusively for staff workers and as such can offer them a better service than an industrial or general union. ASSET declared itself to be the fastest growing trade union in Britain because supervisors and technicians 'are becoming increasingly aware of the need to join a specialist trade union catering for their particular requirements'. The CAWU points out that it 'employs specialist officials who know how to represent clerical and administrative staff' and adds that 'the CAWU is not a satellite of any other body. It is a completely free organisation, owned, managed, and controlled by clerical staff.' In speeches to potential members this point is made even more strongly. A CAWU official stated that in speaking to clerical workers he stresses that they 'will always play second fiddle in a manual workers' union'.

The partially white-collar unions try to counter these claims by arguing that in unity there is strength. The NACSS bills itself as 'the Union that puts real strength behind the staff' and declares that 'employers have extra respect for the N.A.C.S.S., for though it determines its own policies, and maintains its identity as an organisation of staff workers, it is also one of the key sections of the country's strongest Union—the Transport & General Workers' Union'. A BISAKTA official tells white-collar workers in the steel industry that 'we know more about the industry than specialist unions which have members in several industries and we can discuss your problems much better and give more effective representation'.

Finally, just in case the white-collar worker is convinced by these arguments but is reluctant to join a union for fear of what his employer may think, all the unions emphasize those areas in which they are recognized by employers and where relations with them are good. The NACSS informs potential members that 'it has won the respect of management by hard bargaining and fair dealing' and 'has full recognition rights to represent members of the Union in many industries and undertakings'. It also adds that it is possible to 'establish firm, but cordial relationships with employers, benefitting both the staff and the industry'. BISAKTA claims that 'most employers, recognising the need for organisation amongst themselves, are fair-minded enough to allow their staffs the same right' and states that it is 'the recognised union for clerical and supervisory staffs in the steel industry'. NATSOPA published a list of all the firms and employers' associations with which it had agreements and pointed out that 'relations with employers are good, and as long as print workers remain organised this should continue'. The NUJ mentions that it 'had to fight hard for its first newspaper agreement, but that phase of its work is now over' and today 'proprietors' organisations turn naturally to the Union when any question affecting the journalist's working life arises'. In a pamphlet addressed to planning engineers, DATA informs them that it is 'the only trade union which by national agreement with the Engineering Employers' Federation has the right to negotiate' on their behalf. A CAWU official tells potential members in the engineering industry that 'we don't want martyrs; your employers have already recognised us; negotiating machinery is sitting there waiting to be used'.

Impact upon union growth

Much more detail could be given on union recruitment policies. But the purpose here is not to provide a manual on recruiting practices. Rather, it is to determine what effect, if any, these have upon union growth, and sufficient information has now been provided for this to be done.

It is very doubtful if the pattern of aggregate white-collar unionism can be explained to any great extent by the nature of union recruitment policies. There are, as Chapter III indicated, considerable occupational, geographical, and industrial variations in the pattern of white-collar unionism. There are not, as this chapter has indicated, corresponding variations in union recruitment policies. The unions' general approach to recruiting white-collar workers differs little from one occupation to another or one region to another. It is true that most of the unions tend to concentrate their recruiting in certain industries, and, in the main, these are the industries in which the density of white-collar unionism is relatively high. While the latter no doubt helps to account for the former, it is very much a secondary factor. The generally higher levels of white-collar unionism in these industries are mainly explained by other factors—partly, as the previous chapter demonstrated, by the structure of these industries, and partly, as the following chapter will demonstrate, by the attitudes and behaviour of employers with regard to union recognition. In fact, it is precisely because industrial structure and employer attitudes are more favourable to unions in these industries that they have tended to concentrate their recruiting in them.

Although union recruitment policies are not of much significance in explaining variations in the pattern of white-collar unionism, they may nevertheless be important in accounting for its over-all level. The methods by which unions try to recruit white-collar workers have been shown to be more passive than active. It might be argued, therefore, that this is why the general level of unionization among these workers is relatively so low.

But no evidence has been produced which supports this view. In fact, when unions have adopted more aggressive recruiting tactics, they do not seem to have had much impact upon their recruiting performance. The experiences of the union officials who were interviewed for this study indicate that special recruitment drives generally do not produce an appreciable number of new members.[1] The AEU undertook a special recruitment campaign between 1957 and 1967 but its membership grew by only 15·5 per cent during this period as compared with 21·5 per cent during the period 1947–57 when there was no special campaign.[2] The NUGMW launched a special recruitment drive in 1960 and subsequently established several mobile teams of full-time recruitment officials and appointed a national recruitment officer. Yet the union's membership shrank by 0·3 per cent during the period 1960–6 as compared with a 1·1 per cent increase during the period

[1] See *supra*, p. 93.
[2] See Hindell, op. cit., p. 176. The AEU's membership in Great Britain was 721,902 in 1947, 877,641 in 1957, and 1,041,428 in 1967.

1954–60.[1] Even ASSET's 'combines policy' does not seem to have had all that much impact on its recruitment. Its growth from the time this policy was introduced in 1958 up to 1964 was greater than during the period 1951–8, but so was that of most of the other major white-collar unions in private industry.[2]

None of this proves that the recruitment policies of these unions did not have any impact upon their growth. It may be that their growth would have been even less if these policies had not been instituted. But the failure of these policies to make much of a difference in the rate of recruitment suggests that, if they are a factor in union growth, at least they are not very important and are easily outweighed by other factors. Until such time as better evidence becomes available, the most balanced conclusion would seem to be that unions are not much more than catalysts in the recruitment process. Before a group of workers can be successfully organized, there must be some irritating condition resulting in a widespread feeling of dissatisfaction. Unions cannot create this condition. They can only discover where it exists, emphasize it, and try to convince the workers that it can be removed by unionization. Union recruitment is by its very nature largely a passive process.[3]

Whether or not unions have been sufficiently energetic in carrying their appeals to white-collar workers, it has been argued, particularly by American writers, that more white-collar workers would have been recruited if unions had been more skilful in formulating their appeals to them. In Blum's view, American unions have failed to recruit large numbers of white-collar workers at least partly because

instead of fostering a feeling among white-collar employees that management had treated them unfairly and that a union would right their wrongs, labor organizations often unwittingly brought about a contrary opinion (or, at least, did nothing to refute it): that unions had forced management to give too much of industry's earnings to manual workers.

. . . . .

To use effectively whatever bitter feelings exist among white-collar employees concerning salaries, labor organizations must be able to convince these employees that the blame rests squarely on the corporation's shoulders.[4]

[1] See the NUGMW's *Report of the Forty-Fifth Congress*, 1960, pp. 43–4, and the *Report of the Fifty-First Congress*, 1966, pp. 38 and 209–10. The union's membership was 787,228 in 1954, 796,121 in 1960, and 792,995 in 1966.

[2] ASSET's membership increased by 69·9 per cent during the period 1958–64 as compared with 56·4 per cent during the period 1951–8; the AScW's by 72·5 per cent as compared with −11·9 per cent; the CAWU's by 57·4 per cent as compared with 25·4 per cent; the NUJ's by 22·3 per cent as compared with 19·1 per cent; and the NACSS's by 52·6 per cent as compared with 12·4 per cent. For the actual membership figures of these unions see Fig. 7·2 and the notes to this figure in Appendix A.

[3] For a contrary view, see Bernard Karsh, Joel Seidman, and Daisy M. Lilienthal, 'The Union Organizer and His Tactics', *American Journal of Sociology*, lix (September 1953), pp. 113–22.

[4] Albert A. Blum, *Management and the White-Collar Union* (New York: American Management Association, 1964), pp. 29 and 45.

It is Burns's judgement that the unions' approach to the white-collar worker has generally been wrong.

It is an approach that is primarily class-conscious instead of career-conscious, one dedicated to fighting the company and opposing the management rather than improving relations and co-operating with management to improve conditions of work for the worker. Too often the philosophy has been to proletarianize the white collar worker; to ask and induce him to accept the methods and mental outlook of workers in the mass production, maintenance and craft occupations, even though his problems, interests, and goals are not common and coterminus with those of shop workers. The slogan is standardization for the office worker.[1]

Strauss believes that unions would be more successful in recruiting white-collar workers if they used a 'middle-class approach' rather than a 'factory approach'. Instead of trying to convince white-collar workers to give up their 'vain delusions' that they are members of the middle class and hence above trade unionism, the unions should present themselves as the best means by which these workers can achieve their middle-class goals.[2]

It is difficult to prove or disprove this argument. But several observations can be made which cast serious doubt upon its validity. Firstly, the argument is largely based upon the impressions and speculations of its advocates; they have produced little, if any, reliable evidence which conclusively demonstrates that it holds even for America, let alone for Britain and other countries. Secondly, it is based on certain assumptions—that white-collar workers join unions primarily because of their concern for higher salaries, and are prevented from joining primarily because of their concern for their middle-class status—which this study has already shown to be inadequate.[3] Finally, the argument implies that if only the unions would employ good copy writers, they would be rewarded with a large influx of new members. To say the least, this is improbable. The evidence assembled in this study suggests that white-collar unionism is primarily a product of very powerful structural forces. If this is correct, then the density of white-collar unionism is unlikely to be significantly increased simply because a few sentences are changed in the unions' recruiting literature.

UNION STRUCTURES

Although the various recruitment techniques employed by unions do not seem to affect their growth to any great extent, the structures they use to recruit and service members may. Even if the question of union structure is confined to unions recruiting white-collar workers in private industry, it is

[1] Robert K. Burns, 'Unionization of the White Collar Worker', *Readings In Labor Economics and Industrial Relations*, Joseph Shister, editor (2nd ed.; Chicago; Lippincott, 1956), p. 71.
[2] George Strauss, 'White-Collar Unions Are Different!' *Harvard Business Review*, xxxii (September–October 1954), pp. 75–6.
[3] See *supra*, pp. 51–63 and 48–50.

still too broad to be fully discussed in this study. It is intended to examine here only those aspects of union structure which have been claimed to affect union growth. In considering union structure, it is convenient to distinguish between those aspects which concern the internal operation of unions and those which are external to particular unions and concern their relationships with each other and the wider labour movement.

Internal structures

Partially white-collar unions. The aspect of the partially white-collar unions' structure which has been most often examined in relation to their growth is their willingness and ability to represent the special interests of white-collar workers.[1] There can be no doubt that some of the ideals, aspirations, interests, and problems of white-collar workers are different from those of manual workers.[2] Nor can there be much doubt that manual workers often fail to appreciate this. In fact, a strong antipathy has traditionally existed between manual and white-collar workers in British industry. Manual workers often have a strong contempt for white-collar workers, regarding them as 'unproductive', as 'having its cushy', as snobs, as 'bosses' men', as one of 'them' and not one of 'us', and generally as poor material upon which to build trade union organization.[3]

Zweig has quoted a typical workman's view:

I start at 7.30 in the morning, an 'office-wallah' starts at 9. He works in a collar and tie and has clean hands, and I have to dirty my hands. What he does can be rubbed out with a rubber, while what I do stays. He keeps in with the boss class.[4]

Similar sentiments were expressed by *The Bradford News*, an organ of the Independent Labour Party, on the occasion of the decision of the National Union of Mineworkers to press for a special investigation into administrative efficiency in the National Coal Board in 1951.

All miners, and some other men and women who earn their living by hard work, under strict rules, feel suspicious, resentful and jealous of those chaps who sit on their you-know-whats in offices, and push pens. The administrators, technicians, and clerks recognise this, and feel a little nervous, ashamed, or defiant about it, according to how their minds work. . . . Actually, the clerk is an unskilled labourer under modern conditions, and there is no reason for treating him any differently from any unskilled labourer. Usually the qualification on which he gets his first job is good

---

[1] One sociologist has claimed that manual workers' unions have 'a kind of trained incapacity to deal with non-manual people' which he attributes to the fact that these unions 'have developed habits of work and behaviour which reflect working-class culture'. See Seymour M. Lipset, 'The Future of Non-Manual Unionism' (an unpublished paper, Institute of Industrial Relations, University of California, Berkeley, 1961), p. 60.

[2] If documentation is thought necessary, see Runciman, op. cit., especially chaps. 8–11.

[3] On this point see David Lockwood, *The Blackcoated Worker* (London: Allen & Unwin, 1958), pp. 100–5 and 125–32, and Ferdynand Zweig, *The British Worker* (Harmondsworth, Middlesex: Penguin Books, 1952), chap. 21.

[4] Ibid., p. 203.

appearance and address, and manners—the qualification appropriate to a footman or flunkey.[1]

The question of whether or not a clerk is 'productive' is evidently raised so frequently by the manual members of BISAKTA that one of the union's white-collar members was moved to write in the union journal that

The questioner is usually an ill-informed member of the manual labour force, and he is in fact not asking a question at all, but politely suggesting that a clerk is a social parasite living on the 'productive' worker and that if the parasite happens to be a male, then this unmanly scribbling should be left to the women while he gets himself 'a man's job'. Exactly what constitutes 'a man's job' is usually unspecified but presumably it requires a combination of 'brute force and ignorance'.[2]

Sometimes even prominent national officials of manual unions which try to recruit white-collar workers have a very negative attitude towards them. A full-time officer of the AEU, speaking in the prices and incomes debate at the 1966 TUC and commenting on the speeches made earlier by the general secretaries of NALGO and ASSET, had this to say:

Is it not the case that, as distinct from the manual workers in national and local government employment who are decidedly lower paid . . . that the third of a million people that Nalgo represent are enjoying salaries which range from as low as £1,000 per year to as high as £10,000 per year? . . . Is it not true that their lives are cushioned by security, by longer holidays, better superannuation and better sick schemes than the manual workers in these industries? I want to say to Nalgo that if they are really interested in the good of the nation, and bearing in mind that in the main, you know, (and somebody has got to say this) you represent people who produce nothing . . . is it asking too much of you to make a little contribution to solve our nation's problems under our Labour Government. I do not think so.

I now deal with the contribution made by that anarchistic anachronism, Clive Jenkins . . . 'Anarchistic' because he is against everything that is progressive and challenging, and 'anachronism' because he represents people who have run away from the struggle of the workshop floor, who do not want to be associated with manual workers' unions so they join this whatever-you-call-it. In fact, the vast majority of his people are people who have betrayed the manual workers' union . . . and, in my opinion, they are 40,000 Conservatives run by half-a-dozen Clive Jenkinses.[3]

But in spite of these attitudes, and, in some cases, perhaps because of them, most manual unions which also represent white-collar workers have made certain modifications in their structures to help ensure that the special needs and problems of these workers can be more easily articulated and catered for.

Even as traditional a manual union as BISAKTA has made a few structural

---

[1] Cited by David Rhydderch, ' "Fools Rush In" ', *The Clerk* (September–October 1951), pp. 246–7. The author of this article concludes that 'the lesson clerks must learn and learn very quickly is that Unions purporting to represent all and every type of manual workers cannot meet the special needs of clerks'.

[2] See *Man and Metal* (May 1950), p. 73, and (June 1950), p. 89.

[3] *TUC Annual Report*, 1966, p. 476.

concessions to its white-collar members. They are generally placed in separate branches from manual members,[1] and these are brought together in a special section of the union, Section J. This section, unlike the union's other ten sections, has been entitled since 1944 to hold an annual national conference, but this conference has no power to give effect to its recommendations. Like all the other sections, it is not autonomous on any matter and can only offer advice to the union's 'supreme governing and administrative authority', the Executive Council. Section J is allotted two representatives on the twenty-one member Executive Council.[2] Candidates for these positions must be nominated from and by the white-collar membership, but, like the executive candidates from other sections, they are voted upon by all the members of the union. Since the manual members outnumber the white-collar by roughly fifteen to one, they decide, in effect, which of several competing nominees will represent Section J on the Executive Council. In spite of being requested to do so by Section J,[3] BISAKTA has refused to appoint a full-time officer to be specifically responsible for white-collar affairs. In fact, since the union was formed in 1917 only one white-collar member has ever been appointed to a full-time position with the union.[4]

NATSOPA went much further than BISAKTA in providing separate facilities for its white-collar members.[5] The bulk of NATSOPA's membership was concentrated in London and Manchester.[6] In London it was divided into four branches, one of which was exclusively reserved for white-collar members.[7] The union's membership in Manchester was only large enough to justify one branch, but the branch committee was divided into three sub-committees, one of which exclusively represented clerical and administrative members. There was also only a single composite branch in all the other provincial areas of the union. The white-collar membership was not large

[1] This is partly the result of employer insistence. See *infra*, pp. 165–6.

[2] Prior to 1966 Section J was only entitled to one representative on the Executive Council.

[3] See Iron and Steel Trades Confederation, *Quarterly Report* (31 March 1960), p. 11, and (31 March 1964), p. 41.

[4] He was appointed as a Divisional Organiser in 1960 but left the service of the union in 1964. In 1950 the Vice-President of the union, who is elected from and by the Executive Council, was a Section J man, and the Parliamentary Representative in 1964 was also a Section J man.

While this book was being printed, BISAKTA announced a dramatic change in its structure: the appointment of a National Staff Officer and three Staff Organisers who would be specifically and exclusively responsible for white-collar affairs.

[5] The structure of NATSOPA which is described here is virtually identical to that of its successor, SOGAT, Division I.

[6] Roughly 57 per cent of the union's total membership was in London in 1964, while 3 per cent of it was in Manchester. Approximately 80 per cent of its white-collar membership was in London, while 7 per cent of it was in Manchester.

[7] This branch used to be called the London Clerical Branch. But in 1964 its name was changed to the London Branch of Clerical, Administrative and Executive Personnel. See NATSOPA, *Annual Report*, 1964, p. 19. For ease of expression it is still referred to as the London Clerical Branch in the following discussion. The other London branches were as follows: Machine, R & GA, and Ink & Roller.

enough in any of these to warrant a separate section on the branch committee, but white-collar members were generally placed in separate chapels and every attempt was made to see that they were represented on the branch committee in proportion to their numbers in the branch. Finally, in 1964 NATSOPA formed a National Association of Advertising Representatives to function as a separate branch within the union.

Of the twenty full-time officers which the union employed in 1964–5, three were exclusively concerned with white-collar affairs. There was a full-time National Clerical Officer at the union's Head Office in London.[1] The London Clerical Branch had a full-time secretary and assistant secretary and these had always been appointed from among the branch's members.[2] The Manchester Branch did not have a full-time official specially responsible for the white-collar section, but by a coincidence the branch secretary officiating in 1964–5 (who also acted as secretary of the union's North Western District) had been appointed from among the clerical members of the branch.[3] One of the other District Secretaries employed by the union in 1964–5 also had been a clerical worker prior to his appointment. Although District Secretaries had no special responsibility for their clerical members, many of them nevertheless spent a considerable amount of time servicing them.

The white-collar members of the union elected all their own representatives. The London Clerical Branch elected three of its members to sit on the union's Executive Council, while the provincial clerical members elected one of their members to do likewise. Representatives of white-collar members at the union's annual conference, the Governing Council, were also elected from and by these members.[4] For the purpose of electing representatives to attend the annual conferences of the PKTF, the TUC, and the Labour Party, the union's membership was divided into five groups, each entitled to elect one representative to attend each conference. One of these groups exclusively covered the London Clerical Branch.

[1] The position was founded in 1937. Its first incumbent was drawn from among the union's white-collar membership. In 1952 the union decided that strict departmentalization among officers should be discontinued and the National Clerical Officer was reclassified as one of three National Assistant Secretaries. It was understood, however, that while this officer no longer had an exclusive responsibility for the white-collar membership, he still had a special responsibility for it. This officer retired in 1963 and although his replacement was drawn from the London Machine Branch, it was still understood that he had a special but not exclusive responsibility for the white-collar membership. In 1966 SOGAT, Division I, decided once again to appoint a National Clerical Officer. The person who currently fills this position used to be a manual worker in the industry.

[2] For a history of this branch see G. D. Hill, 'Your Branch in Focus: London Clerical', *Natsopa Journal* (January 1959), pp. 8–9 and 21.

[3] The white-collar members in Manchester used to have their own full-time officer. But this position was dispensed with during the last war. See J. Collier, 'Your Branch in Focus: Manchester', *Natsopa Journal* (January 1958), pp. 12–13.

[4] In 1963, 21 out of 81 or 25·9 per cent of the delegates at the Governing Council were representatives of white-collar members, while 11,802 out of 45,832 or 25·7 per cent of the membership was white-collar.

Favourable as the white-collar members' position within the organizational structure of NATSOPA was, in one or two respects it was less favourable than that of the manual members. Although the London Clerical Branch was the largest in the union, it only had three seats on the nineteen-member Executive Council, while the next largest branch, London Machine, had four.[1] Similarly, the London Clerical Branch was only entitled to three representatives on the fourteen-member London Joint Branches Committee which co-ordinated the activities and business of the four London branches, while the London Machine Branch was entitled to five.[2] This under-representation was a sore point with the London Clerical Branch, and on various occasions it tried to get its representation on the Executive Council made equal to that of the London Machine Branch.[3] But the union opposed these moves on the grounds that, because of higher labour turnover, white-collar workers do not have the same length or continuity of service in the industry.[4]

The manual union in which the white-collar members' position has been most favourable is the TGWU.[5] This union has a dual structure. Its membership is divided into thirteen trade groups plus two trade sections, as well as thirteen geographical regions each of which is subdivided into several districts. In general, trade groups deal with questions concerning the wages and working conditions of their members and have primary responsibility for the recruitment of new members, while general administrative matters are dealt with by the regional organization. The lowest level of union government, the branches, also reflect the dual structure of the union. Not only is their coverage restricted to a specific geographical area, it is also generally restricted to the members of a single trade group. Even in those districts where some of the trade groups have so few members that they are placed in composite rather than separate branches, separate sectional meetings are generally held within these branches to deal with specific trade matters.

One of the TGWU's trade groups is occupational rather than industrial in scope. It caters exclusively for white-collar employees and is known as the

[1] In March 1965 the membership of the London Clerical Branch was 9,590 while the membership of the London Machine Branch was 9,272.

[2] It was also laid down that the chairman and secretary of this committee be from the London Machine Branch. The chairman could only vote in the event of a tie. See the union's *Rules*, 1962, p. 172.

[3] See the union's *Annual Report* for 1958, p. 102 and 1960, p. 12.

[4] But the union pointed out to the author that 'Over the years clerical representation at all levels, including the Executive Council and the London Joint Branches Committee, has continued to increase, and since this section has the greater organizational potential both in London and the provinces it is a fair assumption that this increased representation will be a continuing process.'

[5] The TGWU is the largest union in Great Britain and its structure is rather complicated and subject to vary slightly from one region, district, or trade group to another. The following description is of a very general nature. For a more detailed account see the union's *Rules* as well as the *Transport & General Worker's Union Home Study Course* (London: The Union, 1962), especially pts. i and ii.

National Association of Clerical and Supervisory Staffs. To overstress the point slightly, the NACSS is a union within a union. Although the NACSS, like all the other trade groups, is subject to the authority of the General Executive Council of the TGWU, it nevertheless enjoys a large measure of autonomy. In practice, this means that it must get the approval of the General Executive Council before it can call members out on strike or before it implements any policy which might affect the members of other trade groups, but is virtually a free agent with regard to all other trade matters. It is even affiliated in its own right to the CSEU.

The NACSS is governed at national level by a National NACSS Trade Group Committee. The form which the NACSS's government takes at regional level varies somewhat from one region to another. Most regions have a Regional NACSS Trade Group Committee.[1] In some regions, generally those in which the white-collar membership is very small, the NACSS representatives are linked with another Regional Trade Group Committee. There are also a few regions in which a district committee system rather than a trade group system exists. District Committees have the same function as Regional Trade Group Committees except that they generally represent the members of more than one trade group.[2] Where this is the case, NACSS members are represented on District Committees in proportion to their numbers within the district. Regardless of the form which the NACSS's government takes in the regions, the principle is retained of only allowing members of the NACSS to deal with its trade-group business including the election of its representatives.

Although the NACSS has a considerable measure of autonomy, it is also a part of the TGWU and as such is represented on all the administrative and co-ordinating bodies which make up its structure. Approximately 4 per cent of the TGWU's total membership is accounted for by the NACSS,[3] but its representation on these bodies is generally more favourable than this. Each of the regions has a Regional Committee to administer its affairs. Of the 283 people sitting on them in 1964–5, 14 or 4·9 per cent were chosen from and by the NACSS membership.[4] The supreme policy-making authority of the union is the Biennial Delegate Conference. In 1965, 38 or 4·6 per cent of the

---

[1] Although the NACSS is primarily an occupational rather than an industrial trade group, in regions where the NACSS membership is very large, steps are taken to ensure that different industrial interests are represented. For example, in Region 1, the Regional NACSS Trade Group Committee has two advisory committees—one for the Ford Motor Company and another for the road haulage industry. Nationally, *ad hoc* meetings of representatives from specific industries are held from time to time.

[2] Some district committees, especially in the Midlands, cover the members of only a single trade group. They are thus identical to Regional Trade Group Committees except that their scope is restricted to a district rather than a region.

[3] See *supra*, Table 3.6.

[4] All the information contained in this and the following paragraphs concerning the number and backgrounds of representatives and full-time officers was obtained from

820 delegates were chosen from and by the NACSS membership. The main governing body of the union between Biennial Delegate Conferences is the General Executive Council, and each of the trade groups, including the NACSS, is allowed one representative on it. In addition, the General Executive Council has a number of territorial representatives elected by the membership of each region irrespective of trade. In 1964–5 there were twenty-six of these, and three of them happened to be NACSS members. The General Executive Council elects eight of its members to sit on an executive committee, the Finance and General Purposes Committee. In 1964 one of these happened to be an NACSS member.

The NACSS has a full-time national secretary[1] as well as a number of full-time officers at regional level who help to administer its affairs. In 1964–5 there were thirteen regional officers who were exclusively responsible for NACSS affairs,[2] while six others had a special but not exclusive responsibility for them.[3] In addition, although the full-time regional and district secretaries of the TGWU do not have any special responsibility for NACSS members, they nevertheless spend a considerable amount of time servicing them. In fact, some of these officers have been drawn from the NACSS membership. Several of the present district secretaries and three of the thirteen regional secretaries were NACSS members prior to their appointment.[4]

Purely white-collar unions. The aspect of the purely white-collar unions' structure which has been most frequently examined in relation to their growth is their willingness and ability to represent the industrial or sectional interests of their members. All the purely white-collar unions in private industry are 'occupational unions' in the sense that their members are drawn from a particular white-collar occupation or related group of occupations.[5] While the members of any occupational group obviously have many common interests, they also have many that are dissimilar and which are primarily related to the industry or section of the industry in which they work. The major purely white-collar unions in private industry have recognized this and have tried to design their structures in such a way as to make it easier for the different industrial or sectional interests of their members to be articulated and catered for.

DATA places its members in branches according to where they work

correspondence and interviews with the national and regional officers of the NACSS and the TGWU.

[1] The present incumbent was drawn from among the manual members of the TGWU; the previous two were drawn from among its white-collar membership.

[2] All but one of these was appointed from among the members of the NACSS.

[3] All of these had been manual members of the TGWU prior to their appointment.

[4] The full-time secretary of one of the Regional General Workers Trade Group Committees was also a NACSS member prior to his appointment.

[5] See John Hughes, *Trade Union Structure and Government* (London: HMSO, Royal Commission on Trade Unions and Employers' Associations, Research Paper No. 5, 1967), pp. 2–6.

rather than where they live.[1] Branches are therefore more plant than geographically orientated. The Executive Committee of the union is advised of
the particular interests of members employed in the shipbuilding industry,
the aircraft industry, and the nationalized industries, as well as in the largest
chemical employer, Imperial Chemical Industries, by a system of Advisory
Panels which are elected by and from the members in these areas. DATA is
also increasingly co-ordinating the activities of members in large combines
or consortiums. In addition to being responsible for a particular geographical
area, the union's full-time officers have recently been made responsible for
liaison between the representatives of members employed in different factories of particular combines and for bringing them together in conferences
as circumstances demand.[2]

The NUJ's branches generally cover a geographical area. But some of them,
mainly those in the London area, are organized on a functional basis. They
cover journalists working in periodical and book publishing, on trade and
technical magazines, on evening papers, in public relations, in the High
Court of Justice, and in government service, as well as parliamentary
journalists. Freelance journalists are organized in separate branches in areas
where their numbers are sufficient to warrant this, and in separate regional
sections elsewhere. Freelance members are also entitled to elect representatives to a National Freelance Council which advises the union's National
Executive Council on freelance matters. Radio and television journalists are
members of their geographical branches except in London and Dublin where
they have their own branches. There is also a Radio Journalists Council which
advises the National Executive Council on radio and television affairs.[3]

Unlike draughtsmen or journalists, clerical workers are employed in virtually every section of the economy. Since the CAWU has generally tried to
recruit them wherever they were not already members of other unions, it not
surprisingly has found the problem of representing the different industrial
and sectional interests of its members more difficult to solve than has DATA
or the NUJ. Efforts to bring bank clerks and law clerks into the union in 1908
failed, according to the union's official historian, because special branches
could not be formed for them. The membership refused to admit that
clerkdom was divided into sections and that these should be reflected in
union organization and policy.[4] The issue of occupational versus industrial
organization has also resulted in a number of secessions from the CAWU.

[1] For a more complete account of DATA's structure see its *Rules* as well as *Draughtsmen's and Allied Technicians' Association: Its Structure and Work* (Richmond, Surrey: The
Association, 1964).
[2] See DATA's *Report of Proceedings at Representative Council Conference 1966*,
pp. 71–3.
[3] For a more complete account of the NUJ's structure see the union's *Rules* as well as
National Union of Journalists Officers' Guide (London: The Union, n.d.).
[4] Fred Hughes, *By Hand and Brain: The Story of the Clerical and Administrative Workers
Union* (London: Lawrence & Wishart, 1953), p. 23.

In 1920 most of the union's membership in London newspaper offices seceded to form first the London Press Clerks' Association, and then, after a few months, the clerical section of NATSOPA's London Branch.[1] In the same year, the CAWU's organizer for Wales resigned taking most of the Welsh membership with him to found a rival organization, and in 1921 a large proportion of the members employed in trade union offices seceded to join the Welsh breakaway as its London Guild.[2] Finally, in 1937 most of the union's membership in the iron and steel industry broke away or were taken away to become members of BISAKTA.[3]

The CAWU's first major attempt to solve the problem of occupational versus industrial organization took place just after the First World War. Largely as a result of the influence of Guild Socialist ideas upon some of the leading members of the union and the large number of clerks being organized outside the union along industrial lines, the CAWU decided to reorganize itself on an industrial basis in 1920. It established eight national guilds each of which was autonomous on matters concerning only the industries or services it covered.[4] There was also a General Council, composed of delegates from each of the guilds plus the union's national officers, which co-ordinated the guild's activities and ensured their mutual support. But the guild system was doomed almost from the start. Just before it was established, the post-war depression set in and the CAWU's membership not merely declined but slipped away 'in what began to look like a landslide'.[5] The guild system did not prove to be the panacea its advocates had claimed, and it soon came under heavy attack. In 1932 the union finally decided to abolish the guild system and revert to a geographical form of organization.

But as the depression eased during the 1930s and the CAWU's membership began to expand, it found that it was not sufficient simply to place members in branches,[6] group these into geographical areas governed by Area Councils, and let each of these elect a representative to the union's Executive Council. In 1941 it established an Advisory Council for the engineering industry and this became the prototype for several others. Today there are Advisory Councils for the union's membership in engineering, coal, co-operatives, electricity supply, and civil air transport.[7] These function at both regional

[1] Ibid., pp. 67–8 and *infra*, p. 149.

[2] Ibid., pp. 60–2 and 67. In the long run these defections failed to create a rival organization.

[3] See *infra*, pp. 164–5.

[4] A more detailed description of the guild system is scattered throughout Hughes, op. cit., chaps. 5–7.

[5] Ibid., p. 68. The CAWU's membership was 43,000 in 1919, 14,000 in 1921, and 7,000 in 1924. See *infra*, p. 214.

[6] Most of the union's branches are based on a single firm or industry.

[7] At one time there was also an Advisory Council for the membership employed in trade union offices, but this was disbanded because almost all of its membership was concentrated in London and it was not covered by any form of national negotiating machinery.

and national level. There are Area Advisory Councils which give advice to the Area Councils on matters within their own industry and appoint representatives to National Advisory Councils which offer similar advice to the Executive Council.[1] In addition, the CAWU convenes *ad hoc* 'multiple group meetings' where staff representatives working in different branches of large engineering establishments are brought together to discuss common problems. The union also tries to ensure that the sectional interests of its members are looked after by assigning a particular responsibility for certain industries or sections of industries to all its full-time national officers and many of its area officials.

The AScW's structure was similar in broad outline to that of the CAWU. It was organized primarily on a geographical basis: members were placed in branches based on a single establishment, or on a geographical area, or on both; these were grouped into geographical areas governed by Area Committees; and each of these elected a representative to the union's Executive Committee. But the union also made some provisions for ensuring that the different industrial interests of its members were represented. Advisory Committees were established at national and, in some cases, at area level covering members employed in medical research, universities, the chemical industry, the engineering industry, the National Health Service, and the National Coal Board. The function of these committees was 'to give expert advice to the Executive Committee, rather than to make final decisions, although the Executive Committee would seldom reject such advice and will often mandate an Advisory Committee to take a decision'.[2] The AScW also held 'interlocation meetings' to bring together the staff representatives in large multi-plant companies to discuss common problems.

The purely white-collar union in private industry which placed the greatest emphasis on representing the sectional as well as the occupational interests of its members during the post-war period was ASSET. For general administrative purposes, members were placed in branches generally based on a geographical area and these were grouped into districts governed by District Councils. The branches were entirely administrative units, and, in practice, their major function was the collection of subscriptions. They were also responsible for electing representatives to the union's National Executive Council and to its Annual Delegate Conference. The District Councils were responsible for seeing that the branches were properly administered. But neither the branches nor the districts had any direct control over industrial matters.

---

[1] Recently the union has strengthened representation on the Advisory Councils and, in this and other ways, made them more effective. See the union's *Annual Report and Balance Sheet* for 1961, Appendix B; 1962, pp. 8–10; 1963, pp. 8–10; and 1965, pp. 10–11.

[2] 'Democracy in the AScW', *AScW Journal* (May 1959), p. 11. See also 'AScW Organization', *AScW Journal* (March 1962), pp. 13–14 and 24, for a more detailed discussion of the AScW's structure.

For negotiating purposes, the 'group' was the operative unit in ASSET's structure. A group comprised all the union's membership in a particular factory or establishment and had its own grade representatives, chairman, and secretary who functioned as a shop steward. Although subject to the overriding authority of the National Executive Council, the group was, in practice, autonomous on those industrial matters which only concerned its members and was responsible for negotiating with local management. Representatives from all the groups within a single combine or multi-plant company were brought together at least once a year to enable them to exchange information and experiences and to formulate and co-ordinate bargaining objectives. In addition, in such areas as civil air transport, London Transport, railways, and Remploy where its membership was covered by national negotiating machinery, the union established National Industrial Councils. These were the union's 'principal medium for dealing with matters affecting the industry concerned'.[1]

ASSET's full-time officials had a dual responsibility. Each of them was responsible not only for the membership in a particular district, but also for that covered by one or more of the combines or National Industrial Councils, and was expected to study these intimately so as to be aware of their national policies as well as their local problems. The union even went so far as to purchase token shareholdings in the combines in which it had membership so that the specialist officer could attend their annual meeting and, if necessary, speak as a shareholder 'about issues which might be difficult to express as a trade-union officer in factory collective bargaining'.[2]

Impact upon union growth. When the different internal union structures are compared, there seems to be a prima facie case for assuming that some of them would be more attractive than others to white-collar workers. But even granted this, it is very difficult to assess what effect the relative attractions of these unions' internal structures have had upon their growth. For in making such an assessment little, if any, reliance can be placed on differences in the growth of their actual memberships. Such differences are very much influenced by differences in the growth of their potential memberships. Before the growth of one union can be meaningfully compared with that of another, the influence of labour force growth upon union growth must be controlled for. That is, growth-rates must be calculated on the basis of 'real' rather than actual memberships. But the membership densities of most of the unions being considered here cannot be calculated even for a single year, let alone over time. Either the area of potential membership cannot be delimited with any degree of exactness, or the government's

---

[1] See the union's *Rules*, 1964, p. 21.

[2] Clive Jenkins, 'Tiger in a White-Collar?', *Penguin Survey of Business and Industry 1965* (Harmondsworth, Middlesex: Penguin Books, 1965), pp. 58–9.

manpower statistics are not given in sufficient detail to allow this area to be quantified.

Thus no firm conclusions can be drawn about the influence which these unions' internal structures have had upon their growth. But one or two observations can be made which suggest that their influence has been minimal. The potential membership areas of the CAWU and the NACSS are very broadly similar.[1] Although one is a purely white-collar union and the other is partially white-collar, their growth during the post-war period has been almost identical. The CAWU's membership grew by 105·7 per cent during the period 1948–64, while the NACSS's grew by 104·7 per cent.[2] Until very recently BISAKTA would seem to have had the least attractive structure from the white-collar workers' point of view and probably showed the least aggressiveness in recruiting them, but this did not prevent it from establishing a relatively large membership among white-collar workers in the iron and steel industry. Even if it is granted that this occurred in spite of its internal structure,[3] it nevertheless indicates that any negative influence which its structure may have had upon its growth was easily outweighed by other factors.

Whatever the influence of internal structure upon individual union growth, it does not seem rash to conclude that its influence upon aggregative union growth has been negligible. At least it is extremely difficult to see how this factor in any way helps to account for the variations in the pattern of white-collar unionism in private industry. It might nevertheless be argued that the over-all level of unionism among white-collar workers in private industry would have been much higher if they had had more attractive union structures to choose from. But this seems most improbable. The unions catering for white-collar workers in private industry show the same structural diversity as do British unions in general. With the exception of journalists and draughtsmen who are already highly unionized, most white-collar workers in private industry have had the opportunity to join either a purely or a partially white-collar union, and, in many instances, more than one variety of each type. Either these white-collar workers are extremely pernickety regarding internal union structures, or it must be assumed that their reluctance to join trade unions is explained by other factors.

External affiliations

All the major white-collar unions in private industry are affiliated to a large number of other organizations. These range from educational and research

[1] But they are not identical. In addition to clerical workers, the NACSS also tries to recruit supervisors, and, to a lesser extent, certain technical grades.

[2] See *supra*, Table 3.7.

[3] It is argued later in this study that BISAKTA has been relatively successful in recruiting white-collar workers because of the relatively favourable attitude which most iron and steel employers have toward it. See *infra*, pp. 164–7.

bodies such as the Workers' Educational Association, the Labour Research Department, and Ruskin College, through such pressure groups as the National Council for Civil Liberties, the Consumers' Association Limited, and the Movement for Colonial Freedom, to federations of trade unions such as the National Federation of Professional Workers, the CSEU, the PKTF, the TUC, and the International Federation of Commercial, Clerical and Technical Employees, and to such political organizations as the Fabian Society and the Labour Party.[1] It is not possible or necessary to consider here the relationship between all these organizations and the various white-collar unions. Only their relationships with the TUC and the Labour Party will be examined here as these are the ones which have been most frequently mentioned as having an influence on union growth. In addition, the relationships between the various unions representing white-collar workers in private industry will be examined because such relationships have also been claimed to affect union growth.

Affiliation to the Trades Union Congress. All the major unions catering for white-collar workers in private industry are affiliated to the TUC. The CAWU (then the National Union of Clerks) affiliated in 1903; NATSOPA in 1901 before it began to recruit white-collar workers; BISAKTA and the TGWU in the very year they were founded, 1917 and 1922 respectively; DATA (then the Association of Engineering and Shipbuilding Draughtsmen) in 1918; and the AScW in 1942. When ASSET (then the National Foremen's Association) first applied to join the TUC in 1919, its application was turned down because a large proportion of its membership was already represented at the TUC by virtue of holding dual membership in the various craft unions. But ASSET reapplied in 1920, and in 1921 the TUC accepted it into membership.[2] The NUJ affiliated to the TUC in 1920, but it disaffiliated in 1923 after the TUC raised the affiliation fees of member-unions to help support the *Daily Herald.* The NUJ felt it was 'inimical' to its interests that journalists should be identified with the interests of any particular paper. It was not until 1940 that the membership of the NUJ once again decided that the union should affiliate to the TUC.

The question of TUC affiliation raised feelings of disquiet and sometimes outright opposition among certain sections of the memberships of some of these unions. When the motion to affiliate to the TUC was moved at DATA's annual conference in 1918 there was some opposition on the grounds that affiliation was 'premature' and a few delegates wished to be assured that affiliation did not mean that the union was committed to support the Labour Party.[3] The AScW (then the National Union of Scientific Workers) rejected

[1] This is by no means an exhaustive list.

[2] See Alan E. Williams, 'The Foreman's Story: An ASSET History', *ASSET* (January 1954), p. 5.

[3] J. E. Mortimer, *A History of the Association of Engineering and Shipbuilding Draughtsmen* (London: The Association, 1960), p. 61.

a proposal to affiliate to the TUC in the early 1920s,[1] and it was another two decades before this position was reversed by a ballot vote of the membership. Prior to the NUJ's affiliation to the TUC in 1920, the matter had been raised unsuccessfully at five of the union's annual conferences. As a result of affiliation a few members of the union's Parliamentary Branch resigned. There were also attempts at the union's annual conferences in 1921 and 1922 to get it to disaffiliate. After the union did disaffiliate over the *Daily Herald* issue, in 1923, the membership had to be balloted on six occasions before it finally agreed to reaffiliate.[2]

This opposition has led to suggestions that a union's affiliation to the TUC may hinder it from recruiting white-collar workers. Some writers have even gone so far as to suggest that the establishment of a separate central congress for white-collar unions such as exists in Sweden 'might be a valuable aid to the spread of organisation among non-manual employees, since it would demonstrate to many white-collar employees who are reluctant to join unions affiliated with the T.U.C., that there were associations which catered exclusively for their interests'.[3]

But the evidence does not lend much support to such views. The growth rates of the major white-collar unions in private industry as well as of trade union membership in general for the period 1900 to 1964 are shown by Fig. 7.2.[4] The points at which the various unions affiliated to the TUC are marked on the graph. The growth rates of DATA and the CAWU were roughly the same after affiliation as they were before which suggests that it had little impact upon their growth. The growth rates of ASSET and the AScW were slightly less after affiliation than they were before, while that of the NUJ was slightly less after its initial affiliation in 1920 and slightly more after its reaffiliation in 1940. The growth rates of all these unions immediately before and after affiliation tend to follow that of trade union membership in general which suggests that some factor common to all unions rather than something unique to the unions in question such as TUC affiliation was responsible for the change in growth rates. Nor have the growth rates of white-collar unions in other sections of the economy suffered as a result of affiliation to the TUC.[5] As David Lockwood has noted, 'It has yet to be shown

---

[1] Reinet Fremlin, 'Scientists and the T.U. Movement', *AScW Journal* (May 1952), p. 17.

[2] See the references to the TUC in the index of Clement J. Bundock, *The National Union of Journalists: A Jubilee History 1907–1957* (Oxford: Oxford University Press, 1957) for the history of the NUJ–TUC relationship.

[3] B. C. Roberts, 'Introduction', *Industrial Relations: Contemporary Problems and Perspectives*, B. C. Roberts, editor (London: Methuen, 1962), p. 5.

[4] This is a semilogarithmic graph and the slope of any series plotted on such a graph indicates its rate of growth.

BISAKTA is omitted from Fig. 7.2 because it was not possible to obtain its white-collar membership figures for most of the period 1917 to 1964, and, in any case, it affiliated to the TUC and the Labour Party in the very year it was founded.

[5] See D. Volker, 'NALGO's Affiliation to the T.U.C.', *British Journal of Industrial Relations*, iv (March 1966), pp. 66–7.

that TUC affiliation by any non-manual union has led to a decrease in membership.'[1]

Affiliation to the Labour Party. Most, but not all, of the major unions catering for white-collar workers in private industry are affiliated to the Labour Party. The CAWU affiliated in 1907, NATSOPA in 1916 before it began to recruit white-collar workers, BISAKTA and the TGWU immediately after they were formed in 1917 and 1922 respectively, DATA in 1944, and ASSET in 1947. All the attempts which have been made by certain sections of the AScW's membership to get it to affiliate to the Labour Party have been defeated. But in 1945 it established a political fund which was mainly employed for general lobbying activities to further the use of science and the interests of scientific workers. The Labour Party affiliation issue has never been formally raised within the NUJ.

The question of Labour Party affiliation has generally generated more heated feelings among white-collar trade unionists than that of TUC affiliation. More white-collar unions are affiliated to the TUC than are affiliated to the Labour Party.[2] When the CAWU decided to affiliate to the Labour Party in 1907, there was some debate as to whether this should be delayed in case it deterred more conservative clerks from joining.[3] DATA had to ballot its members in 1920, 1923, 1940, and 1944 before a majority of them agreed to allow a political fund to be established and the union to affiliate to the Labour Party.[4] After DATA and ASSET affiliated to the Labour Party, there were attempts by certain sections of their memberships to get them to disaffiliate.[5] Although the question of Labour Party affiliation has never formally arisen in the NUJ, it underlay the debate over affiliation to the TUC. The anti-affiliationists argued that the relationship between the TUC and the Labour Party was so close that TUC affiliation represented an inferential political alignment which journalists could not accept by the very nature of their profession.

Even when white-collar unionists do agree to establish a political fund and affiliate to the Labour Party, their contracting-out rates are generally higher than those of manual unionists.[6] In 1964 the contracting-out rate was 13 per cent in the London Clerical Branch of NATSOPA, 21 per cent in the CAWU,

---

[1] *The Blackcoated Worker* (London: Allen & Unwin, 1958), p. 182 n. 1.

[2] There are also more manual unions affiliated to the TUC than to the Labour Party. In fact, some of these unions are just as opposed to political action as are white-collar unions. See Martin Harrison, *Trade Unions and the Labour Party Since 1945* (London: Allen & Unwin, 1960), p. 325, and A. J. M. Sykes, 'Attitudes to Political Affiliation in a Printing Trade Union', *Scottish Journal of Political Economy*, xii (June, 1965), pp. 161–79.

[3] Hughes, op. cit., p. 21.

[4] Mortimer, op. cit., pp. 447–8, table 15. Harrison, op. cit., p. 23, claims DATA also went to the polls in 1921 over the question of establishing a political fund, but this is incorrect.

[5] Ibid., p. 25 n. 1.

[6] The following contracting-out figures have been obtained from either the union concerned or the Registrar of Friendly Societies.

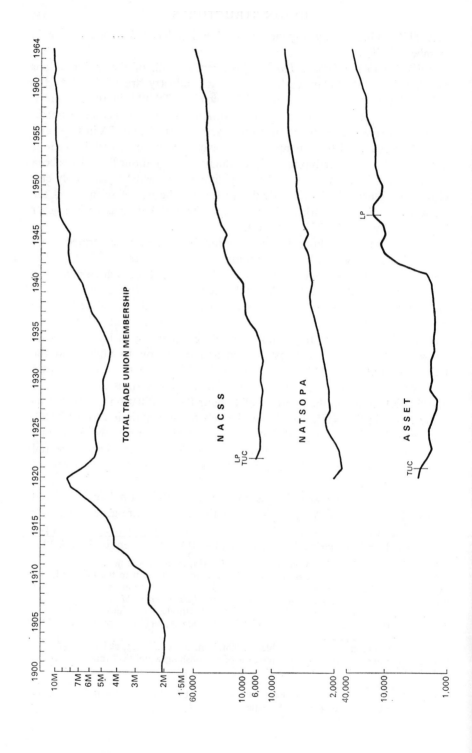

TOTAL TRADE UNION MEMBERSHIP

N A C S S

N A T S O P A

A S S E T

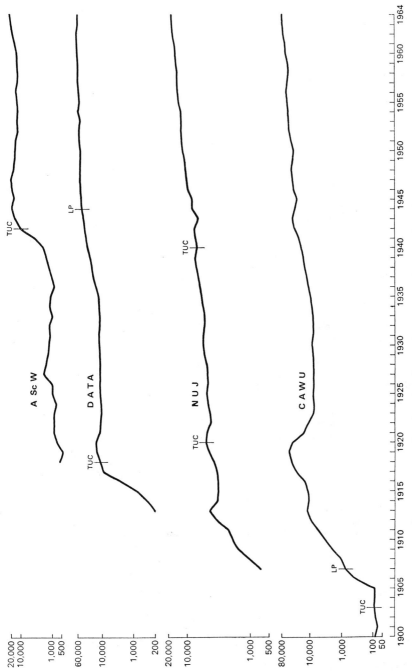

Fig. 7.2. The rate of growth of trade union membership.

48 per cent in ASSET,[1] and 58 per cent in DATA,[2] as compared to 3 to 4 per cent among the total memberships of NATSOPA, BISAKTA, and the TGWU.[3] The higher contracting-out rates among white-collar workers are hardly surprising since it is well known that they are more prone to support the Conservative or Liberal Parties than the Labour Party.[4]

Those writers who have suggested that TUC affiliation may restrict a union's ability to recruit white-collar workers have generally suggested the same, but even more strongly, regarding Labour Party affiliation.[5] Even some of the writers who have argued that TUC affiliation is not an obstacle to recruiting are not so sure about political affiliation. Lockwood notes that the CAWU was very active in the political sphere during the 1930s and suggests that 'it may very well be that clerks outside the union were deterred from joining because of its left-wing policy'.[6] But this is unlikely. The 1930s, as Fig. 7.2 demonstrates, was a period in which the CAWU's membership grew fairly rapidly. It might be argued that it would have grown even more rapidly if the union had not been so politically active, but there is no evidence to support this view. Nor does the evidence lend much support to the view that Labour Party affiliation

[1] This union's contracting-out rate had previously been much higher. In 1960 it was approximately 96 per cent. The reason for this seems to be that prior to 1960 most of its membership existed in a state of limbo in regard to the political fund. That is, they did not pay the political levy, nor did they contract out. The contracting-out form was included on the membership application form, and after 1960 the union refused to accept the application unless the political levy was included with it or the contracting-out section of the form was completed.

[2] DATA's contracting-out rate has been increasing over most of the post-war period. In 1948 it was only 35 per cent. The union's official historian (Mortimer, op. cit., pp. 421–2) claims that this high contracting-out rate is partly explained by the way in which the Association has collected the political levy.

The contribution is levied monthly and a separate stamp is issued for it. On the membership card the monthly political contribution stamp is as prominent as the industrial contribution stamp. It thus serves as a constant reminder to the member that he is paying a monthly levy. If for some reason or other he feels momentarily dissatisfied with the labour movement he may be inclined to 'contract out' of paying the political contribution when the time comes for him to pay his monthly subscription. The method of collecting the political contribution in the A.E.S.D. almost requires from the individual member a conscious reaffirmation, month by month, of his support for the political labour movement.

This assessment seems to be at least partly correct. Towards the end of 1963, the union installed a computer, centralized its financial system, and issued a new membership card which did not distinguish between the political and industrial contributions. By 1966 the union's contracting-out rate had dropped to 47 per cent.

[3] The vast majority of the members who contract out in these unions are white-collar workers. No figures are available for Section J of BISAKTA or the NACSS, but in NATSOPA 86 per cent of the members who contracted out in 1964 were from the London Clerical Branch alone.

[4] See John Bonham, *The Middle Class Vote* (London: Faber, 1954), and D. E. Butler and Anthony King, *The British General Election of 1964* (London: Macmillan, 1965), p. 296.

[5] See, for example, Bernard Donoughue, *Trade Unions in a Changing Society* (London: Political and Economic Planning, 1963), pp. 195–6.

[6] Op. cit., p. 167.

has a detrimental effect on unions' growth rates. DATA's growth rate was roughly the same before and after affiliation which suggests that it had little impact upon the union's growth. The CAWU's growth rate was slightly less after affiliation, while that of ASSET was considerably less. But the CAWU's growth rate immediately before and after affiliation and, to a lesser extent, that of ASSET tend to follow that of trade union membership in general which suggests that some factor common to all unions rather than something unique to the unions in question such as Labour Party affiliation was responsible for the change in growth rates. Finally, it is worth noting that although many draughtsmen are opposed, or at least do not support, the political activities of DATA, they nevertheless join it.

Inter-union relations. In many countries the most bitter jurisdictional disputes have occurred among unions catering for white-collar workers, and this has frequently been offered as at least a partial explanation for why the density of white-collar unionism in these countries is not higher than it is.[1] Whatever the effect of jurisdictional disputes in other countries, their impact upon the growth of white-collar unionism in Britain has been negligible. The reason for this is very simple: there have been few serious jurisdictional disputes among British white-collar unions. Of course, the recruiting interests of these unions overlap at various points and they come into competition for members. There has been competition among the CAWU, the NACSS, and the NUGMW in most industries for clerical workers, as well as between them and BISAKTA in the iron and steel industry and between the CAWU and the National Union of Mineworkers in the coal industry. There has been competition between ASSET and DATA for such grades as planning, process, and methods engineers; between ASSET and the CAWU for such grades as progress chasers, schedulers, and programmers; between ASSET and the AScW for certain scientific and technical grades; and, to a much lesser extent, between the NUJ and the IOJ for journalists, and NATSOPA and the NUPBPW for certain white-collar grades, in the paper, printing, and publishing industry. There has also been competition between ASSET and such manual unions as the AEU, the ETU, the Boilermakers' Society, and BISAKTA for foremen and certain technical grades. But this competition has created relatively little friction and rarely broken into open conflict.[2] Almost all the disputes have been settled peacefully either by the unions themselves or by the Disputes Committee of the TUC.

In fact recent mergers between some of these unions have reduced what

[1] See, for example, *Non-Manual Workers and Collective Bargaining* (Geneva: ILO, 1956), p. 45, and Blum, op. cit., pp. 89–95.

[2] The recognition-jurisdiction dispute which occurred in the steel industry after it was nationalized is an outstanding exception to this generalization, but it is nevertheless an exception. See also G. S. Bain, *Trade Union Growth and Recognition* (London: HMSO, Royal Commission on Trade Unions and Employers' Associations, Research Paper No. 6, 1967), p. 54 n. 76.

little friction exists. NATSOPA and the NUPBPW merged in 1966 to form SOGAT, and the AScW and ASSET merged in 1968 to form the ASTMS. Although the NUJ and the IOJ have not merged, they have agreed on arrangements for dual membership and closer working. In addition, there is a Joint Consultative Committee of Staff Unions in the engineering industry which serves as a forum for the discussion of common problems by the ASTMS, the CAWU, DATA, the NACSS, and the NUGMW. But at least one writer has argued that there is room for further mergers among white-collar unions in private industry. Hindell feels that a merger of the clerical membership of the TGWU and the NUGMW with that of the CAWU would eliminate some needless competition and pool resources of staff and money so that both could be more efficiently deployed, and that this would have a beneficial effect upon membership growth.[1] Even granting that these mergers could be brought about, it is doubtful if they would greatly affect the density of white-collar unionism in private industry. At least, the existence of a single union for the distributive trades does not seem to have greatly boosted its level of unionism. Nor does the existence of a large number of unions for employees in national government seem to have retarded the growth of unionism in this area.

CONCLUSIONS

A great many people believe that the growth of unionism among white-collar workers is largely in the hands of the unions themselves. If only they would make themselves more popular with the general public, devote more time and energy to recruiting, and design structures more attractive to white-collar workers, they would be successful in recruiting these workers. But this belief is not supported by the evidence in Britain. While it is not reliable enough to permit the conclusion that the public image of the trade union movement, union recruitment policies, and union structures have had no effect upon the growth of white-collar unionism, it certainly does not permit the conclusion that their effect has been of great importance. What evidence there is suggests that these factors have been at most of very secondary importance in explaining the growth of white-collar unionism.

If the growth of white-collar unionism is not greatly influenced by the unions, perhaps it is by the employer. An American labour lawyer has noted that:

In an organizing drive, the advantages of communication are markedly with management. Labor has to rely pretty much on appeals via established media of communication, circulars distributed at the place of the employer, home solicitations, and meetings at a hired hall. Management has available to it a complete and accurate mailing list of employees, together with the plant itself, wherein employees can be addressed as a captive audience, or on their own time. Furthermore, during

[1] Op. cit., pp. 197-8.

working hours other than for relief and rest periods, management contacts with employees are more frequent and more sustained. This is a matter about which one could comment at length.[1]

This is also true in Britain, and the following chapter does comment on it at some length.

[1] Robert J. Doolan, 'Attitudes of White-Collar Workers Toward Unionization', *Addresses on Industrial Relations* (Ann Arbor: University of Michigan, Bureau of Industrial Relations, 1959), p. 11.

VIII

THE EMPLOYERS

THE employers' role in union growth has generally been neglected. Even when its importance has been noted, it has not received much systematic or detailed attention. This neglect is not justified. For even the most superficial reflection should indicate that employer policies and practices may profoundly affect the growth and development of trade unionism. Where employers disapprove of trade unions and pursue policies designed to discourage their employees from joining them, trade union growth is likely to be retarded. Conversely, where employers recognize and negotiate with trade unions and encourage their employees to belong to them, trade union growth is likely to be stimulated.

In order to obtain some information on employer attitudes and behaviour with regard to white-collar unionism, a survey of individual employers and employers' associations in private industry was carried out during May–July 1966.[1] The author interviewed twenty-five major firms and fourteen employers' associations, and, in addition, a questionnaire was sent to 142 employers' associations and fifteen firms. All of the organizations approached agreed to be interviewed; the response rate to the questionnaire was 86 per cent. The employers' associations were chosen, with the help of the Confederation of British Industry, as being the most important ones in the industry concerned. The firms were chosen partly because of their size and partly because they were known to have refused or to have granted recognition to white-collar unions.[2] This survey of employers was supplemented by information obtained from interviews during 1965–6 with sixty full-time officials of the major unions catering for white-collar employees in private industry and from documentary sources.

TRADE UNION GROWTH AND RECOGNITION

There are several reasons why the growth of unions is likely to be greater the more willing employers are to recognize them and the greater the degree of

[1] This survey was undertaken on behalf of and under the direction of the Royal Commission on Trade Unions and Employers' Associations, and the findings were published in G. S. Bain, *Trade Union Growth and Recognition* (London: HMSO, Royal Commission on Trade Unions and Employers' Associations, Research Paper No. 6, 1967).

[2] The various firms and employers' associations agreed to co-operate with the Royal Commission and the author on the understanding that their replies would not be attributed to them as organizations. Consequently, material obtained from interviews and questionnaires has been cited in such a manner that the organizations concerned cannot be identified.

recognition[1] which they are prepared to confer upon them. Firstly, workers, especially white-collar workers, tend to identify with management, and they are, therefore, less likely to join trade unions the more strongly management disapproves of them. A NACSS official claimed that before it is possible to recruit many white-collar employees 'you have to be able to show them that their employer is not really opposed, that they won't be disloyal by joining, and that all in all, there is not going to be much of a battle'.

Secondly, the more strongly management disapproves of trade unions, the less likely workers are to join them in case they jeopardize their career prospects. This point is brought out most clearly by the following letter to a union organizer from a technician in a drug-manufacturing company:

As I explained . . . all the members of the technical staff are fearful to have anything to do with our association or any other similar organisation. Apparently the —— Company will have nothing to do with trade unions and most of my colleagues appear to be surprised that I got a job at —— in spite of being a union member. To be quite honest I wasn't asked at the interview if I was a trade union member and to my knowledge they are still unaware of my affiliation.

The evidence which will be presented later in this chapter indicates that the fears of many white-collar workers in this regard are well founded.

Finally and most important, unions are usually accepted on instrumental rather than ideological grounds, 'as something to be used rather than as something in which to believe'.[2] Many employees want to see 'the proof of the pudding' before they join a union but 'the proof of the pudding comes once the union has been recognised'.[3] The less recognition an employer is prepared to give a union the more difficult it is for the union to participate in the process of job regulation and thereby demonstrate to employees that it can provide a service for them. In such circumstances not only are a large number of employees not likely to join the union, but many of those who have already done so are likely to let their membership lapse because the return they are getting on it is insufficient.

There is a considerable body of evidence which supports the argument that recognition is important in fostering union growth. A scholar who studied managerial unionism in the coal industry concluded that it is the 'fact of

---

[1] The assumption is often made that a union either possesses recognition or it does not. But, in reality, union recognition is a matter of degree. On the one extreme, the employer may oppose the union by force or by 'peaceful competition' and there is little or no recognition. On the other extreme, the employer may bargain with the union on any matter it may wish to raise; meet any representatives that the union may appoint; accord the union the necessary facilities to collect subscriptions, hold meetings, and publicize its activities; encourage his employees to join the union; and provide it with essential information for collective bargaining. Between these two extremes, there are many intermediate positions. The variety of employer policies with regard to union recognition should become clearer after reading this chapter.

[2] C. Wright Mills, *White Collar* (New York: Oxford University Press, 1956), p. 308.

[3] Allan Flanders, *Minutes of Evidence 62*, Q. 10,005.

recognition that explains the success of B.A.C.M. [the British Association of Colliery Management]' and the failure of rival organizations.[1]

A sociologist who studied unionization among bank clerks found that about one-fifth of the clerks in his sample who were not in NUBE said they were not members because it was not recognized. 'For one this was an ideological statement, but for the others it was a practical reason, expressing the belief that N.U.B.E. is powerless, or at least less effective than the staff association, because it is not recognised.'[2] He also found that 'the more hostility a bank has shown to the union, the lower has been the union's completeness [membership density]'.[3] This and other evidence he analysed led him to conclude that:

It does seem quite clear that the banks' attitudes, and their relationships with the two organisations, have played an important part in determining the completeness of N.U.B.E. and the staff associations, with recognition or non-recognition being a major factor in the situation. It is hard to doubt that if N.U.B.E. were generally recognised its completeness would be appreciably higher, or that if recognition were withdrawn from the staff associations their completeness would decline.[4]

The best illustration of the importance of employer policies and practices as a factor in union growth is provided in Great Britain by contrasting the public and private sectors of the economy. The density of white-collar unionism in the civil service, local government, and the nationalized industries is extremely high, even among managerial and executive grades.[5] Lockwood has suggested that this is explained by the large-scale bureaucratic administration characteristic of public employment.[6] But while 'bureaucratization' has obviously been very important in encouraging public employees to join trade unions, it has not been the only factor.

An equally and perhaps even more important reason for the high degree of unionism among white-collar employees in the public sector is that their employers have agreed to recognize and negotiate with their unions. In fact, most public employers have gone much further than this and have actively encouraged their employees to join trade unions. Each new entrant to the Civil Service is informed by the Treasury that he is

not only allowed but encouraged to belong to a staff association. Besides being a good thing for the individual civil servant to belong to an association, which can support him in his reasonable claims and put his point of view before the authorities on all kinds of questions affecting his conditions of service, it is also a good thing for Departments and for the Civil Service as a whole that civil servants should be strongly organised in representative bodies. It is only common sense to meet the

---

[1] Brian McCormick, 'Managerial Unionism in the Coal Industry', *British Journal of Sociology*, xi (December 1960), p. 367.

[2] R. M. Blackburn, *Union Character and Social Class* (London: Batsford, 1967), p. 250.

[3] Ibid., p. 249.   [4] Ibid., p. 251.   [5] See Table 3.2.

[6] David Lockwood, *The Blackcoated Worker* (London: Allen & Unwin, 1958), pp. 141–9, and *supra*, pp. 74–5.

wishes of the civil servant about his conditions of service as far as possible, for a contented staff will work much more efficiently than a staff which feels that its interests are being completely ignored by the 'management'. But it is hopeless to try to find out the wishes of a scattered unorganised body of individual civil servants each of whom may express a different view. When they get together in representative associations, their collective wish can be democratically determined and passed on to the 'management' with real force and agreement behind it; the 'management' know where they stand and can act accordingly.[1]

Most local authorities and nationalized industries have made similar pronouncements.

By contrast with the public sector, the density of unionization among white-collar employees in private industry is very low.[2] Lockwood has suggested that this is accounted for by the large number of small firms and the resulting low degree of 'bureaucratization' characteristic of private employment.[3] The present study has already shown that there is a great deal of truth in Lockwood's contention.[4] But again, it is by no means the whole story. Employer policies and practices are also important.

Most private employers, unlike those in the public sector, refuse to recognize and negotiate with white-collar unions, and many of them even pursue policies designed to discourage their white-collar employees from joining unions.[5] A survey undertaken by the British Employers' Confederation (one of the organizations which merged to form the present Confederation of British Industry) in 1963–4 revealed that:

Of 23 Member Organisations which replied to the questionnaire only one was able to state, without reservations, that trade union representation of staff workers is recognised, that this recognition is on a formal basis and that agreements covering the rates of pay, etc. of staff workers are made at national or company level. A few other Member Organisations indicated that staff unions are recognised to a limited extent (e.g. they are recognised only at certain firms or only in respect of certain types of staff workers) but generally such recognition is limited to procedure and does not cover the making of agreements.[6]

While this survey is somewhat limited in scope, its general conclusion is supported by an unpublished Ministry of Labour estimate that some 85 per cent of white-collar employees in manufacturing industries are not covered by collective agreements. In other words, probably not more than 15 per cent of staff workers in manufacturing industries have had their right to union representation recognized by employers.[7]

[1] Cited by Richard Hayward, *Whitley Councils in the United Kingdom Civil Service* (London: Civil Service National Whitley Council, Staff Side, 1963), p. 2.
[2] See Table 3.5.   [3] Loc. cit.   [4] *Supra*, pp. 72–81.
[5] These policies are described *infra*, pp. 131–5.
[6] 'Exchange of Views and Information: Staff Workers' (London: The Confederation, Wages and Conditions Committee, 1964), p. 1. (Mimeographed.)
[7] See also Bain, op. cit., especially pp. 68–72, and table 18.

There can be little doubt that a major reason for the difference in the density of white-collar unionism between the public and private sectors of the economy is the difference in employer policies and practices with regard to union recognition. Variations in such policies and practices also help to account for variations in the density of white-collar unionism within the private sector itself. Chapter III demonstrated[1] that union density among most white-collar workers in engineering and electrical goods, shipbuilding and marine engineering, vehicles, iron and steel, and newspaper publishing, as well as among foremen and overlookers in textiles[2] is relatively quite high. These are also the areas in which at least some form of white-collar union recognition has generally existed for several years.

The Engineering Employers' Federation[3] conceded recognition to the CAWU, the NACSS, and the NUGMW for clerical workers in 1920, 1940, and 1953 respectively, to DATA for draughtsmen and certain allied technical grades in 1924, and to the AScW for certain scientific and technical grades in 1944.[4] It also agreed to recognize ASSET in 1944, but only where the union had majority membership in a particular grade in a particular establishment of a member-firm. The Shipbuilding Employers' Federation recognized DATA in 1941.[5] In 1943 the Iron and Steel Trades Employers' Association adopted a policy of encouraging, but not compelling, member-firms to recognize BISAKTA for clerical workers, laboratory staffs, and departmental foremen, and, to a lesser extent, DATA for drawing-office staffs and the various craft unions for craft foremen.[6] The major proprietorial associations in the newspaper industry recognized the NUJ during and immediately after the First World War. The Newspaper Proprietors Association recognized the NUPBPW and NATSOPA for clerical and certain other administrative workers in 1919 and 1920 respectively, while the Newspaper Society recognized NATSOPA for clerical workers in 1938. Both the Newspaper Proprietors Association and the Newspaper Society recognized the Institute of Journalists in 1943. In the cotton-spinning industry, the British Spinners' and Doublers' Association granted a limited form of recognition to the Textile Officials' Association for supervisory grades in 1950.

Clearly, those areas of private industry in which some form of white-collar

---

[1] *Supra*, especially pp. 33–7 and Table 3.8.

[2] The density of unionization among foremen in textiles is relatively high partly, but not entirely, because weaving overlookers who are really manual workers had to be included in this category for reasons of comparability. See *supra*, p. 32 n. 3.

[3] This Federation covers the majority of firms in engineering and electrical goods, vehicles, certain sections of metal manufacture, and marine engineering (but not shipbuilding).

[4] The concessions of recognition which are mentioned in this chapter are described in much greater detail in Chapter IX.

[5] Since 1964 there have been further concessions of recognition to white-collar unions in the shipbuilding industry. See *infra*, p. 176 n. 3.

[6] Since 1964 the white-collar union recognition situation in the iron and steel industry has been considerably changed by the nationalization of the industry. See *infra*, p. 166 n. 1.

union recognition has generally existed for several years are also those in which the density of white-collar unionism is highest. Unfortunately, the relationship between union membership and recognition cannot be expressed more precisely. Recognition, unlike membership, does not lend itself very well to quantification. There are considerable differences in the degree or quality of the recognition which has been conceded to the various white-collar unions. The Engineering Employers' Federation compelled its member-firms to recognize ASSET only where it had majority membership; this condition still applies for its successor, Division I of the ASTMS. But all the other staff unions in engineering are recognized regardless of the extent of their membership. The British Spinners' and Doublers' Association has recognized the Textile Officials' Association but has refused to enter into formal joint agreements with it. Employers in the public sector have not only recognized the various staff unions, they have also encouraged their employees to join them. It is difficult, if not impossible, to know what weight should be assigned to these and numerous other qualitative differences in the form which white-collar union recognition has taken.

Although recognition cannot be quantified and subjected to statistical analysis, sufficient evidence has been presented here to establish that recognition is very closely associated with membership. But this does not prove that recognition produces membership. It may be that membership is the major factor influencing the employers' decision regarding recognition. Employers may withhold recognition from unions where they do not have sufficient membership to justify its concession and concede it where they do.

'Representativeness' is certainly the criterion which most employers claim to use in deciding whether or not to recognize a union for white-collar employees. Before the Treasury will recognize any staff union, it 'must show that it is representative of the category of staff concerned'.[1] The Engineering Employers' Federation insisted on majority membership as the criterion for recognizing ASSET, and still does for recognizing its successor, Division I of the ASTMS. Similarly, Unilever has claimed that its companies will

recognise a union's right to represent employees and negotiate on their behalf wherever it has established membership amongst a majority of the group which a company is prepared to accept as a 'negotiating group'. At the same time, our companies regard the building up of union membership to the level required for negotiating rights as primarily the responsibility of the unions themselves. Where a union fails to satisfy a company that it has a genuine majority amongst the 'negotiating group', it cannot be said to have earned the right to represent the group.[2]

Lloyds Bank claimed in its evidence to the Donovan Commission that it refused recognition to the National Union of Bank Employees because the bank's 'Staff Association . . . has (by a considerable margin) the greater

---

[1] H.M. Treasury, *Staff Relations in the Civil Service* (London: HMSO, 1965), para. 12.
[2] Unilever Limited, *Minutes of Evidence 46*, p. 1972.

membership'.[1] Another firm 'could only accept trade union representation in the knowledge that at least 80 per cent of our staff are members of the union'. Many of the other employers who were surveyed indicated that they had refused to recognize a staff union because it had not represented a 'substantial proportion' of the employees concerned.

But it is very doubtful if lack of representativeness is the major reason why most private employers refuse to recognize white-collar unions. In applying the criterion of representativeness it is necessary to define three concepts— 'representativeness', 'area of representation', and 'recognition'.[2] In Britain these concepts are usually defined by the employer and in such a way that either it is extremely difficult for the union to 'earn' recognition, or the form of recognition 'earned' is hardly worth having. When this is the case the criterion of representativeness merely becomes a 'respectable' device by which an employer can deny a union recognition.

There is no general agreement as to what 'representativeness' means. Some employers are prepared, and in engineering are obliged, to recognize a union if only one of their staff employees is a member. Other employers will not grant recognition unless a union has recruited 33 per cent of the employees concerned; others expect 51 per cent; and still others interpret 'substantial proportion' as substantial majority and expect unions to have 75 per cent or better. For a few employers the expected percentage tends to be a variable which moves upward as the union's actual membership in the firm increases. Employers who demand an extremely high degree of 'representativeness' would seem to be motivated not so much by their concern that the union should actually be representative of their employees as by their concern that it should not represent them at all.

Employers who claim that they will recognize a representative union, often choose the area over which it will be most difficult for the union to demonstrate its representativeness. Sometimes the firm may have an organizational reason for the choice of this area. But generally it is designed merely to keep the union out. One large company employing approximately 7,000 foremen in forty different establishments claimed it would only recognize ASSET if it could organize a majority of all the foremen and refused to recognize it on an establishment-by-establishment basis. In an interview the company admitted that there was no 'positive' reason for choosing this national area of representation, and that its primary purpose was to put 'a major hurdle in the way of the union'.

Another large company employing roughly 40,000 white-collar employees in seventy-five establishments has agreed to recognize a union for any particular occupational grade, but only if it has majority membership among this grade across the company as a whole. The company's justification for

[1] Lloyds Bank Limited, *Written Evidence*, p. 1.
[2] This is treated in greater detail in Bain, op. cit., paras. 202–4 and 211–12.

this policy was that it had a national salary structure. But it could advance no logical reason in support of such a salary structure or show that the efficiency of the company's operations would be impaired if local salary structures were adopted. In fact, the national salary structure was only introduced fairly recently, about the same time as various unions began recruiting the firm's staff. Moreover, as the company itself pointed out, this salary structure often resulted in overpaying in areas of labour surplus and underpaying in areas of labour shortage. The company's claim that it is not opposed to staff unionism is therefore not altogether convincing.

Some employers will recognize a union for staff employees only if it is representative across the whole industry concerned. Until 1967[1] the Shipbuilding Employers' Federation argued that the recognition of staff unions was a matter of interest to all employers in the industry, for what one firm did in this regard might set a precedent which other firms would be forced to follow. The Federation therefore advised all member-firms to agree only to informal discussions with a staff union over the grievances of an individual member and to refer all claims for recognition on behalf of staff grades to the Federation. For its part, the Federation would only recognize those unions which were representative of a 'substantial proportion' of a particular staff grade throughout the industry as a whole. As a result of this policy the CAWU was refused recognition both nationally and domestically, for while it claimed to have 'a high degree of organization at certain establishments' it did not represent a 'substantial proportion' of the clerical workers employed in the industry as a whole.

When employers say they are prepared to recognize any union which is representative of a particular area of staff employment, this does not necessarily mean that they are prepared to grant 'full' recognition. Many of them will not negotiate with the union; they are only prepared to enter into informal discussions regarding the grievances of individual members.

A leading employers' association covering a key area for future white-collar union growth gives the following advice to member-firms when they find that a substantial proportion of their white-collar employees are organized and 'contact with a staff union seems unavoidable':

It is desirable to confine recognition of a staff union to representations on behalf of members and to exclude *negotiations* on staff salary scales, etc. The difference between representation and negotiation is important. The first do not compel managements to act in the manner desired, while the latter may result in a binding agreement.

Similarly, the Wages and Conditions Committee of the British Employers' Confederation (one of the organizations which merged to form the Confederation of British Industry) took the view in June 1964 that:

Even where membership of staff unions is increasing employers are under no

[1] See *infra*, p. 176 n. 3.

obligation to recognise union representation . . . Even if 'recognition' were granted
to a staff union, this need not include the negotiation of wages and conditions of
employment, but might be limited to informal discussions or to the laying down of
procedure for dealing with requests and complaints.[1]

But the Committee also took the view that:

There is a danger . . . that once a staff union has been recognised, for any purpose
at all, as representing the interests of staff workers, it will be encouraged to press
for the full rights of negotiation. Those members who have already granted full
'recognition' . . . confirmed that official representation of staff workers could be a
source of much difficulty to employers. In the circumstances the Committee agreed
that when discussions were held with staff unions it would be best if possible to
avoid the use of the word 'recognition'.[2]

The possibility that partial recognition might lead to demands for full
recognition has not worried some employers' associations, however, for when
such demands have arisen, they have been refused and even the partial
recognition has been revoked. One employers' association had a procedure
agreement with DATA, but the union 'eventually chose to attempt to use
the Agreement to further a claim for wages which was not the purpose of the
Procedure Agreement. In the circumstances, and in accordance with the
final paragraph of the Agreement, the —— terminated the Agreement.'

These examples indicate that even after a union has demonstrated its
'representativeness', many employers are only prepared to recognize it for
purposes of discussion not negotiation. In fact, discussion rights are often
granted in the hope that they will lessen the demands for negotiating rights.
While it is useful for a union to be able to discuss with management the
grievances of individual members, it is by no means wholly satisfactory.
As the Ministry of Labour's definition of a trade union emphasizes, a major
union function is the negotiation of wages and working conditions. Employers
who refuse to allow a union to negotiate on these matters are thereby preventing it from exercising one of its major functions. Such employers can
hardly claim to be speaking in good faith when they say they will 'recognize'
any union which can demonstrate its representativeness.

Even if employers apply the criterion of representativeness in the fairest
possible manner, there are still grounds for doubting that lack of representativeness is their major reason for refusing recognition. If an employer has no
principled objection to white-collar unionism and his only desire is to ensure
that a substantial proportion of his staff wish to be represented by a union

---

[1] Op. cit., p. 2. This document evidently recorded the views of the Wages and Conditions
Committee only. In giving oral evidence to the Royal Commission, representatives of the
CBI pointed out that it had not been considered by the BEC Council nor approved by its
President or Director. The CBI's present policy was described as 'waiting and seeing', and
neither to stimulate nor to prevent the development of white-collar unions. See *Minutes of
Evidence* 22, p. 822.

[2] Loc. cit.

before he recognizes it, then he should be prepared to give his staff every opportunity to join the union and the union every opportunity to recruit them. If an employer who advances the criterion of representativeness is not prepared to do this, then his claim that he will recognize any representative union is rather hollow, for he is denying the union the means of obtaining recognition.

But few employers are prepared to allow an unrecognized union freedom of access to its potential members by giving it facilities to hold meetings during the lunch break or outside office hours, distribute literature or display notices, collect subscriptions, or process grievances on behalf of individual members. Few employers are even prepared to play a neutral role in the recruiting process, but pursue policies designed to discourage their staff from joining unions.

EMPLOYER POLICIES FOR DISCOURAGING WHITE-COLLAR EMPLOYEES FROM JOINING TRADE UNIONS

If union organizers are to be believed:

The employers will stop at nothing. Every case has to be fought through. They utilise staff associations, give general salary increases while a recruitment campaign is underway, and intimidate and victimise leading members. They also conduct a campaign of demoralisation through the supervisors—'You'll never get recognition', 'You won't be able to do anything, etc.'

Broadly speaking, there are two basic strategies which managers use to discourage their staff employees from joining trade unions—peaceful competition and forcible opposition.[1] These are not mutually exclusive strategies, and often both of them are pursued simultaneously. But it is useful to treat them separately for purposes of analysis.

The strategy of peaceful competition

The strategy of peaceful competition includes a variety of tactics: paying salaries equal to or better than those in unionized firms; granting salary increases during a union recruitment campaign; establishing welfare, profit sharing, and other benefit schemes; offering various types of rewards to 'loyal' employees; giving speeches and interviews designed to convince employees that their interests can be better cared for by management than by a union; granting monthly staff status; and establishing 'company unions'.

It is difficult to document adequately the use of these tactics. Salary increases during recruitment campaigns can be 'explained' by reference to the cost of living or increasing productivity; rewards to 'loyal' employees can be 'justified' on grounds of merit; and the thoughts expressed in speeches and

---

[1] These terms are used by Lloyd G. Reynolds, *Labor Economics and Labor Relations* (Englewood Cliffs, N.J.: Prentice-Hall, 1956), pp. 169–77.

interviews are rarely written down. Moreover, opposition to staff unionism may not be the only reason for following many of the tactics of peaceful competition. While they may be inspired primarily by a strong desire to keep the unions out, they may also be motivated by an employer's sincere wish to treat his staff employees properly and as a 'part of management'. Nevertheless, there are some examples of these tactics being deliberately used to discourage the growth of staff unionism.

An employers' association which 'has refused requests from staff unions for a national procedure agreement or negotiations on several occasions' offers the following service to member-firms:

. . . as a condition of avoiding negotiations with a staff union it is essential that member firms should be offering salaries and conditions which are not open to criticism and the Association is prepared to collect information, national and local, and give advice on such matters. This has been done on a limited and voluntary basis for a number of years and it is intended to extend and improve this service on behalf of members.[1]

An executive in the motor industry frankly admitted that:

ASSET had a fairly substantial membership among our chargehands and as a result we decided to grant some of them staff status and reduce the remainder to operative status.

Other employers were less specific, and simply stated that:

Every possible step is taken to ensure that staff do not reach the frame of mind which will make them think that membership of a union is appropriate.

Although many employers sponsor staff associations or committees to slow down 'the current somewhat sinister trend towards subversive influence from outside',[2] it is not possible to estimate how many of these exist in private industry. But several observations can be made regarding the nature of those which came to light as a result of the survey of employers. Only one was a staff association in the sense that all employees of the company were not automatically members but had to be recruited. The rest were staff committees in the sense that a group of employees was simply elected to represent the views of the staff to management. All were established on the initiative of the employer, in many cases after an approach from a staff union for recognition. Most had only 'consultative and advisory powers' and did not negotiate over salaries and other conditions of employment. Of those companies which allowed their staff committees to negotiate, only one permitted disputes to be submitted to independent arbitration. In all other cases the top executive officer of the company was the final court of appeal.

The best-known device for discouraging staff unionism in private industry

---

[1] Circular Letter from the Association to all Member-Firms, 1964.
[2] M. J. Ruddock, 'Some Problems of Clerical Staff Employment', *Factory Manager*, xxiii (April 1954), p. 90.

is the Foremen and Staff Mutual Benefit Society, a friendly society established in 1899 to provide pensions, life assurance, and sickness benefits to foremen and similar grades of staff in the engineering and shipbuilding industries.[1] The Society has two kinds of members: contributory members or employers; and ordinary members, the eligible employees of contributory members. Contributory members pay at least half of the total contributions in respect of each ordinary member. The FSMBS has over 2,600 contributory members and over 61,000 ordinary members, of whom 8,700 are in receipt of a pension.

Under the Society's rules an ordinary member may not belong to a trade union. In other words, to become a member of the Society an employee must resign any trade union membership which he may hold, or, if he wishes to join a trade union after he has become a Society member, he must resign from the Society. This means he must forfeit his claim to the contributions which the employer has made on his behalf, and that he receives only the surrender value (about 90 per cent) of his own contributions. In short, he must sacrifice 55 per cent of all moneys paid to the FSMBS on his behalf. For many staff employees, especially older ones, this is an obvious deterrent to becoming or remaining a union member.

The Engineering Employers' Federation and the Shipbuilding Employers' Federation advise member-firms to join the FSMBS and to encourage their eligible staff employees to do likewise. Although both Federations are opposed to firms coercing employees into the Society, a few of the employers who were interviewed admitted making an employee's promotion to foreman conditional upon his becoming a member of the Society. No doubt most contributory members do not adopt such measures, but it is clear from the interviews that most of them encourage foremen to join the FSMBS and give it facilities for recruiting and retaining members which are denied to staff unions.

The strategy of forcible opposition

The second strategy which employers use to oppose staff unionism is forcible opposition. This strategy is implemented by such tactics as: overlooking union members for promotion and pay rises, transferring active unionists from department to department, threatening to discontinue any 'extras' presently being paid above the union rate, sending management officials to union recruitment meetings to note the names of those employees attending, and dismissing leading union members. It is also difficult to document the use of these tactics, for threats are generally communicated verbally and victimization of leading members can often be 'justified' on grounds

---

[1] For a more complete account of this organization see FSMBS, *Written Evidence*; ASSET, *Minutes of Evidence 53*, pp. 2248–51; and *The FSMBS: British Industry's Friendliest Most Sincere Union-Hating Outfit* (London: ASSET, 1966).

such as inefficiency or insubordination. Only cases which trade unionists claim to be examples of forcible opposition can be cited here; the reader must judge for himself whether the facts substantiate these claims.

After recruiting approximately 40 per cent of the weekly paid clerical staff of a private bus company, the CAWU approached the firm for recognition late in 1965. But the company refused to recognize the union, even for discussion purposes, until it had recruited at least 75 per cent of the staff involved. Moreover, the company's general manager sent the following memorandum to each of his staff employees:

> On my return to the office today I was very surprised to read a letter from the above Union seeking formal recognition of this Union as a negotiating body for my weekly paid staff.
>
> Up to this time I have always assumed that the existing direct methods of negotiation between members of my staff and the management have been perfectly adequate and that the general relationship between management and staff has been a very happy one within this Company.
>
> For the moment, the letter has been formally acknowledged as I feel it is only right that I should know the general opinion of all my staff in this matter, because any step which I would take must have far reaching consequences. I am asking you therefore to complete the enclosed form so that I shall know the numbers of my staff involved. This particular matter has been brought up at a rather unfortunate time, because recent discussions I have had with the Company Chairman have proved to be quite fruitful and there was to be a general review within the next two weeks and considerably wider in application than ever previously, embracing as it would have done the junior staff under 21 years of age. For the moment this will have to be suspended until I am aware of your views with regard to this Union.
>
> Your replies will be handed to myself personally and will be treated in strict confidence.

The union claimed that this was an attempt to intimidate the staff. The company denied the charge and said it was entitled to know which members of the staff were union members. In spite of a boycott of the firm by the local Trades and Labour Council, a publicity campaign waged by the union in the local press, and attempts by the Ministry of Labour to obtain a settlement of the dispute, the company still refused to recognize the union.

During 1963 ASSET organized all of the thirty foremen employed at a Scottish factory of an optical manufacturing company. The firm refused to recognize the union and the foremen consequently staged a half-day protest stoppage. The company retaliated by dismissing all the foremen. Three months later, and after the intervention of the Scottish TUC, the firm rehired all but four of the foremen. The four men who were not rehired consisted of the union's local group secretary, treasurer, and chairman, plus the person who had first requested ASSET to recruit the company's foremen. Three of the men had sixteen years' service and the other had thirteen years'. ASSET claimed this was a case of victimization. The company denied this charge. It claimed that a reorganization had resulted in fewer employees being required and that it had the right to rehire 'the best people to serve the company'.[1]

It is not possible, of course, to give even a rough estimate of the extent to which the methods of peaceful competition and forcible opposition are used. But it is obvious from the above examples and many more which could be given that such methods are used by a considerable number of employers to discourage their white-collar employees from joining trade unions.

EMPLOYER BELIEFS REGARDING WHITE-COLLAR UNIONISM

The fact that most employers who claim not to recognize white-collar unions because of their lack of representativeness also try to ensure by one means or another that they do not become representative, suggests that this is not their major reason for withholding recognition. This conclusion is supported by the findings of the survey of employers. It indicates that there are more fundamental reasons why most private employers refuse to recognize white-collar unions. Some employers withhold recognition from certain unions because they consider them inappropriate for the occupation, firm, or industry concerned; other employers refuse to recognize any form of white-collar unionism because they believe it is unnecessary or because they fear it will have certain 'dire consequences'.

The 'appropriateness' of a union

Certain unions have been refused recognition because employers did not consider them 'appropriate' to represent a particular industry or category of staff. Before nationalization most iron and steel employers felt that BISAKTA was the appropriate union to represent the industry's clerks, laboratory staffs, and foremen, and they refused to recognize ASSET, the CAWU, or the AScW for these grades.[2] The British Spinners' and Doublers' Association granted recognition to the Textile Officials' Association because it was considered more appropriate than ASSET. The British Federation of Master Printers refused to recognize NATSOPA for clerical workers partly because it felt that a purely white-collar union with a wider industrial scope such as the CAWU would be more appropriate to represent these workers. Some companies have recognized the TGWU or the NUGMW for all their employees, both manual and non-manual, and have refused recognition to all other applicants because they did not wish to have a multiplicity of unions.

[1] ASSET also claimed that the company, as a government contractor, was in breach of clauses 4 and 5 of the Fair Wages Resolution, and it referred the firm, through the Minister of Labour, to the Industrial Court. The Industrial Court found that the firm was in breach of clause 5 (which concerns the posting up of copies of the Fair Wages Resolution) but not of clause 4 (which obliges contractors to recognize the freedom of their workpeople to be members of trade unions).

[2] See *supra*, p. 126 n. 6.

Still other employers have refused to recognize DATA or ASSET because they felt these unions were 'so politically motivated, that they would only be a disruptive force'.

Employers have applied the criterion of 'appropriateness' most often in deciding whether or not to recognize manual workers' unions on behalf of staff grades. Before most employers' organizations considered any of the manual workers' unions 'appropriate' to represent white-collar employees, these unions were required to make certain structural modifications: the Newspaper Society required NATSOPA to establish an autonomous clerical section; the Iron and Steel Trades Employers' Association demanded that BISAKTA establish separate branches for staff workers; the Engineering Employers' Federation insisted that the TGWU establish a separate organization, the NACSS, and that the NUGMW establish a separate clerical department with its own national officer and notepaper.

In particular, employers have used the criterion of 'appropriateness' in refusing recognition to manual unions on behalf of supervisory staffs. Most employers have traditionally argued that while they have no objection to supervisory workers retaining their membership in a central branch of a manual workers' union in order to maintain their rights to accumulated benefits or in case they are demoted to the tools, it is not desirable to have these unions actively representing and negotiating on behalf of foremen. This argument has been well stated by the Overseas Employers' Federation:

> Employers . . . argue against supervisory staff being members of a rank and file union, on the grounds that supervisory staff must obviously be in a position to exercise discipline, which must inevitably result in situations in which there is a conflict between their duty to the employer and their loyalty to their union and fellow members. Management would rightly regard it as prejudicial if action taken by the supervisors in the course of their duty could be called into question by the union, which can give directions to a supervisor by virtue of his membership in the union.
>
> .   .   .   .   .
>
> This does not mean that he cannot join a union, but because of his relation to management, it is inappropriate for him to join the same bargaining unit as those whom he supervises and, in effect, sit on both sides of the bargaining table at once: he remains free to join a union whose objectives are not in conflict with his responsibilities.[1]

This question has been most fully debated in the shipbuilding and engineering industries. The major manual workers' unions, particularly the Boilermakers' Society and the AEU[2], have for several years been demanding the right to represent any supervisory grades which they have in membership. They claim it is up to the supervisor to choose which union he wishes to represent him, and, in any case, they are anxious 'to offset the infiltration of

---

[1] *Supervisory Staff and Trade Union Membership* (London: The Federation, 1963), pp. 2–3.

[2] Now the AEF. See p. xv.

less desirable forms of organisation' among supervisory grades (presumably a reference to ASSET).

The Boilermakers' Society first sought negotiating rights from the Shipbuilding Employers' Federation on behalf of foremen in 1950. In 1958 the union established a supervisory branch in each district, removed these branches from the jurisdiction of the rank and file District Committees, and placed them under the control of the full-time District Delegate who was made responsible to the Executive Council on all matters concerning foremen. The Shipbuilding Employers' Federation argued that in practice this structural modification did not mean a great deal for since the District Delegate was under the control of the District Committee on all other matters, it was still possible for the District Committee to bring pressure to bear on him and thereby indirectly control the supervisory branches. The employers pointed to several instances where in spite of this modification in the union's structure, it had been possible for foremen to be taken before District Committees and fined for 'acting contrary to the interests of the Society'. The Federation therefore felt that the Boilermakers' Society was not an appropriate organisation to represent supervisors and on several occasions refused the union recognition for supervisory grades. In 1967, the Federation revised this policy, but only after the Boilermakers' Society agreed to place all their supervisory membership in a central branch under the control of national rather than district officials.[1]

In 1963 the Executive Committee of the AEU decided to open a supervisory branch in each district, to remove these branches from the jurisdiction of the District Committees, and to make them directly responsible to the full-time Divisional Organizer. For some time the AEU pressed its claim for negotiating rights for foremen in individual engineering firms, and in November 1965 it requested such rights from the Federation itself. But the Federation refused the request because it did not consider that a manual union was appropriate for representing foremen.[2]

Staff unionism is unnecessary

Some employers refuse to accept that any union is appropriate to represent staff employees because they believe themselves better able than any 'outside organization' to look after the interests of these employees. These employers argue that their 'door is always open' and that they are prepared to give their personal consideration to any grievances which their staff employees may have. In any case, they claim that the terms and conditions of employment being observed by the firm for its staff employees are equal to, if not superior

[1] See infra, p. 176 n. 3.

[2] The NUGMW and the NACSS (Tgwu) have also requested negotiating rights for foremen from the Engineering Employers' Federation. The Federation has refused both these requests because it felt that the concession of such rights could not be confined to these two unions alone, but would have to be extended to other manual unions as well.

to, those negotiated by trade unions. Thus trade union representation for these workers, if not undesirable, is at least superfluous.

This general attitude was expressed by a medium-sized chemical firm which refused recognition to both the AScW and the NACSS because:

At the present time our staff receive treatment over and above a standard likely to be negotiated by any staff union.

It was expressed even more fully by the personnel manager of a large department store chain who refused to recognize USDAW because:

It is our company's policy . . . that all employees have the right to approach the management direct with any complaint or query which may arise, and which might affect the cordial relationship which exists between us. I cannot see any purpose, therefore, in our meeting to discuss the introduction of a third party into the relationship.

Another firm gave an even more intimate relationship with its staff as the reason for refusing to recognize the NACSS:

We regard our Staff as being members of 'The Family'. There is no need for them to be represented by a Union.

While still another company refused to recognize the NACSS because:

We already have a Staff Committee which provides the necessary facilities for staff to make known their views.

The 'dire consequences' of staff unionism

Employers' fear of the results of staff unionism is perhaps their most fundamental reason for refusing recognition. The 'dire consequences' which employers believe will result from staff unionism include restrictions on management's decision-making freedom, dissension and conflict among the members of the staff and between the staff and management leading to a decrease in morale and to divided loyalties, and practices which tend to promote mediocrity.

Restrictions on management's decision-making freedom. The most general fear is that ultimately staff unionism will restrict managements freedom to make decisions. A food manufacturer argued that after unions are recognized:

Management's freedom to act without consultation in areas previously regarded as management's prerogative is restricted.

A brewers' association refused to recognize the NACSS because:

The members of the Association feel that recognition of a white-collar union would seriously impair their responsibility for managing their own businesses.

Similarly, a wholesaler refused to recognize USDAW on the grounds that:

A few of my staff may be members of a trade union and I do not interfere with their right to do so. Conversely I do not expect them to interfere with my right to decide to run my business as I think fit, consistent with any duties I may have as a good employer.

Dissension and conflict leading to a decrease in morale and to divided loyalties. Some employers feel that white-collar unionism will result in dissension and conflict not only between themselves and their staffs who are regarded as 'part of management', but also among individual members of the staff. It is claimed that this will lead to a decrease in morale and divided loyalties and thereby reduce the over-all efficiency of the firm's operations. This view is particularly common with regard to supervisors and employees engaged on 'confidential' work, but many employers hold it in respect of all staff employees.

In its most general form this view is expressed by statements such as these:

The introduction of white-collar unions is a disturbing influence; some employees wish to be members, others do not, with the result that there is a divided camp with consequent jealousies, lack of team spirit, and a drop in morale.

If staff members are encouraged to join trade unions they must inevitably be liable to a conflict between their loyalty to the company and their responsibility to the union.

With particular reference to foremen, the argument takes the form:

I do not see how management or a part of management such as foremen can be part of an anti-management organisation such as a trade union, and still be an effective member of the management team.

We are reluctant to recognise a union for supervisors. We cannot give an entirely rational answer to why we are reluctant, but on the whole we feel that you are putting key people into a position whereby they are going to have a conflict of loyalty.

Practices which tend to promote mediocrity. Other employers believe that white-collar unions will introduce practices which will promote mediocrity and stifle ambition. Some employers think that staff unions, like manual unions, will introduce 'restrictive practices' such as limitations on the interchangeability of personnel and the closed shop, and that these will 'tend to restrict the ability of the employer to engage the best staff available for the job'.

But a more common belief is that white-collar unions will introduce practices which will prevent the employer from treating his staff employees on their merits as individuals. This fear is expressed in such statements as the following:

The real disadvantage is that any minimum scale of salaries and conditions tends to destroy incentive, initiative and ability and can result in a levelling down.

Unionisation, with consequent 'rate for the job', tends to restrict reward for individual merit, and to discourage interchangeability of work. Employees therefore become less versatile and possibly less ambitious.

Membership of a white-collar union would militate strongly against the prospects of a brighter individual in making his way up the ladder of success and would reduce all staff members to mediocrity. It would be difficult indeed to promote or to increase the remuneration of the 'better man or woman'.

We feel strongly that although we would recognise a staff union if it is the wish of the majority of the staff—we would not negotiate over salaries of staff as such negotiations might well lead to the underpayment of the efficient and the over-payment of the inefficient.

It has been argued elsewhere that most of these employer beliefs regarding white-collar unionism have little basis in fact.[1] But in the present context it matters little whether they do or not. What is important is that employers think they do and as a result refuse to recognize white-collar unions.

CONCLUSIONS

This chapter began by showing that union recognition is very closely associated with union membership. But this was not sufficient to prove that recognition produces membership. It was also necessary to demonstrate that white-collar unions are generally refused recognition not because they lack representativeness but because employers believe they are inappropriate, unnecessary, or will have certain 'dire consequences'.

But this is still not sufficient to prove that recognition produces membership. White-collar unions have been able to obtain recognition in a few areas in spite of the generally unfavourable attitudes and behaviour of employers. This may have been because they had sufficient membership strength to force employers to concede recognition. Hence before it can be said that recognition produces membership it is also necessary to demonstrate that these concessions of recognition were not made primarily because of the membership strength of these unions.

It is obviously impossible to examine every concession of recognition which individual employers have made to white-collar unions. Fortunately, it is also unnecessary to do this in order to explain why white-collar union recognition has generally come about. The vast majority of white-collar union recognition has resulted from employers' associations granting recognition on behalf of their member-firms or at least providing a framework within which recognition could fairly easily be obtained from individual firms. Employers' associations have many functions but, from the trade unionists' point of view, one of their most important has been to act as relay stations for transmitting minimum terms and conditions of employment, including union recognition, throughout an entire industry.

Employers' associations in private industry have granted recognition to

[1] Bain, op. cit., chap. 5.

white-collar unions in newspaper publishing, engineering, shipbuilding, iron and steel, and cotton spinning. Almost all these concessions of recognition were made during and immediately after the First World War, 1917–24, and immediately prior to and during the Second World War, 1938–45. In contrast, since 1945 only two employers' associations have conceded recognition to white-collar unions. The clustering of these concessions during two fairly short periods suggests that certain environmental factors may have been conducive to promoting union recognition. Consequently, in the following chapter every major concession of recognition to a white-collar union in private industry is considered in relation to the climate of its period.

IX

GOVERNMENT ACTION AND THE SOCIAL CLIMATE

The climate of the period

THE First World War enormously enhanced the power and prestige of the trade union movement. Between 1913 and 1920 the number of trade unionists more than doubled, giving the movement a total membership of over 8 million. More important, the density of union membership also more than doubled—from around 20 per cent in 1913 to almost 48 per cent in 1920, a figure which has yet to be surpassed.[1] Nor were all those who were joining trade unions manual workers; many white-collar employees were also taking collective action. Unions were formed among bank and insurance clerks; many white-collar unions affiliated to the TUC; various white-collar groups, including teachers, bank clerks, and insurance agents, threatened or undertook strike action; and civil servants demonstrated against the government. By 1920 almost three-quarters of a million white-collar employees belonged to trade unions,[2] and these unions were adopting an increasingly militant outlook.

The effect of the war on the status of the unions was of even greater importance than its effect on union membership. With the outbreak of war the government was compelled to seek the co-operation of the trade union movement to ensure that production would not be retarded by strikes or restrictive practices. On the whole, the movement was willing to co-operate, and it was soon acting as adviser to the government on labour matters. Trade unionists were given a share in the management of industry by being appointed to control boards which were responsible for allocating raw materials, deploying labour, and similar duties. A trade unionist was made a member of the War Cabinet, a Ministry of Pensions and a Ministry of Labour were formed with trade unionists as their heads, and altogether eight Labour men were given office in the wartime government. As the trade unions were brought into the

[1] See *supra*, Table 3.1, and A. G. Hines, 'Trade Unions and Wage Inflation in the United Kingdom, 1893–1961', *Review of Economic Studies*, xxxi (October 1964), pp. 250–1. Hines's density figures are understated because in computing them he uses the total occupied labour force which includes groups outside the scope of trade unionism such as employers, self-employed, and members of the armed forces.

[2] Sidney and Beatrice Webb, *The History of Trade Unionism* (London: Longmans Green, 1920), p. 503.

administration of government and industry, their position advanced to one of responsibility and respect and they were increasingly accepted as an essential element in the country's industrial and social organization.

The years immediately preceding the war had been marked by intense labour unrest. As the war went into its later stages and people began to think about reconstruction problems, they realized that industrial relations would have to be reconstituted on a new basis or massive labour unrest would re-occur in the post-war period. In 1916 the government established a committee under the chairmanship of J. H. Whitley to make recommendations 'for securing a permanent improvement in the relations between employers and workmen'. The Whitley Committee concluded that an essential condition for securing such an improvement was 'adequate organization on the part of both employers and workpeople'. It therefore recommended that in well-organized industries joint industrial councils representing both trade unions and employers' associations should be set up to give regular consideration to workers' problems, while in industries in which organization was inadequate to sustain collective bargaining, minimum wage-fixing machinery should be established. The government accepted these recommendations and instructed the Ministry of Labour to encourage employers and unions to establish machinery which would facilitate consultation and negotiation between them on industrial and labour problems.

The principle of trade union recognition which the Whitley Committee asserted was reaffirmed by the National Industrial Conference, the House of Commons, and the Mond-Turner talks. The National Industrial Conference of 1919 was held at the suggestion of the government to consider post-war labour problems and represented both employers and unions. It reported that 'the basis of negotiation between employers and workpeople should . . . be the full and frank acceptance of the employers' organisations on the one hand and the trade unions on the other as the recognised organisation to speak and act on behalf of their members'.[1] In 1923 the House of Commons debated a resolution stating '. . . that local authorities, banks, insurance and shipping companies, and other employers of professional and clerical workers should follow the example of the Government in recognising the organisa-tions of these workers'. It received widespread support from members representing all shades of political opinion and was passed on a free vote without a division.[2] The Mond-Turner talks of 1928–9 resulted in a frank admission by the participating employers that it was 'definitely in the interests of all concerned in industry that full recognition should be given to . . . unions . . . as the appropriate and established machinery for the discussion and negotiation of all questions of working conditions'.[3]

---

[1] Cited in Henry Clay, *The Problem of Industrial Relations* (London: Macmillan, 1929), p. 155.

[2] See 162 *H.C. Deb.* 5 s., 18 April 1923, cols. 2160–2200.   [3] Clay, loc. cit.

Whitleyism created an atmosphere which was more favourable to the recognition of unions than that of any previous era. As one astute observer of this period of industrial relations has remarked, Whitleyism

constituted a public and official recognition of trade unionism and collective bargaining as the basis of industrial relations, that is perhaps surprising, when it is recollected that large groups of employers were still refusing to recognise the unions when war broke out.

.   .   .   .   .

Collective bargaining ... was authoritatively pronounced normal and necessary, and was extended, potentially if not actually, over the whole field of wage-employment for the market.[1]

Finally, the war by causing a labour shortage, a rise in the cost of living, and the introduction of compulsory arbitration, accelerated a shift from local to national bargaining.[2] The labour shortage greatly enhanced the bargaining power of the unions and they were able with advantage to play off one employer or regional association against another. In order to counter these tactics, many employers began to negotiate on a national basis, a policy which happened to coincide with a traditional objective of most unions— the standardization of conditions of employment throughout an industry. The trend to national bargaining was also promoted by the rising cost of living and the existence of compulsory arbitration. As the war progressed, the arbitration tribunals soon became swamped with numerous local applications for wage increases, most of them supported by precisely the same argument— the rising cost of living. In order to reduce the number of claims and thereby simplify the work of the tribunals, the government encouraged employers and unions to settle wage claims on a national basis.

It was in this favourable environment of Whitleyism, and of increasing union membership, militancy, status, and employer willingness to engage in national bargaining, that many of the unions representing white-collar employees were recognized. The NUJ was recognized by the Newspaper Proprietors Association in 1917, by the Newspaper Society in 1918, and by the Scottish Daily Newspaper Society in 1921; the Newspaper Proprietors Association recognized the NUPBPW for circulation representatives in 1919, and NATSOPA for clerical workers in 1920; and the Engineering Employers' Federation recognized the CAWU in 1920 and DATA in 1924.

Recognition of these unions came just in time, for this favourable environment was soon to change. The two decades following 1920 were, on the whole, difficult ones for the unions and were characterized by severe depression, falling wages, massive unemployment, and drastically declining trade union funds and membership. The unsuccessful General Strike of 1926

---

[1] Clay, op. cit., pp. 154 and 177.
[2] See Allan Flanders, 'Collective Bargaining', *The System of Industrial Relations in Great Britain*, Allan Flanders and H. A. Clegg, editors (Oxford: Basil Blackwell, 1954), pp. 272–8.

resulted in a loss of prestige for the unions and in the passage of the Trade Disputes and Trade Union Act which introduced certain restrictions on strike action and political action by trade unions. After the recognition of DATA by the Engineering Employers' Federation in 1924, it was fifteen years before another major private employer or employers' association was to concede recognition to a union representing white-collar workers.

Recognition of white-collar unionism in the printing industry

Recognition of the NUJ. The NUJ was founded in 1907. For the first decade of its existence it followed a not very successful policy of trying to secure recognition and improvements in wages and working conditions on a firm-by-firm basis, but the outbreak of war in 1914 changed all this. As newspaper proprietors reduced wages and staffs causing real wages to fall and unemployment to rise, the union realized that 'the method of local action and individual approach had achieved its maximum possibilities'.[1]

During August 1917 the NUJ submitted an application for a general increase in salaries to the several associations of newspaper proprietors covering the whole of Great Britain. The Newspaper Federation, representing the daily papers of the north and the midlands and a rather indeterminate body of weekly papers, conceded this 'war bonus' to the NUJ in October; the Newspaper Proprietors Association, covering the national dailies of Fleet Street, granted the war bonus plus the principle of minimum salary scales in December; the Newspaper Society, acting for most of the English and Welsh weeklies, conceded the war bonus in April 1918; and the Southern Federation, negotiating for the dailies of the south, followed suit almost immediately. During 1919, the Northern Federation, the Newspaper Society, and the Southern Federation followed the lead of the Newspaper Proprietors Association by granting the principle of minimum salary scales. Before long, most of the individual Scottish proprietors began to follow these minimum rates and in 1921 the Scottish Daily Newspaper Society, covering the Scottish dailies, signed an agreement with the NUJ. The Scottish Newspaper Proprietors Association, formed in 1923 to act for the Scottish weeklies, agreed to follow the minimum rates in 1943.

No formal recognition or procedure agreement was ever signed by the NUJ and the employers' associations, although clauses concerning the procedure to be followed in settling disputes were inserted in later agreements. Recognition was established simply by the various federations of newspaper proprietors meeting the NUJ and granting its demand for a war bonus.

The strength of a union, as determined by the size of its membership and its willingness and ability to engage in industrial warfare, is one of the most obvious factors which might induce an employer to grant recognition. In 1917 the membership of the NUJ was almost 3,500 and it was estimated that

[1] F. J. Mansfield, *'Gentlemen, The Press!'* (London: W. H. Allen & Co., 1943), p. 218.

the union then represented almost 40 per cent of all working journalists.[1] Although the union was not anxious to engage in strike action, it had called a few successful strikes against individual firms in the years prior to 1917. In 1917–18 the Welsh journalists were threatening to strike if the employers did not grant recognition, and the union executive was threatening 'to ally itself with other trade union forces in the newspaper industry, with the object of securing by other means the justice which is denied through friendly negotiation'.[2] Moreover, the union's bargaining power was somewhat enhanced by the diversity of employers' associations which enabled the union to play off one proprietorial group against another. The granting of the war bonus by the Northern Federation was useful to the union in convincing the Newspaper Proprietors Association to do likewise, while both these precedents were of great value in persuading the Newspaper Society and the Southern Federation to concede.

Despite this, the union was not yet well enough organized, nor was its membership sufficiently large, militant, or strategic to force the employers to grant recognition. By 1917 the union had been in existence only ten years, had no full-time officers, possessed negligible reserve funds with which to finance industrial action, and prior to its affiliation to the Printing and Kindred Trades Federation in July 1919, could not have expected any extensive help from the manual workers in the industry. Almost 1,500 of its 3,500 members were serving in the armed forces, the majority of journalists were far too genteel to participate in a strike and, even if they did, striking journalists were easily replaceable since the job could be undertaken by 'any one who has passed the sixth standard'.[3] As one officer of the union wisely remarked, 'The employers have not the slightest reason to fear a general, or even a district, strike.'[4]

A more significant factor than the strength of the union was the sympathetic attitude of a few of the key proprietors. An early president of the union claimed that it 'had many friends among the "executives" who sat in the Council of the N.P.A. to decide our economic fate'.[5] A few of the employers had risen from the ranks of journalism and had great affection for their origins. The greatest friend of the union was Lord Northcliffe, the owner of *The Times* and the *Daily Mail* and the most dominant figure of his day in British journalism. He backed the NUJ from the start: he argued that 'newspaper workers should adopt the methods of other professions, and form a society for mutual protection and encouragement';[6] he placed a column of the leader page of the *Daily Mail* at the disposal of the union for an article on

[1] F. J. Mansfield, '*Gentlemen, The Press!*' (London: W. H. Allen & Co., 1943), p. 298.

[2] Letter from NUJ to Newspaper Society, December 1917, cited ibid., p. 268.

[3] Speech in 1913 of H. M. Richardson, General Secretary of the NUJ, 1918–36, cited ibid., p. 297.

[4] Ibid., p. 204.   [5] Ibid., p. 224.

[6] Letter from Lord Northcliffe to Horace Sanders, Secretary, Central London Branch, NUJ, 2 October 1912, cited ibid., pp. 170–1.

its objectives; and when asked by the NUJ to use his influence to encourage the Newspaper Proprietors Association to recognize the union, he replied:

You know that the union will have my support in any reasonable negotiations with the newspaper proprietors. I am one of the few newspaper owners who have been through the mill of reporting, sub-editing and editing, and I have very vivid and resentful recollections of underpaid work for overpaid millionaires.[1]

It is difficult to explain fully the granting of recognition to the NUJ without reference to the sympathetic attitudes of a few of the leading newspaper proprietors of the day. No doubt these attitudes were conditioned by the environment of the era—the wartime trend to national bargaining and Whitleyism—but the fact nevertheless remains that they were favourable and almost certainly hastened the recognition of the NUJ.

The most important factors promoting the recognition of the journalists' union were the related developments of the consolidation among employers' associations and Whitleyism. In the early stages of the war wage negotiations were undertaken on an association-by-association basis. Many of the unions, particularly the Typographical Association (now the National Graphical Association) had improved their positions by obtaining concessions from one employers' association and then forcing these upon other associations. Partly to ensure that they would not be forced to follow agreements which they had not helped to make and partly to obtain the greater degree of policy co-ordination demanded by the wartime conditions, the proprietors began to unify their forces. A Newspaper Conference was established in 1914 and met weekly throughout the war to co-ordinate the actions of the proprietors' associations in their relationship with the government and also in their dealings with the unions. In 1916 the Newspaper Society reconstituted itself to act as a central co-ordinating body for the various regional associations. This process continued until by 1921 all the newspaper proprietors of England and Wales were represented by only two federations: the Newspaper Proprietors Association, covering the national dailies, and the Newspaper Society, covering all the provincial dailies and weeklies. By 1917 the proprietors were as anxious to bargain nationally, at least with the manual printing unions, as the unions themselves.

This trend toward national co-ordination of policy-making and bargaining by employers was reinforced by the Whitley spirit. Beginning in 1916, several conferences were held in the printing industry to discuss ways of reducing friction between employers and unions. While these conferences were in progress the Whitley Report was published. Since most of the newspaper proprietors eulogized its recommendations in their editorials, they could hardly reject them in practice. As the NUJ was quick to inform them, 'the whole

[1] Letter from Lord Northcliffe to F. J. Mansfield, President of NUJ in 1918, 15 December 1917, cited ibid., p. 226.

trend of things is in the direction of settling wages and conditions by bodies representing employers and workers, and what nearly every newspaper now advocates (take the articles on the Whitley Committee proposals as an example) cannot logically be refused to newspaper staffs'.[1] As a result of the above conferences and the stimulation given by the Whitley Reports, a Joint Industrial Council was formed, covering the various printing unions and all the provincial dailies and weeklies. The first objective of this JIC was 'to secure complete organisation of employers and employees throughout the trade'. In an industry as highly and extensively organized as printing, it was only logical that this meant all employees, including journalists. Logical or not, the manual workers through the offices of the PKTF, insisted that the NUJ should participate in the JIC.

Clearly, the recognition of the NUJ by the newspaper proprietors was very much a product of the First World War era. The union could claim to be fairly representative of journalists and thus had a good claim to recognition. But it was not bargaining from a position of strength, and, if it had been forced to rely strictly upon its own resources and undertake industrial action to try and force employers to grant recognition, it is highly unlikely that the union would have been successful. The liberal attitude of a few key employers and the increasing willingness of proprietors to engage in national bargaining because of the war, Whitleyism, and the bargaining tactics of some manual unions were the really crucial factors bringing about the recognition of the NUJ.

Recognition of the IOJ. The history of the recognition of unionism among journalists would not be complete without some mention of the Institute of Journalists. The IOJ was founded in 1884 primarily as a professional body to look after the interests of both working journalists and newspaper proprietors. During the war it became interested in negotiating with the employers over the wages and conditions of journalists, and in 1920 it was certified as a trade union. During the 1917–19 negotiations the employers suggested that a joint approach should be made to them by the NUJ and the IOJ, but the former refused. When the JIC was established, the employers also tried to have the IOJ included on the trade union side of the Council, but the PKTF gave solid backing to the NUJ and refused to accept the IOJ into membership. The employers then refused to recognize the IOJ on the grounds that they already bargained with a union affiliated to the PKTF for the grades covered by the Institute.

A twenty-year campaign by the IOJ for recognition ensued, and finally, in 1943, both the Newspaper Proprietors Association and the Newspaper Society gave way and recognized the Institute. Recognition of the IOJ came at the same moment as the NUJ was causing consternation in the employers' ranks by campaigning for the closed shop. Bundock has argued that the employers recognized the IOJ in the hope of being able to play off one

[1] Statement of NUJ to Newspaper Federation, 15 October 1917, cited F. J. Mansfield, '*Gentlemen, The Press!*' (London: W. H. Allen & Co., 1943), p. 264.

organization against the other and thereby undermine the NUJ's strength.[1] Strick has suggested that the IOJ was recognized in order to facilitate the merger talks of the NUJ and the IOJ which were then current and were being encouraged by both the employers and the PKTF.[2] While there is not sufficient evidence available to determine which of these interpretations is correct, it is at least clear that the employers were not forced to recognize the IOJ because of its industrial strength.

NPA recognition of the NUPBPW for circulation representatives and NATSOPA for clerks. In 1919 the Printing Trades Guild of the CAWU (then the National Union of Clerks) began to recruit clerical workers in the printing industry. By 1920 about 1,500 printing clerks belonged to the CAWU, and in March of that year the Newspaper Proprietors Association agreed to pay the union's minimum salary scales thereby recognizing the union. Almost simultaneously, the printing clerks became dissatisfied with the degree of autonomy they were allowed under the CAWU's rules and the vast majority of them seceded and formed the London Press Clerks' Association. In July 1920 the Association merged with NATSOPA, and soon afterwards the NPA recognized NATSOPA for clerical grades.[3] A few months earlier, in September 1919, the NPA and the NUPBPW (then the National Union of Printing and Paper Workers) had signed an agreement covering circulation representative and clerical grades employed in circulation, distribution, and competition departments. Although the CAWU has only a handful of printing clerks in membership, it is still recognized by the NPA and is a signatory to the National Clerical Workers (London) Agreement. But it does not take any part in negotiating this agreement.

The factors explaining the NPA's recognition of the NUPBPW and NATSOPA for white-collar workers are, in general terms, the same as those explaining the granting of recognition to the NUJ and they need not be repeated. It might be thought that the manual strength of NATSOPA and the NUPBPW was used to encourage employers to recognize these unions for white-collar workers. Although the device of manual leverage was to become important in later negotiations, there is no evidence to suggest that it was used in 1919–20. It should be remembered that the Newspaper Proprietors Association recognized a union with no manual connection, the CAWU, when it had roughly the same clerical membership as NATSOPA.

It only remains to explain why the NPA should have recognized the NUPBPW and NATSOPA for white-collar workers in 1919–20, while the Newspaper Society and the Scottish proprietors did not do so at this

[1] Clement J. Bundock, *The National Union of Journalists: A Jubilee History, 1907–1957* (Oxford: Oxford University Press, 1957), chap. 22.

[2] H. C. Strick, 'British Newspaper Journalism 1900 to 1956: A Study in Industrial Relations' (unpublished Ph.D. thesis, University of London, 1957), p. 284 and section 3.

[3] During 1964 NATSOPA established a National Association of Advertising Representatives, but so far the NPA has refused to recognize it.

time.[1] The explanation is twofold. First, the history of industrial relations in printing indicates that the NPA has always had a more favourable outlook towards trade unionism than the Newspaper Society or the Scottish proprietors' associations. This is due partly to the impact on the NPA of such personalities as Lord Northcliffe and partly to differences in the membership composition of these organizations. The NPA is composed of large London firms while the Newspaper Society and the Scottish associations are composed of much smaller provincial employers who tend to have a more restrictive outlook towards industrial relations. Second and more important, in 1920 virtually all the white-collar membership of the two unions was concentrated in London, that is, among the firms of NPA members. Even today most white-collar union membership in the printing industry is situated in the capital.

Recognition of the CAWU and DATA in the engineering industry

The other major development in white-collar union recognition during this period occurred in the engineering industry. The Engineering Employers' Federation[2] recognized the CAWU (then the National Union of Clerks) in 1920 and DATA (then the Association of Engineering and Shipbuilding Draughtsmen) in 1924.

The CAWU was founded in 1890. The union made its first systematic attempt to organize engineering office staffs in 1913, and in the following year it called its first strike. Throughout the war the union continued to call strikes against individual employers and, in addition, referred numerous cases to arbitration. Between 1914 and 1919 the union's membership increased from 10,000 to 43,000, and approximately 10,000 of these were employed in the engineering industry.[3] In December 1919 the Federation met the union to ascertain its objectives and policies, and on 9 August 1920 a memorandum of agreement was arrived at regarding the terms on which the Federation agreed to recognize the CAWU. After being discussed by the members of both organizations, it was signed and put into operation on 15 December 1921.[4]

---

[1] The Newspaper Society recognized NATSOPA for clerical workers in 1938 (*infra*, pp. 158–61) but still has not granted recognition for circulation representatives. Neither NATSOPA nor the NUPBPW ever formally requested recognition for white-collar workers from the Scottish Daily Newspaper Society, the Scottish Newspaper Proprietors Association, or the Society of Master Printers of Scotland.

[2] In 1920 the Engineering Employers' Federation was known as the Engineering and National Employers' Federations, and in 1924 as the Engineering and Allied Employers' National Federation.

[3] The total membership figures were supplied by the CAWU. The membership figure for the engineering industry is from Roy Grantham, 'How to Negotiate', *The Clerk* (January 1965), p. 4.

[4] The procedure agreement was amended in October 1946 to make it mandatory for employers to exhaust the procedure before introducing any downward alteration in wages or working conditions. See p. 151 n. 1; p. 169 n. 3; p. 172 n. 1; p. 174 n. 2; and p. 179 n. 3.

The draughtsmen's union was founded in 1913. By 1917 it had around 9,000 members, held its first national conference which elected a full-time General Secretary, and tried without success to meet the Federation for the purpose of negotiating a war bonus. In 1918 the union became a registered trade union affiliated to the TUC, and, although the Federation once again refused to meet the union for a national discussion on wages, two of the Federation's local associations recognized the union. Early in 1919 the union called its first strike. In December the Federation met the union to determine its aims and policies. Additional discussions were held the following year, but nothing came of them. By 1920 the union had close to 15,000 members on its books, and it decided to establish minimum rates below which no member of the Association would accept new employment. Finally in 1923 the union called several more strikes, the largest being at the English Electric plant at Rugby. After the English Electric dispute had lasted almost six weeks the Federation agreed to recognize the Association if it would call off the strike. This was agreed to by DATA in June 1923, and after fairly lengthy negotiations a procedure agreement was made operative as of 17 March 1924.[1]

The rapid build-up of membership in the CAWU and DATA during the war and the willingness of these unions to harass individual employers by strikes and by references to arbitration has led some people to argue that union strength was the most crucial factor forcing the Federation to grant recognition. Thus the General Secretary of the CAWU during this period claimed 'the union, started a guerilla campaign . . . [which] . . . resulted in a gradual general recognition, first by individual firms, then District Associations, and lastly by their National body'.[2] Similarly, the editor of the draughtsmen's journal at this time argued that DATA's experience showed that the Federation 'only recognise a union when compelled to do so by a demonstration of its industrial strength'.[3] While the industrial strength of these unions undoubtedly was a factor in getting the engineering employers to concede recognition, this strength was not as great nor as significant as the above remarks would suggest.

By the time the CAWU was recognized in 1921, the union was, in the words

---

[1] The 1924 procedure agreement covered draughtsmen employed in drawing-offices or in designing, calculating, estimating, and filing departments, and tracers, but excluded chiefs, principal staff assistants outside the jurisdiction of the chiefs, and apprentices. The scope of the agreement was enlarged to cover apprentices and young persons in 1938, planning engineers who previously had been employed as draughtsmen in 1944, all planning engineers in 1949, and draughtswomen in 1956.

The draughtsmen's procedure agreement also contained the 'general alterations clause' which was later to be inserted in the procedure agreements of most of the other staff unions in engineering. See p. 150 n. 4; p. 169 n. 3; p. 172 n. 1; p. 174 n. 2, and p. 179 n. 3.

[2] H. H. Elvin, 'Engineering for Engineering Clerks', *The Clerk* (February 1925), p. 19.

[3] Cited by J. E. Mortimer, *A History of the Association of Engineering and Shipbuilding Draughtsmen* (London: The Association, 1960), p. 106.

of its President, 'travelling through fog and storm'.[1] With the contraction of war industries and the onslaught of the post-war depression, its membership plummeted from 43,000 in 1919 to 14,000 in 1921, and eventually bottomed at 7,000 in 1924. By 1921 the union was virtually bankrupt; it was racked with factional conflict; and a majority of the branches in Wales and in the printing trades had seceded.

DATA was much better organized than the CAWU. This at least partly explains the inclusion of the 'general alterations clause' in DATA's procedure agreement and its omission until 1946 from that of the CAWU. But DATA's strength relative to that of the Federation was not impressive. Between 1920 and 1924 membership of the Association declined by close to a third, and the large expenditure occasioned by the unemployment among draughtsmen in 1921–2 seriously weakened the union's financial position. Moreover, in the depressed years of the early twenties the employers began to take the offensive. In 1921 they forced both manual and staff unions in the industry to accept wage cuts, and, in the following year, the Federation was strong enough to lock-out all the manual unions and force them to sign the Managerial Functions Agreement which clearly established management's right to exercise its 'prerogatives'.[2] The Kilmarnock strike, which occurred within a few months of the signing of the procedure agreement, best illustrates the draughtsmen's vulnerable position. After this strike had lasted almost four months the Federation threatened DATA with a national lockout of its members and demanded the unconditional return to work of the strikers. In the face of this threat the union gave way and even had to accept the victimization of some of the strikers. Clearly, DATA was in no position in 1924 to force recognition upon an unwilling Federation.

Whatever may have been the industrial power of these two unions in the early twenties, it was not sufficient to convince the individual employers and local associations, against whom the brunt of the 'guerilla campaign' was directed, that the Federation should be allowed to concede recognition. In June 1917 and February 1919 the Federation inquired of local associations whether they were in favour of recognizing staff unions. On both occasions the vote was overwhelmingly in the negative. In August 1919 the Federation sent out a third letter of inquiry which actually recommended the recognition of staff unions and drew the attention of the local associations to the National Industrial Conference's favourable recommendation on union recognition.[3] In spite of this urging, the local associations agreed by only a bare majority to give the Federation the authority to grant recognition to the CAWU and DATA. After the Federation negotiated the memorandum of agreement

---

[1] Cited by Fred Hughes, *By Hand and Brain: The Story of the Clerical and Administrative Workers' Union* (London: Lawrence & Wishart, 1953), p. 68.

[2] For a more complete discussion see Arthur Marsh, *Industrial Relations in Engineering* (Oxford: Pergamon, 1965), pp. 74–9.

[3] Circular Letter from EEF to Local Associations, 2 August 1919.

with the CAWU in August 1920, a number of individual employers and local associations felt that the Federation had committed a 'great tactical blunder' by recognizing the union at a time when its strength was declining, and they threatened to secede unless recognition was withdrawn.[1] The Federation refused to revoke the CAWU's procedure agreement, but it decided to withhold recognition from DATA 'until circumstances make this course necessary'.[2] In order to pacify its dissident members, the Federation decided not to recognize DATA at the same time as the CAWU, but to wait until a tighter labour market and further industrial action by DATA would make it easier to justify recognition of this union to the local associations.

In view of the opposition of many local associations, the CAWU and DATA probably would not have been recognized at this time except for the leadership exercised by the Federation. If the war had not greatly increased the Federation's role in industrial relations, the Federation would probably have been unable to exercise successfully such leadership. Before the war all negotiations in engineering were carried out on a domestic or district basis, and the Federation only became involved if matters were referred to it through procedure. During the war a system of national bargaining for manual workers began to develop as a result of industry-wide arbitration awards, the emphasis which wartime governments placed on common action by employers and unions, and employers' desire to discourage competitive local wage settlements. These developments greatly increased the power and influence of the central body over the local associations and made it much easier for the Federation to get them to follow its lead on recognition.

The increased power and influence of the Federation as a result of wartime development suggests why it was able to lead a reluctant membership to grant recognition, but it does not explain why the Federation should wish to take this lead. The explanation of the latter is composed of two elements: the existence of a public opinion favourable to trade union recognition, and a belief by the Engineering Employers' Federation in the wisdom of a policy of union containment by conciliation.

Although Whitleyism itself had little impact on the engineering industry, the environment of opinion created by Whitleyism was most important in increasing the willingness of engineering employers to recognize staff unions. The Whitley Reports urged employers to recognize unions. This sentiment was reaffirmed by a unanimous recommendation of the National Industrial Conference.[3] At the second meeting of the Conference in the spring of 1919, the trade union side called upon the Federation to conform with this unanimous recommendation by recognizing the staff unions in the engineering industry. The Federation's representative at the Conference replied that lack

[1] Various letters of Local Associations to EEF.
[2] Circular Letter from EEF to Local Associations, 15 June 1923.
[3] *Supra*, p. 143.

of union recognition in engineering was a thing of the past.[1] During the summer the Federation sent a copy of the Conference's recommendation to all local associations and asked them for authority to recognize staff unions.[2] In the autumn the trade union side of the Conference informed the Federation that the question of staff union recognition in engineering would be raised again at the Conference's next meeting. In preparation for this the Federation decided to meet the staff unions in December to determine the 'conditions under which it might be possible to recognise the clerks' and draughtsmen's unions'.[3] In the period of idealism following the publication of the Whitley Reports, the Federation found it increasingly difficult to maintain a good public image while at the same time denying recognition to staff unions.

The pressure of public opinion upon the engineering employers was reinforced by the logic of the Federation's own industrial relations policy. The Federation's experience with manual workers' unions had strengthened its belief in the policy of trying 'to contain union claims, not by dramatic conflict, but by conciliation procedure—by the Provisions for the Avoidance of Disputes'.[4] The employers realized that the strength of the staff unions was on the decline due to the post-war depression and that the unions were in no position to force the Federation to grant recognition. The Federation felt, however, that it would be a most 'short-sighted policy' to withhold recognition from these unions until the economic situation improved and their strength increased.[5] Far better to recognize the unions now while the Federation was in a good bargaining position and was still able to get them to agree to procedural machinery which would tend to minimize strikes and contain union demands.

The results of the recognition negotiations justify the Federation's strategy. The Federation merely agreed to recognize formally the union's right to negotiate with individual firms and local associations, a right which many of the firms and local associations had already acknowledged. It refused to allow the staff unions to bargain nationally over wages[6] or to recognize the role of white-collar shop stewards or staff representatives in collective bargaining. In return the unions agreed to respect the workers' freedom to join or not to join a union, not to undertake joint action with manual workers'

[1] Mortimer, op. cit., p. 66.

[2] Circular Letter from EEF to Local Associations, 2 August 1919.

[3] From EEF documents.

[4] Marsh, op. cit., p. 43. The Engineering Employers' Federation recognized the manual unions in 1898 after completely defeating them by a lock-out lasting thirty weeks. In a sense, national recognition was merely a by-product of a policy of containment designed to allow managements maximum freedom to run their establishments as they thought best, while at the same time minimizing disruptions of production due to employee discontent.

[5] Report of a Federation meetings, 27 May 1921.

[6] National negotiations for white-collar workers in engineering did not occur until the Second World War.

unions, and to submit all grievances to a system of 'employer-conciliation'[1] before striking. Although the granting of formal recognition was to prove of great importance to the staff unions, it appeared at the time that the unions had paid a very high price for very little. It is not surprising that the procedure agreements were 'viewed with great suspicion' by many members of the CAWU and DATA.[2]

Thus in engineering, as in printing, the recognition of unions catering for white-collar workers was very much a product of the times. The ability of the CAWU and DATA to harass individual employers and to disrupt production obviously encouraged the employers to grant recognition. But if the war had not increased the power and influence of the Federation over its constituent associations, and if the pressure of public opinion and the logic of the strategy of union containment by conciliation had not convinced the Federation of the wisdom of granting recognition, it is highly unlikely that the CAWU and DATA would have obtained recognition in the engineering industry at this time.

THE PERIOD 1938 TO 1945

The climate of the period

The trade union movement, which had reached its peak membership of 8·3 million in 1920 and had fallen by 1933 to little more than half this level, began to recover as the depression eased in the later thirties. By 1938 the trade union movement had over 6 million members and by 1946 over 8·8 million. During the Second World War the unions gained not only in membership, but also in prestige just as they had done during the First World War. The Labour Party was strongly repesented in the Churchill Coalition, supplying two of the five members of the War Cabinet plus four other Ministers. As in the First World War, a trade unionist, Ernest Bevin, was appointed as Minister of Labour and National Service. In addition, trade union representatives were on a host of official bodies including: the National Joint Advisory Committee, the Joint Consultative Committee, the National Production Advisory Council, the Regional Boards for Industry, and the Local Joint Production Committees. The trade union movement was 'no longer prepared to be treated as a poor relation' but demanded and received 'an honourable recognition of its willingness and suitability for participation in the planning and execution of the production programme'.[3]

---

[1] 'Grievances arising are taken by trade unions to panels of employers at Local and Central Conference level. These panels have the dual responsibility, both of representing the member firms involved, and of conciliating between the firm and the trade union or unions concerned. Engineering carries with it the air of an industry in which employers act as judge and jury in their own cause on matters in procedure' (Marsh, op. cit., p. 13).

[2] Circular Letter from the Secretary of the EEF to members of the Management Committee, 2 May 1923.

[3] H. M. D. Parker, *Manpower* (London: HMSO, 1957), p. 67.

In view of the contribution the trade unions were making to the war effort, many trade unionists felt that the government should give more positive support to collective bargaining. The comments of one General Secretary are fairly representative of trade union feelings at this time:

It should not be necessary at this time of day, for any trade union to have to struggle for recognition for we have it on the authority of the Prime Minister himself that without the co-operation of the trade union movement during this war, our country might well face disaster.

It is my opinion that whilst we are prepared if necessary to sacrifice everything to preserve our democracy against Nazi and Fascist aggression, we must also, in the words of Sir Walter Citrine at the last Trades Union Congress, 'Keep an eye on the would-be tinpot Hitlers here'.

. . . If, indeed, with the enemy on the doorsteps and with our cities being blasted into ruins by the bombs of the enemy, there can still be found reactionary employers so feudal minded as to consider a bona fide trade union as one of their first enemies, there is something radically wrong.[1]

Such attitudes resulted in questions regarding union recognition in particular firms and industries being raised in the House of Commons, and eventually in discussions between the TUC and the Minister of Labour as to the possibility of introducing legislation to compel employers to recognize trade unions.

As a result of pressure from several unions,[2] the TUC began to examine the whole question of union recognition. They felt that there were three possible ways of dealing with the problem: an amendment to the Essential Works Orders making union recognition by a firm a condition of its being scheduled as essential under these Orders,[3] an amendment to the Conditions of Employment and National Arbitration Order (Order 1305)[4] making it possible to refer the question of union recognition to the National Arbitration Tribunal, and the introduction of legislation along the lines of the American Wagner Act.[5] After a fairly lengthy correspondence on this topic with the Minister of Labour during 1942, the TUC discussed the matter with him in person in February 1943. They agreed that the problems of defining what was meant by union recognition, a bona fide trade union, and representative membership were so great as to make it impossible to deal with the recognition problem by legislation. Although the war did not produce legislation on union recognition, the possibility of its introduction helped to create an environment in which it became more difficult for employers to refuse to recognize trade unions.

The Minister of Labour was reluctant to deal with the recognition problem by legislation, but he was not unwilling to handle the problem by other

[1] T. W. Agar, General Secretary of ASSET, 'Editorial', *The Foreman* (April 1941), pp. 1–2.

[2] See references to trade union recognition in the *TUC Annual Report* for 1942, 1943, and 1944.

[3] *Infra*, p. 157.   [4] *Infra*, p. 158.

[5] Most of this information is drawn from 'Trade Union Recognition' (an unpublished paper circulated to Regional Industrial Relations Officers by the Ministry of Labour, 1943).

means. He encouraged firms to recognize unions by using the Ministry's conciliation services and by employing 'the good services of the Supply Departments concerned with the firms' contracts ... to regularise the position'.[1] He also fostered union recognition by establishing Courts of Inquiry to investigate the causes and circumstances of a number of major recognition disputes. Since the Industrial Courts Act was passed in 1919, there have been nine Courts of Inquiry into recognition disputes. Four of them were set up during the Second World War, and all of these found in favour of the unions concerned.[2] In recommending that the employers should concede recognition, these Courts were influenced not only by the strength of the unions' arguments but also by the exigencies of the wartime situation. As the chairman of three of these Courts of Inquiry stated in one of his Reports:

We appreciate that Mr. King [the Managing Director of the firm concerned] is quite sincere in his belief that he is entitled to refuse to have any dealings with a Trade Union. . . . In peace time if he chooses to try to exercise this right and a trade dispute occurs in consequence the National Interest may not be gravely involved. In war time we think that however strongly individuals may desire to run their works in their own way, it is their duty to their country to fall into line with the vast majority of other good employers and assist the Government in the accepted methods of conciliation.[3]

Trade union recognition was also encouraged during the war by the passage of the various Essential Works Orders. These Orders enabled the Minister of Labour to prohibit workers from leaving employment in essential firms, as long as he was satisfied that their terms and conditions of employment were not less favourable than those generally recognized by trade unions and employers' organizations in the appropriate industry. Since the Essential Works Orders required firms to have 'recognized' conditions of employment before they could be scheduled as essential, the Orders encouraged the establishment of voluntary negotiating machinery. Altogether fifty-six JICs or similar bodies were revived or newly established in the years 1939 to 1946. In addition, the system of statutory wage regulation was extended by the passage of the Catering Wages Act in 1943 and the Wages Council Act in 1945. By 1946 the Ministry of Labour estimated that almost 90 per cent of the labour force was covered either by joint voluntary negotiating machinery or by statutory machinery.[4]

[1] *TUC Annual Report*, 1943, p. 118.
[2] *Report by a Court of Inquiry in the Matter of a Trade Dispute Apprehended at Briggs Motor Bodies Ltd., Dagenham*, Cmd. 6284, 1941; *Report by a Court of Inquiry into a Dispute Between Richard Thomas and Company Limited and the National Association of Clerical and Supervisory Staffs*, 30 June 1941 (*infra*, pp. 163–4); *Report by a Court of Inquiry into a Dispute Between Trent Guns and Cartridges, Limited, Grimsby and the National Union of General and Municipal Workers*, Cmd. 6300, 1941; and a *Report by a Court of Inquiry Concerning a Dispute Between the Clerical and Administrative Workers' Union and Certain Colliery Companies in South Wales and Monmouthshire*, Cmd. 6493, 1943.
[3] Cmd. 6300, p. 10.
[4] Cited in Allan Flanders, 'Collective Bargaining', op. cit., p. 285.

Another institution which promoted union recognition during the war was the National Arbitration Tribunal established in 1940 by Order 1305. This stipulated that there should be no stoppages of work and that, in the event of voluntary negotiation failing to settle a dispute, it should be submitted by either side, through the Ministry of Labour, to the National Arbitration Tribunal for a binding award. Although a recognition dispute could not be dealt with by the Tribunal under Order 1305, it was possible for any union, recognized or unrecognized, to request the Minister to refer a firm to the Tribunal for an award on wages and working conditions.[1] Simply by being involved in the determination of these conditions, the unions were given a form of implicit recognition. More important, when faced with the possibility of having a wage structure imposed upon them by a third party, many employers felt it was better to recognize the union and determine the firm's wage structure by collective bargaining. The National Arbitration Tribunal had many functions, but, from the trade unionists' point of view, its major one was 'to compel people who would not be reasonable enough to negotiate to face up to the question in the light of publicity, fact and reason before a body which would give a decision after hearing the case'.[2]

In this wartime atmosphere of growing union power and prestige, of demands for legislation compelling employers to recognize unions, and of increasing state intervention in industrial affairs, several more white-collar unions were recognized by employers: NATSOPA by the Newspaper Society in 1938, the NACSS by the Engineering Employers' Federation in 1940 and Richard Thomas in 1941, BISAKTA by the Iron and Steel Trades Employers' Association in 1943–5, and ASSET and the AScW by the Engineering Employers' Federation in 1944.

Recognition of NATSOPA by the Newspaper Society[3]

After receiving recognition for clerks from the Newspaper Proprietors Association in 1920, NATSOPA began to concentrate its clerical organizing in general printing and provincial newspapers. Agreements covering clerical workers in these areas were signed with Allied Newspapers of Manchester in 1924 and the *Newcastle Chronicle* in 1925. During these negotiations officials of the Newspaper Society acted on behalf of the firms concerned, but the Society itself was not a party to the agreements. Around this time NATSOPA also entered into discussions with the London Master Printers

[1] See Moshe Reisse, 'Compulsory Arbitration as a Method of Settling Industrial Disputes, with Special Reference to British Experience Since 1940' (an unpublished B.Litt. thesis, University of Oxford, 1963).

[2] A trade union official speaking at the Trades Union Congress of 1946. Cited by Allan Flanders, 'Collective Bargaining', op. cit., p. 284.

[3] Most of the information on this topic has been obtained from historical documents supplied by the Newspaper Society, relevant issues of the *NATSOPA Journal*, the union's Executive Council Minutes and Annual Reports, and James Moran, *NATSOPA: Seventy-Five Years* (Oxford: Oxford University Press, 1964), especially pp. 99–103.

Association, an affiliate of the British Federation of Master Printers, in an attempt to secure an agreement for all clerical workers in London weekly and periodical houses. The union's participation in the General Strike brought these talks to an end.

After the General Strike the matter of clerical recognition remained fairly dormant until 1932 when the union tried to extend the Manchester and Newcastle agreements to several other provincial newspaper houses. Most of these employers refused to grant recognition, and NATSOPA raised the whole question of clerical recognition with the Newspaper Society. Since its membership overlaps in some areas with that of the British Federation of Master Printers, the Newspaper Society referred the matter to the Joint Labour Committee of both organizations. But the employers' associations were no more willing to grant recognition than their individual members had been.

During the next four years the question of clerical recognition was frequently referred to the industry's Joint Industrial Council. In April 1937 the JIC expressed 'the hope that no employer will place an embargo on any employee who desires to do so joining a trade union'.[1] In October the Joint Labour Committee of the Newspaper Society and the British Federation of Master Printers replied that while they could not deny the right of clerical workers to join a trade union, they felt it was 'not desirable that clerical workers be members of an operatives' trade union', and they threatened to withdraw from the JIC if NATSOPA took any aggressive action to enforce its demands on this question.[2] NATSOPA felt the employers did not have the right to dictate to their employees which union they should join, and they threatened to strike. The dispute had now reached crisis proportions and the JIC appointed a Special Committee to go into the whole question of clerical recognition. The Special Committee was able to bring the parties together in March 1938, but the employers still refused to grant recognition.

NATSOPA then decided to ignore the British Federation of Master Printers[3] and to concentrate its attention on the Newspaper Society. This decision was probably prompted by two considerations. Most of the union's provincial clerical membership was situated among member-firms of the Newspaper Society. More important, the member-firms of the Newspaper

[1] Cited by George Issacs, 'Harmony or Discord in the Printing Industry', *NATSOPA Journal* (January 1938), p. 17.

[2] 'Organization of Clerical Workers in the Printing Industry', *NATSOPA Journal* (May 1938), p. 1.

[3] After the war, NATSOPA once again turned its attention to the British Federation of Master Printers. But in spite of a number of threatened stoppages, the Federation has yet to concede the union's request for clerical recognition. See NATSOPA's *Annual Report*, 1946, pp. 47–8; 1947, p. 43; 1948, p. 56; 1949, pp. 51–2; 1950, pp. 66–7; and 1951, pp. 58–9. See also Moran, loc. cit., and the *Report of a Committee of Investigation into a Dispute Between Waterlow & Sons Ltd. and the National Society of Operative Printers and Assistants*, 17 November 1948.

Society are more vulnerable to strikes than are those of the British Federation of Master Printers. General printers can stockpile their product and make up lost production to some extent; newspaper proprietors can do neither, and they therefore view strikes with greater apprehension than almost any other group of employers.

During the summer of 1938 NATSOPA tendered strike notices in several provincial newspaper houses. The Special Committee once again brought the two sides together. In July the Newspaper Society stated that its weekly members were still opposed to granting recognition, but it would be prepared to negotiate an agreement covering its daily members. NATSOPA accepted this offer and, after rather lengthy negotiations, an agreement was signed in December with effect from 17 November 1938.

The agreement was very restrictive in scope; it applied only to provincial daily newspaper houses and not to weekly houses; it excluded shorthand-typist-telephonists employed in editorial departments and employees engaged in a confidential capacity; and it covered only wages, specifically omitting hours and overtime provisions.[1] In addition, the union agreed to establish an autonomous clerical section and not to allow any joint action between the manual and clerical sections to be taken until the entire conciliation procedure of the JIC had been exhausted. The union felt that the agreement was most unsatisfactory, but they accepted it because 'it gave recognition of the right of clerical workers to join a trade union of their choice'.[2]

The union's industrial strength was the major factor persuading the Newspaper Society to recognize NATSOPA for clerical workers. NATSOPA participated in the general expansion and strengthening of unionism which began in the mid-thirties as the depression eased. The total membership of the union increased from 22,000 in 1933 to 28,000 by 1938, and in the latter year the London Clerical Branch had over 4,700 members. Clerical membership in the provinces was also increasing, and in 1937 a full-time national clerical officer was appointed. But it was not NATSOPA's strength among provincial clerical workers which forced the Newspaper Society to grant recognition. In 1944, the first year for which such figures are available, provincial clerical membership was only a little over 900 and in 1938 it was probably much less. What was significant in promoting clerical recognition was the printing clerks' strategic alliance with the printer. The union was prepared to call out not only its clerical membership in provincial newspaper houses but, more important, its manual membership. Moreover, NATSOPA would undoubtedly

---

[1] The agreement between NATSOPA and the Newspaper Society operative in 1964 covered substantive matters in addition to wages, but the other restrictions still applied. NATSOPA tried to extend the agreement to cover advertising representatives, but the Newspaper Society refused to do this on the grounds that the union did not have sufficient members among this occupational category to be representative of them. They also refused to recognize the NUPBPW for circulation representatives on similar grounds.

[2] George Issacs, 'Must We Fight Again?' *NATSOPA Journal* (December 1938), p. 21.

have called for and received the support of the other manual workers' unions in the industry through the PKTF. Faced with such pressure, the Newspaper Society could do little but give way. Thus the granting of clerical recognition to NATSOPA by the Newspaper Society resulted from the strength not of clerical but of manual unionism.

Recognition of DATA by the Shipbuilding Employers' Federation

DATA approached the Shipbuilding Employers' Federation[1] for recognition in 1918 and again in 1937, but on both occasions the Federation refused even to meet the Association in order to discuss the matter.[2] Towards the end of 1940 the union made another approach to the Federation for recognition. In considering this application the Federation felt that the recognition of the draughtsmen's union would be undesirable for several reasons:

There is obviously considerable objection on the part of shipbuilding and ship-repairing firms to any outside control of draughtsmen, who are regarded by firms as key men and constitute an important part of their responsible staff, being remunerated purely according to ability and qualifications. In these circumstances it was felt that the status of draughtsmen as staff employees would be adversely affected by recognition of their trade union, particularly bearing in mind that executive posts are generally filled from the drawing office. Quite apart from this, however, it was thought that any scale of minimum rates laid down by a union would tend to become standard rates, to stifle incentive for advancement, and militate against the best interests of the draughtsmen.[3]

In view of this the employers felt that the interests of draughtsmen would best be served by their joining the Foremen and Staff Mutual Benefit Society,[4] and the Federation therefore refused to grant recognition to DATA.

The union then approached the Minister of Labour, Ernest Bevin, and asked for his help in securing recognition from the Shipbuilding Employers' Federation. Bevin agreed to help, and in December 1940 the Ministry wrote to the Federation requesting their reasons for refusing to grant recognition to DATA, and pointing out that such a refusal was 'likely to create some trouble'.[5] The Federation furnished the Ministry with a statement of its attitude on the recognition of DATA and requested a meeting with the Ministry before it undertook any further action. Such a meeting took place and shortly afterwards the employers agreed to meet DATA for an informal discussion on the question of recognition. This meeting occurred in March

[1] During 1966 the Shipbuilding Employers' Federation merged with the Shipbuilding Conference (which was mainly a trading association for shipbuilders) and the Repairers' Central Council (which was mainly a trading association for repairers) to form the Shipbuilders' and Repairers' National Association.

[2] Mortimer, op. cit., pp. 45 and 181.

[3] Circular Letter No. 303/40 from the Shipbuilding Employers' Federation to Local Associations, 26 November 1940.   [4] Supra, pp. 132–3.

[5] Letter from the Ministry of Labour to Shipbuilding Employers' Federation, 31 December 1940.

1941, and in July the President of the Federation was able to report that the Executive Committee 'was practically unanimous after their meeting with the Draughtsmen in feeling that there was no reason for delaying any longer the recognition of their right to look after the interests of draughtsmen and tracers in the industry'.[1] It was agreed not to enter into any formal procedure agreement, but merely to circulate a letter to union branches and local associations indicating the general lines upon which disputes should be handled. In December 1941 DATA negotiated its first national wage agreement with the Shipbuilding Employers' Federation.[2]

In explaining the granting of recognition to DATA, the Federation claimed it was taking into account the extent to which the union was organized in the shipbuilding industry, and the existence for many years of a recognition agreement covering draughtsmen in the engineering industry to which many of the Federation's members with marine engineering departments were subject. No doubt these factors did condition the decision of the Federation to grant recognition to DATA. But the Federation was aware of both these factors in 1937 and 1940 when it refused even to meet the Association for discussions, and, therefore, they do not explain why the Federation should have changed its mind between 1940 and 1941. Nor does the industrial strength of the draughtsmen's union explain the Federation's change of outlook. In spite of claiming to have 70 per cent of the qualified draughtsmen in shipbuilding in membership, there was no talk in the union of taking strike action to bring pressure upon the Federation, and indeed there had been relatively few strikes among draughtsmen in shipbuilding since the union was founded in 1913.

The only element which was present in the spring of 1941 when the Federation agreed to meet DATA, that was not present in the autumn of 1940 when they refused to do so, was the influence of the Ministry of Labour. Although there is no record of what was discussed at the meeting between the Federation and the Ministry, it is fairly clear that the Ministry's influence was crucial in getting the Federation to agree to meet the union. Moreover, the very possibility that the Ministry might take further action on the matter was a factor which the Federation now had to take into consideration. Even if the employers' attitude on this question had evolved to a point where the Federation would have recognized the union in any case—and such a sudden unprompted change of attitude within the space of six months is most unlikely—then at the very least the Ministry's influence was a catalyst in the recognition process.

[1] Minutes of the meeting of the Central Board of the Shipbuilding Employers' Federation held at Carlisle, 25 July 1941.
[2] Although the Ship and Boat Builders National Federation, an association covering employers in the small ship (up to 150 feet in length) and boat-building industry, does not recognize DATA, it follows the agreements which DATA and the Shipbuilding Employers' Federation negotiate.

Recognition of white-collar unionism in the iron and steel industry

There were two major developments in the recognition of white-collar unionism in the iron and steel industry during this period: Richard Thomas and Company Limited[1] recognized the NACSS in 1942, and the Iron and Steel Trades Employers' Association recognized the Iron and Steel Trades Confederation (better known as the British Iron, Steel and Kindred Trades Association or BISAKTA) for staff grades in 1943-5. One of the most difficult struggles for recognition during the war occurred at Richard Thomas. It illustrates the lengths to which the Minister of Labour was willing to go in order to promote union recognition during the war, and it is worth considering in some detail.

Recognition of the NACSS by Richard Thomas.[2] During the late thirties, the NACSS began recruiting the white-collar employees of Richard Thomas. By the autumn of 1939 the union had approximately 50 per cent of the staff employees in the company's West Wales works in membership, and it requested recognition. In January 1940 the company replied that it did not feel that the union 'could improve the pleasant relationship which existed between it and the clerical staffs', and it refused to grant recognition.[3] The Ministry of Labour then tried to get the company to meet the union, but the Ministry's efforts were unsuccessful. In May the local branch requested permission to strike, but the union refused because of the general agreement not to undertake such action during the war. Order 1305 was passed in July, and almost immediately the NACSS submitted a claim to Richard Thomas for graduated salary scales and improved working conditions. The company refused these demands and the union then referred the claim, through the Minister of Labour, to the National Arbitration Tribunal.

At the first hearing in November, the Tribunal suggested to the employers that since the NACSS represented a majority of their staffs, they should seriously consider recognizing the union and negotiating the points at issue. After being allowed to consider this matter for a week, the employers still refused to grant recognition. Consequently the Tribunal held a further hearing in December and ordered that graduated minimum salary scales should be established for the company's staff. The award was a victory for the NACSS, but its value to the union was limited. The Tribunal only awarded the principle of minimum salary scales, it did not, and could not, force the company to negotiate with the union regarding the level of these scales.

---

[1] Later part of Richard Thomas and Baldwin Limited and now part of the British Steel Corporation.

[2] Most of the material for this section has been drawn from the *Report by a Court of Inquiry into a Dispute Between Richard Thomas and Company Limited and the National Association of Clerical and Supervisory Staffs, 30 June 1941.* This was supplemented by an interview on 7 November 1966, in Cardiff, with the late Mr. R. C. Mathias, who was then a Regional Secretary of the TGWU, and at the time of this dispute was secretary of the staff branch at Richard Thomas. [3] Ibid., p. 1.

The company was thus able to implement the award without consulting the union. The union then claimed that the salary scales were unsatisfactory and, when in February 1941 the company refused to meet them to discuss the matter, the NACSS requested that the Minister of Labour refer the questions of the level of the salary scales to the National Arbitration Tribunal.

Meanwhile, a member of the union was suspended by the company for alleged insubordination. As a result the branch struck and refused to return to work until the company recognized the union. The strike quickly spread to thousands of manual workers in the tinplate works and in the steel works, and soon the scale of the strike made a return to work imperative in the national interest. The Ministry of Labour conciliated, and the strikers agreed to return to work on the understanding that the company would give favourable consideration to the question of recognition. But such consideration was not forthcoming and the staff were invited to join a company-sponsored staff association. The union once again referred the whole matter to the Minister of Labour and as a result a Court of Inquiry was established. In June 1941 it reported strongly in favour of the union's case for recognition, but the company still refused to recognize the NACSS. Finally, Bevin threatened to use the government's emergency powers to take over the firm for the duration of the war if it did not recognize the union. Faced with this prospect, Richard Thomas gave way and recognized the NACSS in January 1942.

The struggle of the NACSS for recognition at Richard Thomas shows very clearly how unions were able during the war to use the Ministry of Labour and the National Arbitration Tribunal to bring pressure upon employers to grant recognition. Most employers were not prepared to go to the lengths which Richard Thomas were to avoid granting recognition, and they gave way either as a result of conciliation or a threatened referral to the National Arbitration Tribunal. If they did not, however, and a situation arose which might disrupt production and thereby affect the national interest, the Minister had shown that he was prepared to establish a Court of Inquiry[1] and, as a last resort, even compel the employer to grant recognition. It was a lesson which no doubt was not lost on other employers.

Recognition of white-collar unionism by the Iron and Steel Trades Employers' Association.[2] The growth and recognition of staff unionism at Richard Thomas in 1939–42 was the first major breakthrough for unions catering for staff employees in the iron and steel industry, but it did not represent the first attempt to organize staff employees in this industry. The CAWU (then the National Union of Clerks) began recruiting iron and steel clerks before the First World War, and, after several manual unions merged in 1917 to form the Iron and Steel Trades Confederation or BISAKTA, this organization also

---

[1] *Supra*, p. 157.
[2] A great deal of the following material was obtained in interviews with various employers and trade unionists who, for fairly obvious reasons, asked not to be identified.

became interested in recruiting clerical workers. In 1920 these two unions came to an agreement whereby all clerical employees in the industry would join the CAWU, and it would affiliate to BISAKTA in respect of this part of its membership with the right to representation on BISAKTA's Executive Council. In a sense, clerical trade unionists in the iron and steel industry held membership in both organizations. The CAWU was responsible for recruitment, day-to-day administration, and negotiations; BISAKTA was responsible for certain administrative details and expenses, and had the right to be consulted on general policy matters regarding iron and steel clerks.[1]

The new alliance was not particularly successful in recruiting clerical workers. In 1919 there were four to five thousand clerical trade unionists in the industry, but by 1927 this number had dwindled to 338, and by the end of 1936 it had only risen to 399.[2] During 1936 the CAWU submitted a claim for improved salaries and working conditions to Colvilles Limited, but the company refused to recognize the union. With BISAKTA's approval the CAWU struck. The company then agreed to the establishment of a committee consisting of representatives of the Iron and Steel Trades Employers' Association, BISAKTA (but not the CAWU), and the employees concerned. The committee was to examine the whole situation created by the strike and to evolve a procedure for dealing with future staff disputes at Colvilles. It was agreed that any conclusions arrived at by the committee would 'not prejudice the right of the N.U.C. . . . to be recognized as acting on behalf of the staff'.[3] Very little documentation on the committee's proceedings is available, but it is clear that as a result of its deliberations BISAKTA was recognized for clerical workers at Colvilles, and the union became anxious to amend the 1920 agreement between itself and the CAWU. It seems likely, especially in view of later developments in the industry, that BISAKTA's change of attitude was brought about by a realization that the employers were more prepared to recognize it for staff workers than the CAWU. Whatever the reason, BISAKTA terminated the 1920 agreement on 30 June 1937 and took over most of the clerical membership in the iron and steel industry.

As white-collar unionism became more prevalent in the industry, the Iron and Steel Trades Employers' Association began seriously to consider the matter, and late in 1943 they laid down the following policy. The question of whether or not to recognize staff unionism was to be left to each individual firm to decide. If a firm decided in favour of granting such recognition, however, then it was to be guided by the following principles: recognition should not be granted for confidential employees or department heads; negotiations affecting staff grades should be kept separate from those affecting manual

[1] *CAWU Annual Report and Balance Sheet*, 1919, p. 19.

[2] Sir Arthur Pugh, *Men of Steel* (London: Iron and Steel Trades Confederation, 1951), p. 416, and the Iron and Steel Trades Confederation, *Quarterly Report* (31 March 1937), p. 48.

[3] Ibid., p. 49.

workers; staff employees should be left free to join or not to join the union as they saw fit; and recognition should be confined to those unions already established in the industry for manual workers, with the possible addition of DATA. Finally, it was decided that there would be no national negotiations for staff grades, but, if a firm wished, the Association would act on its behalf in negotiations with a union for any specified grade of staff.

In February 1945 this policy was formalized in three identical procedure agreements which the Iron and Steel Trades Employers' Association signed with BISAKTA for clerical workers, laboratory staffs, and departmental foremen.[1] These procedure agreements were entirely permissive and in no way forced an employer to recognize the union. Each agreement only applied to a firm after it had decided to grant recognition to BISAKTA for that specific staff grade. In spite of the permissive nature of the procedure agreements, most of the large firms in the industry adopted those for clerical workers and laboratory staffs, but not so many subscribed to the agreement for foremen. Among the firms which had signed the national procedure agreements, however, few actually entered into negotiations with BISAKTA for these grades; they merely tended to listen to what the union had to say regarding staff salaries and conditions and then made a unilateral announcement on these matters. Although there were no national procedure agreements for the other unions catering for staff employees in the industry, most firms negotiated with DATA and some negotiated with the various craft unions for craft foremen.

At the time of obtaining recognition, BISAKTA had only about 500 to 1,000 staff workers in membership. But other white-collar unions were beginning to make considerable headway. The CAWU still had a foothold in the industry which it was using as a base upon which to expand, and the NACSS, with the help of the government, had broken through in south Wales. Most important, ASSET, which the employers regarded as communist-controlled, had mounted an intensive recruitment campaign among foremen

---

[1] The white-collar union recognition situation in the iron and steel industry has been completely changed by the Iron and Steel Act of 1967 which nationalized a major section of the industry and obliged the British Steel Corporation to negotiate with any workers' organizations appearing to them to be appropriate. After consulting the TUC, the Corporation conceded recognition to BISAKTA, the National Union of Blastfurnacemen, the NUGMW, the TGWU, the Amalgamated Union of Building Trade Workers, and the National Craftsmen's Co-ordinating Committee (DATA is a member of this body) for 'staff, foremen, and supervising/technical grades' but excluding management grades above the level of foremen. The Corporation announced that the unionization of managerial grades up to but excluding departmental heads would be actively encouraged and that it would be prepared to recognize any organization on behalf of these grades which could demonstrate it was representative of them and free of influence from higher management. The ASTMS and the CAWU also claimed recognition from the Corporation and undertook industrial action to lend weight to their claim. In July 1968 a Court of Inquiry was set up to consider this matter, and it recommended that both these unions should be recognized. This recommendation is now under consideration by the Corporation. See the *Report of a Court of Inquiry Under Lord Pearson Into The Dispute Between the British Steel Corporation And Certain Of Their Employees*, Cmnd. 3754.

in south Wales and the north-east coast. In 1943 it called a strike at Dorman Long on Tees-side, and referred a claim against the company for increased wages to the National Arbitration Tribunal.[1] Shortly afterwards BISAKTA challenged ASSET's right to recruit in the iron and steel industry and the whole matter was referred to the Disputes Committee of the TUC.[2]

In view of these developments, the employers began to regard the growth of staff unionism in the industry as inevitable and felt that in such circumstances it was better to recognize, as one employer put it, 'the devil you know rather than the one you don't'. They argued that since all of BISAKTA's membership was in the iron and steel industry, the union's future progress was entirely dependent upon the prosperity of this industry and it was therefore likely to pursue 'reasonable' and 'statesmanlike' policies. 'Outside' unions such as ASSET, the CAWU, and the NACSS had only a small proportion of their membership in the iron and steel industry and were therefore in a position to follow 'militant' and 'irresponsible' policies in this industry without affecting the over-all progress of their organization. In short, the employers felt that over the years BISAKTA had been 'welded and educated into responsibility', and it was thus the best union to recognize for staff grades. Consequently, while the question of which union had the right to recruit staff workers in the iron and steel industry was being considered by the TUC, the Iron and Steel Trades Employers' Association tried to bolster BISAKTA's claim by granting them procedure agreements to cover these grades.

The employers granted these procedure agreements to BISAKTA not because of the union's strength among staff grades, but because of its weakness in this area. The procedure agreements were designed to serve a twofold purpose. In the first place, they provided a shield behind which an employer could take refuge if approached for recognition for staff grades by an 'outside' union. Without having to recognize BISAKTA, an employer could inform such a union that his Association's policy as formalized in the national procedure agreements only allowed him to recognize BISAKTA or other 'internal' unions. In addition, the procedure agreements ensured that if a firm decided to recognize BISAKTA for staff grades, it did so in a manner consistent with all the other firms in the industry which had also granted such recognition. The agreements thus prevented the union from playing off one employer against another.

Recognition of the NACSS, ASSET, and the AScW by the Engineering Employers' Federation

During and immediately after the First World War, when the Engineering Employers' Federation was granting recognition to the CAWU and DATA,[3] several more staff unions were being formed. The Association of Supervisory

---

[1] *Report of National Executive Council of ASSET*, 1945–6, p. 6.
[2] See *TUC Annual Report*, 1945, pp. 27–9.   [3] *Supra*, pp. 150–5.

Staffs, Executives and Technicians (then the National Foremen's Association) was founded in 1917 and in the following year the Association of Scientific Workers (then the National Union of Scientific Workers). In 1922, when several unions amalgamated to form the Transport and General Workers' Union, a white-collar section was also established within this organization. In the depressed years of the twenties and early thirties, the white-collar membership of these unions did not grow appreciably, and what little membership they had was concentrated in public employment. With the economic recovery in the later thirties and the outbreak of war, the member- ship of these unions began to grow both in the public and private sectors of the economy, and it was not long before they began to demand recognition from private employers, especially those in engineering.

Recognition of the NACSS. Of the fourteen unions which amalgamated to form the TGWU in 1922, at least five had white-collar workers in their ranks. The structure of the new union thus allowed for an administrative, clerical, and supervisory trade group to service and recruit this type of worker. At the time of the amalgamation almost all of the union's 6,000 white-collar members were concentrated in the Port of London Authority and in London Transport. This situation remained unchanged until 1935 when the union's white-collar membership began to grow, especially amongst the clerks of a few of the larger engineering firms. At the beginning of 1938 the TGWU approached the Engineering Employers' Federation for a procedure agreement similar to the one signed with the CAWU, but the Federation refused. The employers argued that a manual union 'was not an appropriate union for organizing clerical and supervisory staffs', and, in any case, if they recognized the TGWU for white-collar workers, they would soon be forced to recognize all the other manual unions for these grades as well.[1]

The TGWU then decided to reorganize the structure of the union in such a way that the Federation would not be involved in recognizing the right of a manual union to represent staff workers. Early in 1939 the administrative, clerical, and supervisory group of the union was reconstituted as the National Association of Clerical and Supervisory Staffs. The NACSS was still a part of the TGWU, but it was claimed that the relationship was similar to that between an individual union and the TUC or to that between a subsidiary company and a holding company. The new structure was devised not only because the union felt there was some substance to the employers' claim that manual and staff affairs should be kept separate, but also because it felt that the new structure 'would overcome the difficulties that appear to prevent certain classes of non-manual workers from joining our ranks'.[2]

In May 1939 the NACSS entered into discussions with the Federation over

---

[1] *Proceedings of a Conference Between the EEF and the NACSS*, London, 28 September 1939, p. 2.
[2] Secretary of the NACSS in the *TGWU Record* (May 1939), p. 299.

recognition. The union argued that the new structure met the employers' demands regarding the separation of staff and manual matters, and that by recognizing the NACSS they would not be recognizing a manual union for staff grades and thereby setting a precedent for manual unions to follow.[1] The NACSS gave an understanding not to be associated with the manual side of the TGWU and not to be a party to any dispute in which manual workers were engaged. It also assured the employers that the word 'supervisory' in its title referred to inspectors in passenger transport firms and not to engineering.[2] As a result of these discussions the Federation decided it would enter into a procedure agreement with the NACSS similar to the one negotiated with the CAWU in 1920, subject to two conditions: the union would act completely independently of the TGWU, and supervisors would be specifically excluded from the scope of the agreement. An agreement along these lines was signed on 23 April 1940.[3]

In granting recognition to the NACSS the Federation was aware that the union's membership in engineering was very small and confined to a few large firms. It was also not altogether convinced that the NACSS was in practice a separate and distinct entity from the TGWU since it shared the same offices and had a representative on the latter's executive. Yet it nevertheless recognized the NACSS for clerical workers.

Its reasons for doing so were twofold. The Federation still thought it was wise to continue the policy of union containment by granting recognition to a union in return for its agreement to submit all disputes to a system of 'employer conciliation'.[4] If a procedure agreement was not granted, the Federation argued to its local associations, firms would be 'in a somewhat vulnerable position should they become involved in a dispute with their clerical workers because there will be no official point of contact between the Association and the Union or between the Federation and the Union, and in the absence of any agreed procedure the clerical workers may look for support to the industrial side of their Organization'.[5] More important, the Federation felt that

to recognise one staff union as entitled to negotiate on behalf of clerical staff workers, and to refuse such recognition to other staff unions, is to place the employers in a position of appearing to dictate to their staff clerks as to which trade union they

---

[1] Actually, the NACSS did not have a fundamentally different structure from the old administrative, clerical, and supervisory trade group. The difference between the two organizations was simply one of name. The NACSS's constitutional position in relation to the TGWU is the same as that of the old white-collar trade group and that of the other trade groups within the TGWU.

[2] *Proceedings*, op. cit., p. 6.

[3] This agreement was amended on 14 May 1947 to make it mandatory for employers to exhaust the procedure before introducing any downward alteration in wages or working conditions. See p. 150 n. 4; p. 151 n. 1; p. 172 n. 1; p. 174 n. 2; and p. 179 n. 3.

[4] *Supra*, pp. 154–5.

[5] Circular Letter No. 64 from EEF to Local Associations, 28 March 1940.

must belong if they desire to raise a question through a union. It would also have the effect of creating a monopoly for the National Union of Clerks, thus leaving the Federation open to a charge of discriminating in favour of that particular union.[1]

Thus the NACSS's battle for recognition was actually won in 1920 when the Federation recognized the CAWU. For as soon as the NACSS could demonstrate that it had some membership in the engineering industry and that at least in a formal sense it was a separate organization from the TGWU, the precedent of 1920 forced the Federation to recognize the NACSS as well.

Recognition of ASSET.[2] While the recognition of the NACSS did not establish any major new principles and was therefore readily conceded by the Engineering Employers' Federation, the same was not true of the recognition of ASSET. The union was formed among engineering foremen in 1917 and had a membership which, for the next twenty-two years, fluctuated between 1,000 and 3,000. With the outbreak of the Second World War the union's membership began to grow, especially in engineering, and in May 1940 the General Secretary of ASSET wrote to the Engineering Employers' Federation 'to offer the loyal co-operation of our entire membership' and to request recognition for foremen.[3] The offer of loyalty was no doubt appreciated, but the Federation was not so overwhelmed that it responded by granting the union's request. In fact, it even sent a circular to member-firms instructing them to withold recognition of this union.

ASSET's first major breakthrough in the engineering industry came in 1941. By the beginning of that year it had recruited a large majority of the foremen at the two member-firms—Harland and Wolff Limited and Short and Harland Limited—of the Belfast Marine Engineering Employers' Association, and it approached the Association for recognition and the right to negotiate over wages. In accordance with the instructions issued by the national Federation, the Belfast Association refused to recognize or negotiate with the union. ASSET, with the support of the manual unions, then threatened a stoppage of work, got the Ministry of Labour and the Admiralty to bring pressure to bear upon the employers, and requested the Government of Northern Ireland to refer the matter to arbitration. As a result of these developments the Belfast Association turned the whole matter over to the national Federation. In view of the situation facing the Association, the Engineering Employers' Federation decided in August 1941 that the Association should maintain its refusal to recognize ASSET but the two member-firms should be allowed to recognize this union if they so desired. The firms then conducted a referendum among their foremen and since this resulted in a vote in both firms of about 70 per cent in favour of recognition, recognition was granted.

[1] Circular Letter No. 64 from EEF to Local Associations, 28 March 1940.
[2] Unless otherwise noted, the material for this section was drawn from EEF sources.
[3] Letter from ASSET to EEF, 27 May 1940.

Following this victory, the union once again approached the Federation for recognition on behalf of foremen and technical staffs,[1] and during the spring of 1942 informal discussions were held between the two organizations. But the Federation argued 'that as foremen are fundamentally part of the management, their conditions of employment cannot properly be the subject of negotiations by a trade union organization', and they therefore still refused to recognize ASSET.[2]

Not having sufficient strength to obtain recognition by means of industrial activity, ASSET transferred the struggle for recognition to the social and political arenas. It requested the help of the TUC whose General Secretary, Sir Walter Citrine, informed the Federation in October 1942 that the union had 'the fullest support of the Trade Union Congress' in its fight for recognition and hinted that the TUC was prepared to make this matter a major political issue.[3] Meanwhile ASSET submitted a claim for salary increases for foremen to the Witton, Birmingham, plant of the General Electric Company. Since the firm would not agree to negotiate a general claim for foremen, the union submitted a separate claim for each of its 280 members in the firm to the National Arbitration Tribunal at the beginning of December. This number of cases was sufficient to keep the Tribunal busy for well over a year, and by completely clogging the arbitration machinery would endanger production. It was rumoured in the press that arms output was threatened and that Bevin might intervene, and on 17 December the Federation discussed the possibility of it being adversely criticized in the Press because of its attitude towards the recognition of ASSET.[4]

On 28 December Citrine again wrote to the Federation, this time suggesting that they should recognize ASSET in those firms where the union had majority membership among the grades for which it catered. On 23 January 1943 ASSET held a mass meeting in London at which the main speaker was Sir Stafford Cripps, a socialist and the Minister of Aircraft Production. During the meeting it was announced that Cripps had invited ASSET to set up a committee to advise the Ministry of Aircraft Production on technical production matters. The Engineering Employers' Federation had an observer at this meeting who reported to them that the General Secretary of ASSET 'pointed out that this was tantamount to "recognition" and now they had this much from so important a Ministry they need not worry unduly about other quarters'. Five days later, on 28 January, the Federation decided to explore

---

[1] During 1942 the union changed its name from the National Foremen's Association to the Association of Supervisory Staffs and Engineering Technicians and began to recruit both foremen and technicians. In 1946 the union changed its name to the Association of Supervisory Staffs, Executives and Technicians.

[2] Letter from EEF to ASSET, 29 May 1942.

[3] Letter from Sir Walter Citrine to EEF, 7 October 1942.

[4] See *News Chronicle*, 1 December 1942; *Daily Telegraph*, 30 November 1942; and Minutes of the EEF Management Board, 17 December 1942.

the possibility of recognizing ASSET along the lines suggested by Citrine in his letter of 28 December.

ASSET then withdrew the 280 cases from the National Arbitration Tribunal, and negotiations to draft a procedure agreement began. There were numerous differences of opinion between the employers and the union over the details of the agreement, but it was finally signed on 1 January 1944. It was unlike any other procedure agreement in the engineering industry. It applied only where the union had a majority membership in a particular grade in a particular establishment operated by a member-firm of the Federation. It was agreed that every effort would be made to settle disputes without reference to ASSET. To ensure that no officials of the union would interfere with the employer–foremen relationship within an individual establishment, no provision was made for a works conference.[1]

During this period ASSET's membership, although increasing, was not impressive. At the beginning of 1942 the union had 2,500 members, and by the end of 1943 it had almost 10,000, but only about 4,000 were in engineering and most of these were in aircraft production.[2] The union could hardly claim to be representative, yet the Federation recognized it. The reasons for doing so were clearly pointed out by the Director of the Federation in a speech to his General Council on 28 January 1943:

> On the approach to the ASSET question the inclination of every man in this room is to say that no foremen ought to be made a member of a trades union and that no trades union should be recognised as having the right to speak for them. On the other hand we have to recognise that the war has brought in to management circles a whole host of people who are never likely to find a permanent home there. They will go back to the tools, and in the circumstances it is not reasonable to expect that during this interim period they should forego all their trades union inclinations.
>
> Again there is the question of public policy. There is very little doubt with the Trades Union Congress in the field, Government sentiment against us, the Minister of Aircraft Production in principle openly espousing the cause of ASSET [that] it only remains for ASSET to present one case where public opinion can be effectively challenged, and the verdict will be against the Federation. Public policy in war-time has a much stronger appeal to the popular mind than industrial reservations.

Given ASSET's lack of membership in the engineering industry, and the intense feeling of management on the question of the unionization of foremen, ASSET might not yet be recognized by the Engineering Employers' Federation if it had not been for the leverage the union was able to exercise because of the wartime situation.[3]

---

[1] On 1 February 1966 the 1944 agreement was amended to provide for a works conference stage in the procedure. The general alterations clause which is contained in the procedure agreements of all the other staff unions in engineering was never included in ASSET's agreement. See p. 150 n. 4; p. 151 n. 1; p. 169 n. 3; p. 174 n. 2; and p. 179 n. 3.

[2] *Reports of National Executive Committee of ASSET*, 1942–3, 1945–6.

[3] It became increasingly difficult after the war for unions to use statutory institutions to

Recognition of the AScW. The AScW was founded in 1918 and for the next two decades it restricted its membership to qualified scientists in universities and research establishments and acted in most respects simply as a professional association. Beginning in 1938 several industrial branches were formed and an increasing emphasis was placed on the trade union side of the Association's work. In 1940 the Association re-registered itself as a trade union[1] and amended its rules to enable unqualified assistants working in scientific and research departments to join the Association. The war resulted in a vast increase in the number of scientists and ancillary grades employed by industry and government, and the AScW's membership began to grow at a phenomenal rate. In 1939 there were fewer than 1,500 members in the Association; by 1946 there were over 17,000.

During 1941 the AScW submitted a claim for a salary increase to Napier Motors Limited and the resulting negotiations led to an informal conference being held between the union and the London Association of the Engineering Employers' Federation. At this conference the London Association suggested to the AScW that they should approach the national Federation with a view to obtaining a procedure agreement to cover their engineering membership. The union was active in several of the larger London electrical firms and the London Association was anxious that a procedure agreement be established to contain the AScW's demands.[2] Following the London Association's suggestion, the AScW wrote to the Engineering Employers' Federation in December requesting a procedure agreement. In February 1942 the Federation refused the union's request on the grounds that 'a close personal relationship exists between managements and their technical staffs and conditions of employment could be determined only through this personal relationship'.[3]

During the next few months several disputes arose between the AScW and

exert pressure upon employers for wage increases or recognition (*infra*, pp. 175–6). For example, in July 1952 ASSET submitted a claim to the Engineering Employers' Federation for a substantial increase in its members' salaries. The Federation refused to grant the claim because ASSET'S procedure agreement did not provide for national negotiations on wages, but was operative only where the union had majority membership in an individual grade in an individual establishment. In January 1953 ASSET requested the Minister of Labour to refer the dispute to the Industrial Disputes Tribunal for a binding award. Since there was no national joint negotiating machinery in the engineering industry for settling the wages of the workers covered by the claim, it was necessary, under Order 1376, for ASSET to demonstrate that it represented a 'substantial proportion' of these workers before the Minister could refer the dispute to the Tribunal. ASSET could not do this, and the Minister was unable to refer the dispute to compulsory arbitration.

[1] The AScW first registered as a trade union in 1918, but in 1926 it deregistered 'on the grounds of decreasing membership and the difficulties of recruiting'. See Reinet Fremlin, 'Scientists and the T.U. Movement', *AScW Journal* (May 1952), pp. 15–18; (October 1952), pp. 15–17.

[2] Letter from London Association to EEF, 18 July 1942.

[3] Cited in *Negotiations with the Engineering and Allied Employers' National Federation or a Procedure Agreement and Recognition Agreement*, an AScW pamphlet, 1943.

individual engineering firms, and in September the union reported these to the Ministry of Labour. The Ministry suggested that voluntary negotiating machinery should be established and they promoted a meeting between the union and the Engineering Employers' Federation to discuss this matter. At this meeting the Federation made it clear that its major objection to recognizing the AScW was that many of the union's members occupied executive or managerial posts in industry and the employers could not consent to such employees' salaries and working conditions being determined by negotiations with a trade union. The AScW pointed out that they were only interested in negotiating on behalf of the 'ordinary non-executive grade of technical or scientific worker'. They assured the Federation that they were prepared to exclude managerial and supervisory grades from the scope of any procedure agreement which might be signed, in the same way that such grades had been excluded from the DATA procedure agreement of 1924.[1] In view of this the Federation decided on 29 October that they were prepared to meet the AScW to negotiate an agreement.

The negotiations began in February 1943, and lasted on and off for the next fifteen months. The main points of difference centred around two issues: the specific grades to be excluded from the agreement, and whether a 'general alterations clause' similar to that in the DATA agreement of 1924, preventing employers from altering salaries and working conditions before they had exhausted the procedure, would be included in the agreement.[2] Negotiations temporarily broke down in December, but in March 1944 the AScW requested that negotiations be resumed. Finally on 11 May 1944 a procedure agreement was signed by the two organizations.

The Federation recognized the AScW not as a result of any great activity on the part of the Association, but largely as a by-product of recognizing DATA and ASSET. By the end of 1942 the AScW had only 3,400 members in the engineering industry, had never called a strike, and had yet to refer a case to the National Arbitration Tribunal. In fact, the union possessed so little strength that during the lengthy negotiations of 1943–4, it was forced to accept every major amendment to the draft procedure agreement which the Federation put forward. As in the case of the NACSS[3] the AScW obtained recognition largely as a result of precedents which had been set or were about to be set by other unions. As soon as the AScW made it clear that they were not interested in negotiating for managerial grades and were prepared to accept recognition on the same qualified basis as DATA, it became most

[1] *Supra*, p. 151 n. 1.

[2] The AScW was forced to accept the procedure agreement in 1944 without the inclusion of the general alterations clause, but in March 1947 the clause was added to the agreement. Moreover, the 1944 agreement did not provide for a works conference stage in the procedure. The agreement was amended to provide for such a stage on 17 December 1964. See p. 150 n. 4; p. 151 n. 1; p. 169 n. 3; p. 172 n. 1; and p. 179 n. 3.

[3] *Supra*, pp. 168–70.

difficult for the Federation to refuse the AScW recognition. As one local association pointed out to the Federation, the AScW 'represents a fairly compact and homogeneous body of employees in much the same way as the Draughtsmen do, and therefore it is difficult to see on what grounds they are excluded from a form of recognition which is granted to the Draughtsmen's Union'.[1] Even more important, at the same time as the AScW was trying to obtain a procedure agreement, ASSET was mounting its intensive public campaign for recognition. By the end of 1942 the Federation was on the brink of granting recognition to ASSET not only for technical grades but also for supervisory workers. Not to have granted recognition to the AScW as well would have been curiously illogical and would not have withstood public scrutiny.

THE PERIOD 1946 TO 1964

The climate of the period

The government replaced Order 1305 by Order 1376 in 1951 and Order 1376 by the Terms and Conditions of Employment Act in 1959. Each successive measure made it more difficult for unions to use statutory provisions to exert pressure upon employers for recognition. Under Order 1305 a union only had to be a party to a dispute over the terms and conditions of employment which should exist in a firm or industry for the dispute to be referred to compulsory arbitration. But under Order 1376 a union also had to be a recognized party to the joint voluntary negotiating machinery existing in the firm or industry concerned, or, in firms and industries where such machinery and recognition did not exist, the union had to represent a 'substantial proportion' of the employees concerned. Finally, under the Terms and Conditions of Employment Act a union cannot refer a dispute to compulsory arbitration. It can only request that the Industrial Court order an employer to observe terms and conditions of employment not less favourable than those contained in an agreement negotiated by organizations representing a substantial proportion of the workers and employers in the industry concerned. Even to do this, a union must be a party to the agreement; that is, the union must be generally recognized throughout the industry.

It is true that the government has taken some steps over the post-war period to encourage trade union recognition and collective bargaining, but none of them gives more than moral support to the principle of trade union recognition. In 1946 it strengthened the House of Commons Fair Wages Resolution by inserting a clause requiring all government contractors to recognize the freedom of their workpeople 'to be members of trade unions'. There is nothing in the Fair Wages Resolution, however, which forces an employer to recognize and bargain with a union. In 1949 and 1950 the

---

[1] Letter from London Association to EEF, 18 July 1942.

government ratified ILO Conventions No. 87 and 98 which state that workers shall have the right to 'join organisations of their own choosing' and enjoy 'adquate protection against acts of anti-union discrimination'.[1] But ratification does not make these conventions the law of the land. 'An Act would be required for that', as Professor Wedderburn has pointed out, 'and none has been passed.'[2]

Perhaps it is not surprising that in a period in which the legislative framework has become increasingly unfavourable to union recognition, no significant concessions of recognition have been made to unions catering for white-collar workers in manufacturing. While some individual firms have granted recognition to such unions during this period, only two employers' associations have done so: the British Spinners' and Doublers' Association to the Textile Officials' Association in 1950 and the Engineering Employers' Federation to the NUGMW for clerical workers in 1953.[3] In the first case, the nature of the recognition was so restricted as to make it unimportant; in the second, the outcome was determined by events which occurred during the Second World War.

Recognition of the Textile Officials' Association by the British Spinners' and Doublers' Association[4]

During the Second World War the wages and working conditions of textile operatives were improved on several occasions, but very few of these improvements were passed on to mill officials and supervisors. The relative economic position of textile officials therefore seriously deteriorated and they formed local associations to represent their views to the employers. These local associations began to band together, and in 1947 they merged with ASSET. Following the merger, ASSET established a National Sectional Council for the Textile Industry, appointed a full-time official to administer this Council,

---

[1] See C. Wilfred Jenks, *The International Protection of Trade Union Freedom* (London: Stevens, 1957).

[2] K. W. Wedderburn, *The Worker and the Law* (Harmondsworth, Middlesex: Penguin Books, 1965), p. 16.

[3] Since 1964 there has been another major concession of recognition to white-collar unions in manufacturing, and it supports the general argument of this chapter. For several years the Shipbuilders' and Repairers' National Association (see *supra*, p. 161 n. 1) refused to recognize unions representing clerical or supervisory grades (see *supra*, p. 129) but in 1967 it gave way and granted recognition. There is not room here to give all the details, but it is clear that the major factor bringing about this change of policy by the Association was a recommendation of the Geddes Committee. This Committee was established by the government in 1965 to examine the competitive position of the shipbuilding industry. It reported in 1966 and recommended, among other things, that there was a 'need for new national negotiating and consultative machinery for shipbuilding' which would 'be comprehensive embracing the shipbuilding employers on the one hand and *all* the unions operating in the industry on the other' (my italics). See *Shipbuilding Inquiry Committee 1965–1966 Report*, Cmnd. 2937, 1966, especially paras. 404–5. See also *supra*, p. 166 n. 1.

[4] The information for this section has been obtained mainly by correspondence and interviews with the parties concerned.

and provided him with an office in Manchester.[1] In 1948 the union approached the British Spinners' and Doublers' Association (then the Federation of Master Cotton Spinners' Association) for recognition.

But since the employers regarded ASSET as a communist-dominated union, they not only refused to recognize it but also encouraged their employees to resign from it and establish a separate organization. Many of the officials responded in 1949 by forming the Textile Officials' Association, a registered trade union unaffiliated to the TUC.

In February 1950 the British Spinners' and Doublers' Association recognized the Textile Officials' Association as 'the body which should be entitled to represent to the Federation the views and interests of its members', but stipulated 'that such recognition shall not extend to the entering into of formal joint agreements between the two bodies'.[2] In practice this has meant that the employers' association listens to what the union has to say, and sometimes responds by issuing recommendations to its member-firms regarding the 'appropriate' terms and conditions of employment for officials. But the British Spinners' and Doublers' Association refuses even to make recommendations regarding officials' salaries.[3] The employers argue that it is not possible to discuss meaningfully national minimum salary scales because of the wide variations in the responsibilities and qualifications of officials due to differences in the size and organizational structure of firms. But it is doubtful if this is more true of textiles than of other industries.

The British Spinners' and Doublers' Association granted recognition to the Textile Officials' Association to encourage its growth at the expense of ASSET's. At the same time, the form of recognition was designed to enable employers to keep themselves informed of the views of their officials without actually negotiating with them.

Recognition of the NUGMW for Clerical Workers by the Engineering Employers' Federation

In April 1940 the Engineering Employers' Federation recognized the NACSS (Tgwu).[4] This encouraged the NUGMW to approach the Federation for recognition on behalf of staff grades, and in September 1941 the two organizations met to discuss the matter.

The NUGMW argued that their 1922 Procedure Agreement with the

---

[1] *ASSET* (September 1947), p. 114.

[2] Cited in Allan Flanders, 'Collective Bargaining', op. cit., p. 255 n. 1.

[3] The British Spinners' and Doublers' Association has been willing to recommend that 'Assistant Overlookers who are engaged on the supervision of operatives as well as on maintenance and setting of processing machinery . . . should receive a wage not less than the average full staff wage earned by the highest paid grade of operative, under their supervision, on the standard number of machines', but it has not been willing to recommend specific minimum salary scales for the various staff positions. (See Circular Letter from British Spinners' and Doublers' Association to Chairman of Member-Firms, 12 March 1952.)

[4] *Supra*, pp. 168–70.

Federation[1] did not explicitly state that its scope was restricted to manual workers and that therefore the union was entitled under this agreement to raise questions concerning their engineering members whether they were manual, clerical, or supervisory employees. The Federation refused to accept this argument, but agreed to recognize the NUGMW for clerical workers if it would establish a separate organization similar to the NACSS. It was not possible to recognize the NUGMW itself for clerical workers for 'to admit the principle of recognition to one industrial union to negotiate on behalf of clerical staffs would at once open the door to similar claims by other industrial unions and this would create a position of chaos so far as negotiations covering clerical staffs were concerned'.[2] The NUGMW was not prepared to establish a separate organization, however, and claimed that union officials dealing with manual questions were also quite competent to handle staff affairs. Neither side would change its position and the meeting ended in a stalemate.

The matter lay more or less dormant until early in 1945 when the NUGMW began to press various London engineering firms for white-collar negotiating rights. The union threatened to refer certain of these firms to the National Arbitration Tribunal, and this resulted in an informal meeting between the union and the Federation and eventually, in October, to a formal conference between the two organizations. The NUGMW was now prepared to sign a separate agreement for clerical workers, establish separate branches for staff workers which would comprise a separate department within the union, appoint a national officer to administer the affairs of this department who would not participate in manual negotiations in engineering, assure the employers that there would be no joint action between the clerical and manual sections of the union, and even design distinctive notepaper for the use of the union's clerical department. In short, the NUGMW was prepared to conform to the same arrangements that had been made with the TGWU, except that it would not agree to establish a completely separate organization with its own name, constitution, and executive.

In spite of the unwillingness of the NUGMW to establish a separate organization, the Federation decided to recognize the union's 'clerical department', and in November 1945 the Management Board approved a draft procedure agreement for the NUGMW similar to the one signed with the NACSS. The draft agreement was also approved by the NUGMW. Before the agreement was signed by either organization, however, the National Engineering Joint Trades Movement (which was composed of the Confederation of Shipbuilding and Engineering Unions, the AEU, and a few other unions) requested the Federation to recognize the right of either itself or its individual member-unions to negotiate with federated firms, local associations, or the Federa-

[1] The Managerial Functions Agreement of 1922 which applies to all the manual workers' unions in the industry.
[2] Minutes of Meeting of the Management Board, 25 September 1941.

tion itself on behalf of all foremen and staff grades. The NEJTM's claim was prompted by the increased encouragement which the Federation and its member-firms were giving at this time to staff grades to join the Foremen and Staff Mutual Benefit Society,[1] the rules of which made union membership incompatible with membership of the Society. The Federation considered that since the NUGMW was a member of the CSEU, its claim was covered by that of the NEJTM. The Federation therefore postponed the ratification of the NUGMW's draft agreement pending consideration of the 'wider' claim. Negotiations on the wider claim took place with the NEJTM during 1946, but no agreement was reached and the unions let the matter drop.

After these negotiations ended, the NUGMW did not press the Federation to ratify the draft agreement, for the union was no longer willing to accept the 'restrictive' clause in the agreement prohibiting joint action by manual and staff workers.[2] Questions raised locally by the NUGMW in respect of clerical workers therefore continued to be dealt with on an informal basis until October 1952, when the NUGMW wrote to the Federation requesting that the 1945 draft agreement be made operative. After once again receiving assurances that clerical members would not be represented by an officer negotiating for engineering manual workers and that distinctive notepaper would be used by the clerical section, the Federation signed the procedure agreement on 17 June 1953.[3]

At the time of obtaining recognition, the NUGMW had fewer than 1,000 white-collar members in the engineering industry. In fact, the small number of white-collar workers in the union—less than 5,000 out of a total membership of almost 800,000—probably explains why it was so reluctant to establish a separate organization for them.[4] In spite of the union's small white-collar membership, the Federation felt 'it would be illogical . . . to refuse to extend to the National Union of General and Municipal Workers the same facilities as had been extended to the Transport and General Workers' Union'.[5] However, the two cases were not strictly comparable. In 1940 the Federation recognized an organization for clerical workers which, at least in a formal sense, was separate from any manual union, while in 1953 it recognized a department within a manual union for these grades. The Federation may well argue that in practice there is little to choose between the respective white-collar structures of the TGWU and the NUGMW. Nevertheless, the TGWU's structure formally respects the Federation's principle that manual unions should not represent staff workers, while the NUGMW's does not. The recognition of the NUGMW for clerical workers did more than just duplicate an existing precedent. It also created a precedent—one which in principle

[1] *Supra*, pp. 132–3.   [2] EEF documentary sources.
[3] The agreement was amended on 6 December 1962, to include the general alterations clause. See p. 150 n. 4; p. 151 n. 1; p. 169 n. 3; p. 172 n. 1; and p. 174 n. 2.
[4] From NUGMW documentary sources.
[5] Circular Letter No. 130 from EEF to Local Associations, 8 July 1953.

weakens the Federation's case against recognizing other manual unions for staff grades.

CONCLUSIONS

The industrial strength of trade unions, as determined by the size of their membership and their willingness and ability to engage in industrial warfare, is commonly believed to be the major, if not the only, factor encouraging employers to recognize these organizations. One student of trade union growth argues that

It is an axiom of trade unionism that 'employers recognise strength'. Non-manual unions have always found it difficult to demonstrate their strength by conducting a strike, yet in the face of a determined employer few other tactics are effective.[1]

The Labour Correspondent of *The Times* claims 'the history of trade unionism has shown that the only way to secure recognition from a reluctant employer is to strike for it'.[2] Similarly, the TUC maintains that unions have generally obtained recognition by overtly exercising their strength in the form of strike action and that this strength 'has been developed without the help of any external agency'.[3]

Some sociologists have argued that white-collar unions are recognized not so much as a result of their industrial strength as of the process of bureaucratization which makes recognition in the employer-managers' own self-interest. For 'if the bureaucratic rules are to be acceptable and friction in their operation is to be reduced to a minimum, they should clearly have been formulated in consultation with organised groups representative of all the main interests involved'.[4]

The evidence presented in this chapter supports neither of these arguments. None of the major concessions of recognition to white-collar unions in private industry came about because the employer-managers of bureaucratic organizations felt that their administrative burdens would thereby be lessened. In fact, the employer-managers of many of the larger and more bureaucratic firms have often been those who are most opposed to recognizing white-collar unions.[5] If employer-managers do realize the help which white-collar unionism can be to them, this would seem to occur only after it has been recognized and functioning in their organizations for some time and its effectiveness in this regard has been demonstrated.

---

[1] Keith Hindell, *Trade Union Membership* (London: Political and Economic Planning, 1962), p. 170.

[2] 'Recognition the Real Aim Behind Bank Unions Dispute With Employers', *The Times* (2 December 1963), p. 5.

[3] *Selected Written Evidence Submitted to the Royal Commission* (London: HMSO, 1968), p. 172.

[4] R. K. Kelsall, D. Lockwood, A. Tropp, 'The New Middle Class in the Power Structure of Great Britain', *Transactions of the Third World Congress of Sociology*, iii (1956), p. 322. See also Kenneth Prandy, *Professional Employees* (London: Faber, 1965), p. 147.

[5] See, for example, *supra*, pp. 128–9.

Nor did the major concessions of recognition to white-collar unions in private industry generally come about wholly or even primarily because of their industrial strength. The industrial strength of these unions was generally a factor in getting employers' associations to concede recognition, but it was rarely the most important factor. In fact, in only one instance—the Newspaper Society's recognition of NATSOPA for clerical workers in 1938—was the industrial strength of a union the major reason for its obtaining recognition, and even in this instance it was the strength of the manual membership rather than the white-collar membership which was crucial. In all other instances, employers' associations granted recognition to these unions long before they had sufficient strength to force the employers to do so, and generally even before the unions represented a substantial proportion of the employees concerned.

The Iron and Steel Trades Employers' Association recognized BISAKTA for staff grades and the British Spinners' and Doublers' Association recognized the Textile Officials' Association largely to encourage the growth of these unions at the expense of others which the employers considered to be less desirable. The NUJ, NATSOPA, and the NUPBPW obtained recognition from the newspaper proprietors as did DATA from the Shipbuilding Employers' Federation, and the CAWU, DATA, and ASSET from the Engineering Employers' Federation, largely as a result of government policies necessitated by war. Both world wars resulted in government policies which made it easier for unions to exert pressure for recognition and harder for employers to resist it. Finally, the NACSS, the AScW, and the NUGMW were recognized by the Engineering Employers' Federation almost solely because of the precedents it had established by recognizing the CAWU, DATA, and ASSET. In short, most white-collar union recognition in private industry has come about, directly or indirectly, as a result of government policies and the favourable climate they created for trade unionism.

There is not room here to give all the details, but it is clear that government action and the favourable climate which it produced were also the major factors bringing about the recognition of white-collar unions in the public sector of the economy. The bureaucratization of the civil service may have made unionization 'a virtual necessity with or without the accompaniment of Whitleyism'.[1] But there can be little doubt that the change in the government's negative attitude towards the unionization of its own employees was brought about after the First World War not because it suddenly became aware of the administrative advantages of trade unionism but because of the recommendations of the Whitley Reports. In Professor Clay's words, the government 'could hardly now refuse to adopt for itself the treatment it prescribed for other employers'.[2]

[1] Kelsall, *et al.*, loc. cit.
[2] Op. cit., p. 162. See also B. V. Humphreys, *Clerical Unions in the Civil Service* (Oxford: Blackwell, 1958), especially chaps. 5–8.

The government has also placed the industries which it has nationalized under a duty to recognize and bargain with appropriate trade unions, and this largely explains the recognition of white-collar unions in the coal-mining, road transport, civil air transport, electricity, and gas industries.[1] Whitleyism also helped NALGO to obtain limited recognition and negotiating rights from a few local authorities immediately after the First World War. But it was not until the Second World War and the passage of Order 1305 that NALGO was able to persuade all the local authorities of the wisdom of granting recognition and negotiating rights by referring several of them to the NAT.[2]

[1] See O. Kahn-Freund, 'Legal Framework', *The System of Industrial Relations in Great Britain*, op. cit., p. 54.
[2] See Alec Spoor, *White-Collar Union. Sixty Years of NALGO* (London: Heinemann, 1967), especially chaps. 9, 16, and 17.

X

CONCLUSIONS

MOST of this study has been taken up with examining the relationship between the industrial and occupational pattern of white-collar unionism and a range of factors which might conceivably affect this pattern. Its findings can be briefly summarized. No significant relationship was found between the growth of aggregate white-collar unionism and any of the following factors: (*a*) such socio-demographic characteristics of white-collar workers as their sex, social origins, age, and status; (*b*) such aspects of their economic position as earnings, other terms and conditions of employment, and employment security; (*c*) such aspects of their work situation as the opportunities for promotion, the extent of mechanization and automation, and the degree of proximity to unionized manual workers; and (*d*) such aspects of trade unions as their public image, recruitment policies, and structures. While the evidence regarding some of these factors was not sufficiently reliable to permit them to be discounted completely, it was satisfactory enough to reveal that at most they have been of negligible importance.

But the findings of this study are by no means entirely negative. It also found that the growth of aggregate white-collar unionism was significantly related to the following factors: employment concentration, union recognition, and government action. The relationship between these key independent variables and between them and the dependent variable can be usefully summarized in a two-equation descriptive model.[1]

$$D = f(C, R) \qquad (1)$$
$$R = g(D, G) \qquad (2)$$

where D = the density of white-collar unionism;
C = the degree of employment concentration;
R = the degree to which employers are prepared to recognize unions representing white-collar employees; and
G = the extent of government action which promotes union recognition.

The first equation specifies that the density of white-collar unionism is a

---

[1] The term 'model' is used here simply to mean 'a number of co-ordinated working hypotheses which give a simplified and schematized picture of reality'. See Maurice Duverger, *Introduction to the Social Sciences* (London: Allen & Unwin, 1964), pp. 243–4.

function of the degree of employment concentration and the degree to which employers are prepared to recognize unions representing white-collar employees. The more concentrated their employment the more likely employees are to feel the need to join trade unions because of 'bureaucratization', and the more easily trade unions can meet this need because of the economies of scale characteristic of union recruitment and administration. While employment concentration is a favourable condition for the growth of white-collar unions, it is not by itself sufficient. Employers must also be prepared to recognize these unions. The greater the degree to which employers are willing to do this the more likely white-collar employees are to join unions. This is because they are less likely to jeopardize their career prospects by joining, they can more easily reconcile union membership with their 'loyalty' to the company, and they will obtain a better service as their unions will be more effective in the process of job regulation.

But the degree to which employers are prepared to recognize unions representing white-collar employees is to some extent dependent upon the membership density of these unions. This is why the second equation is necessary. It specifies that the degree of recognition is a function of the density of white-collar unionism and the extent of government action which promotes union recognition. Employers generally do not concede recognition to a union before it has at least some membership in their establishments. The only exception to this is when employers recognize a union prior to it having obtained any membership in order to encourage its growth at the expense of other 'less desirable' unions. Even in these cases, recognition is at least partly a function of membership density—that of the 'less desirable' unions. But while a certain density of membership is a necessary condition for any degree of recognition to be granted, the findings of this study suggest that it is generally not a sufficient condition. The industrial strength of white-collar unions, as determined by the size of their membership and their willingness and ability to engage in industrial warfare, has generally not been sufficient in itself to force employers to concede recognition. This has also required the introduction of government policies which have made it easier for unions to exert pressure for recognition and harder for employers to resist it.

There are several respects in which this model might be thought to be incomplete. Bureaucratization and the density of white-collar unionism have been claimed to be interdependent; not only does bureaucratization encourage the growth of trade unions, but trade unions by demanding the standardization of working conditions are alleged to further bureaucratization. Inasmuch as bureaucratization is associated with employment concentration, this argument implies that employment concentration and the density of union membership are also interdependent. But the findings of this study suggest that the degree of interdependence between bureaucratization and unionization is very slight.[1] Employment concentration and the bureaucratization associated with it are primarily a function of the techniques of production and as such are exogenous to the industrial relations system. Even if the degree of interdependence between these variables is stronger than the findings of this study suggest, this could easily be allowed for by simply adding a third equation to the model:

$$C = h\,(D, T) \tag{3}$$

where $T =$ the techniques of production.

Some writers have argued that white-collar unions are recognized as a result of the process of bureaucratization which makes recognition in the employer-managers' own self-interest. Inasmuch as bureaucratization is associated with employment concentration, this argument implies that white-collar union recognition is determined by employment concentration, and that the second equation should be rewritten as

$$R = g\,(D, G, C). \tag{4}$$

But if employer-managers do realize the help white-collar unionism can be to them, this would seem to occur only after it has been recognized and functioning in their organizations for some time and its effectiveness in this regard has been demonstrated. For the findings of this study suggest that the degree to which employers are prepared to recognize white-collar unionism can be adequately explained by its density and the extent of government action which promotes recognition.[2]

Some of these same writers have also argued that the more opposed employers are to recognizing white-collar unionism, the more they will try to resist the administrative pressures which lead to bureaucratization and eventually to the unionization of their staff employees.[3] Inasmuch as bureaucratization is associated with employment concentration, this argument implies that the degree of employment concentration is determined by the extent to which employers are prepared to recognize unions representing white-collar employees, and that the third equation should be rewritten as

$$C = h\,(D, T, R). \tag{5}$$

But while employers may be able to slow down the trend towards bureaucratization, the problems posed by governing large numbers of employees prevent them from reversing or even stopping this process. It thus seems safe to conclude that this refinement to equation three, like the equation itself, is superfluous.

Finally, it might be argued that the extent of government action which promotes union recognition is not an exogenous variable as the model suggests, but is determined by the industrial and political strength of the trade union movement, of which the density of union membership is a rough

---

[1] *Supra*, pp. 80–1.   [2] *Supra*, pp. 180–2.   [3] *Supra*, pp. 75–7.

quantitative index. Even granting this, the extent of such action by the government is still exogenous from the point of view of this model. For if the extent of government action is determined by the density of union member-ship, then it is determined by the density of *total* union membership and not by the density of *white-collar* union membership, the variable of concern to this model. The density of white-collar union membership comprises only a small part of the density of total union membership, especially in the period when the government action which promoted union recognition occurred, and it therefore seems safe to treat the latter as an exogenous variable from the point of view of this model.

It may even be that the extent of government action is also largely an exogenous variable from the point of view of the industrial relations system. This cannot be established very firmly, but the evidence gathered for this study suggests that at least the government policies which have promoted union recognition in Britain were not introduced because of pressure from the trade union movement.[1] In fact, the primary purpose of these policies was not to promote union recognition, but to deal with the social and economic exigencies created by world wars. In some instances these policies infringed the right to strike and the free movement of labour and were only most re-luctantly agreed to by the trade union movement. In a sense, their favourable effect on union recognition was simply a by-product, and, in many cases, an unexpected by-product. In short, if the world wars had not occurred, it is most improbable that these policies would have been introduced, and, given the wars, some of them would have had to be introduced even if there had not been a trade union movement.

This two-equation descriptive model of the growth of aggregate white-collar unionism in Britain is therefore claimed to be complete: the number of equations is just enough to determine all the endogenous variables, given the exogenous variables. This does not mean that the model gives a 'complete' explanation of the growth of aggregate white-collar unionism. 'To attempt to account for the unique or even the rare event', as Moore has noted, 'is to set an impossibly high standard for theory'.[2] This study has therefore con-centrated on the systematic and repetitive features of union growth rather than its exceptional or deviant aspects. All that is claimed on behalf of the model is that the variables it includes are those which have a systematic in-fluence on aggregate union growth, while those it excludes behave in a random manner. If the equations in this model were to be estimated, they would both have to contain an error term which would represent not only the errors of measurement in the variables, but also the influence of the omitted variables which have a sporadic and unsystematic influence on union growth.

[1] *Supra*, Chap. 9.
[2] W. E. Moore, 'Notes for a General Theory of Labor Organization', *Industrial and Labor Relations Review*, xiii (April 1960), p. 387.

A model is generally constructed for the ultimate purpose of solving the equations simultaneously to obtain the values of the variables that are contained in them, thereby making a prediction. Unfortunately, given the nature of available statistical data and technique, not all the variables in this model can be satisfactorily quantified and the system of equations cannot be solved. While this may make the model less useful, it does not make it less valid. Although not practically quantifiable, the model is nevertheless conceptually quantifiable and operational in nature. It gives an adequate explanation of the growth of aggregate white-collar unionism in Britain, and, in addition, has some important implications for research on this subject as well as for the function of unions in modern industrial society, and for the future growth of white-collar unionism.

The model claims that the growth of aggregate white-collar unionism in Britain can be adequately explained by three strategic variables—employment concentration, union recognition, and government action. This in no way implies that other factors, including some of those discounted in this study, are not of importance in accounting for less aggregative patterns of union growth. For example, while the strategic variables may explain the existence of unionism *per se* among a given group of workers, which *particular* union is successful in organizing the group may be determined by union structures and recruitment policies. Similarly, the explanation of why one worker in a given environment joins a union while another worker in the same environment does not, may well be found in the different personality or attitude structures of the two individuals. But the strategic variables predominate, and unless they are held constant any explanation of these less aggregative patterns of union growth is likely to be obscured or distorted. Regrettably, most of the studies which have tried to ascertain the determinants of the individuals' propensity to unionize by means of attitude surveys have not controlled for these strategic variables.[1]

It is becoming increasingly fashionable to argue that with industrial progress, greater affluence, and more enlightened management, unions are losing their function. No less a social critic than John Kenneth Galbraith sees unions as having 'a drastically reduced function' and as being 'much less essential for the worker' in the modern industrial system.[2] Much of this argument assumes that the major, if not the only, function of trade unions is their

---

[1] See J. R. Dale, *The Clerk in Industry* (Liverpool: Liverpool University Press, 1962), chap. 4; Kenneth Prandy, *Professional Employees* (London: Faber, 1965), especially chaps. 5, 6, and 8; R. M. Blackburn, *Union Character Social Class* (London: Batsford, 1967), especially chap. 4; E. W. Bakke, 'Why Workers Join Unions', *Readings in Labor Economics and Industrial Relations*, Joseph Shister, editor (New York: J. B. Lippincott & Co., 1956), pp. 30–7; Joel Seidman, Jack London, and Bernard Karsh, 'Why Workers Join Unions', *Annals of the American Academy of Political and Social Science* (March 1951), pp. 75–84; and K. N. Vaid, 'Why Workers Join Unions', *Indian Journal of Industrial Relations*, i (October 1965), pp. 208–30.

[2] *The New Industrial State* (London: Hamish Hamilton, 1967), chap. 23.

ability to achieve economic benefits for their members. Even granting the highly controversial contention that unions possess such ability, the model seriously challenges this assumption. It suggests that white-collar workers value trade unions and join them not so much to obtain economic benefits as to be able to control more effectively their work situation.[1] As their employment becomes more concentrated and bureaucratized, individual white-collar workers find that they have less and less ability to influence the making and the administration of the rules by which they are governed on the job. In order to rectify this situation, they join trade unions and engage in collective bargaining. Given that employment concentration and bureaucratization will continue, trade unions will be just as necessary and useful to the white-collar workers of the twentieth century as they were to the 'sweated' manual workers of the nineteenth century.

The final implication of the model concerns the future growth of white-collar unionism. The model suggests that white-collar unions will continue to grow in the future as a result of increasing employment concentration, but that their growth will not be very great unless their recognition by employers is extended. The model also suggests that the strength of these unions will generally not be sufficient in itself to persuade employers to concede recognition; this will also require the help of the government. In short, the future growth of white-collar unionism in Britain is largely dependent upon government action to encourage union recognition.

The Government, following a recommendation of the Donovan Commission,[2] established a Commission on Industrial Relations in February 1969 which, among other things, is empowered to hear recognition disputes and to make recommendations for their settlement. In order to ensure that employers respect the Commission's rulings and bargain with unions in 'good faith', the Government also intends to give the Commission the power to recommend that a union should have the right of unilateral arbitration.[3] The CIR has got off to a somewhat uncertain start. But given that it creates an environment which makes it easier for unions to exert pressure for recognition and harder for employers to resist it, then the argument advanced in this study suggests that there will be a significant increase in the degree of white-collar unionism in Britain during the 1970s.

[1] On this point see Allan Flanders, 'Collective Bargaining: A Theoretical Analysis', *British Journal of Industrial Relations*, vi (March 1968), pp. 24–6.
[2] Report of the *Royal Commission on Trade Unions and Employers' Associations* (London: HMSO, 1968), chap. 5, and the White Paper, *In Place of Strife*, Cmnd. 3888, 1969.
[3] In order to allow the CIR to begin work without delay, it was established as a Royal Commission. Provisions to put it on a statutory basis and to give it the power described here will be included in an Industrial Relations Bill which the Government intends to present to Parliament as soon as possible.

APPENDIX A

NOTES TO TABLES AND FIGURES

TABLE 2.1

Table 2.1 is largely based on Guy Routh, *Occupation and Pay in Great Britain* (Cambridge: Cambridge University Press, 1965), pp. 4–5, table 1. His work, in turn, is based upon the *Census of Population* of Scotland and England and Wales for 1911, 1921, 1931, and 1951. For a detailed account of the methods Routh used to compile his table, see p. 6, n. 1, and Appendix A of his book.

The following modifications were made to Routh's figures to derive Table 2.1:

(*a*) In order to obtain a separate category for salesmen and shop assistants the following occupations were abstracted from the 1951 Census: 715, 730–741, 749, and 755. For 1921 and 1931 the comparable occupations were abstracted. In 1911 a distinction between employers and proprietors in the distributive sector of the economy was not always drawn. Consequently, they were subdivided on the basis of the 1921 ratio.

(*b*) The new salesmen and shop assistant category (with the exception of occupation number 755) was subtracted from Routh's semi-skilled group. Then this new semi-skilled category, the unskilled, and the skilled categories were added together to give the 'all manual workers' group.

(*c*) The 'insurance agent and canvassers' category (code number 755 in the 1951 Census) was subtracted from Routh's clerical workers to give the 'clerks' in Table 2.1. As mentioned in (*a*) above, occupation 755 was also included in the salesmen and shop assistant group.

(*d*) The figures in Table 2.1 do not always agree exactly with Routh's, due to rounding.

The occupations in the 1961 Census were classified as follows:

(*a*) *All manual workers.* The members of the following occupations were included in this group after subtracting all persons designated as 'employers and managers' and 'foremen and supervisors': 000–007, 010–015, 020–021, 030–034, 040–045, 050–056, 060–078, 080–085, 090–093, 100–108, 110–113, 120–124, 130–135, 140–143, 150–154, 160–161, 170–174, 180–188, 191, 193–211, 235, 250, 251 (officers–men divided according to 1951 ratio and men assigned to this group), 252, 254–264, 266–267, and 320–321 (officers–men divided on the 1951 ratio and men assigned to this group).

(*b*) *Salesmen and shop assistants.* The members of the following occupations were included in this group after subtracting all persons designated as 'employers and managers': 232, 233, 234, 237, and 239.

(*c*) *Clerks.* The members of the following occupations were included in this group after subtracting all persons designated as 'employers and managers': 220 and 221.

(*d*) *Foremen and inspectors.* The members of all manual occupations listed in (*a*) who were designated as 'foremen and supervisors' were included in this group. The members of all white-collar occupations designated as 'foremen and supervisors' were included with the occupations they supervised.

(e) *Lower professionals and technicians.* The members of the following occupations (including those designated as 'employers and managers' and 'foremen and supervisors') were included in this group: 190, 192, 265, 282–287, 294, 295, 310, and 312–314.

(f) *Higher professionals.* The members of the following occupations (including those designated as 'employers and managers' and 'foremen and supervisors') were included in this group: 280, 281, 288–293, 296–299, 311, and 320–321 (officers–men divided on 1951 ratio and officers assigned to this group).

(g) *Managers and administrators, employers and proprietors.* In 1961, as in 1931, both these groups were combined. The members of all occupations designated as 'employers and managers' (except those following an occupation in the higher or lower professional groups) were included in this category, plus all the members of the following occupations: 222–223, 230–231, 236, 238, 251 (officers–men divided according to 1951 ratio and officers assigned to this group), 253, and 270–278. This total group was then divided according to the 1951 ratio.

(h) As in previous years, the 'totally economically inactive' and the 'inadequately described occupations' were excluded from all occupational groups.

Thus all occupations which are generally considered to be non-manual have been included in the white-collar group except for the following marginal groups: fire-brigade officers, photographers, storekeepers, radio operators, and telephone and telegraph operators. Thus, if anything, the white-collar totals are slightly understated.

Table 2A.1 is the master table derived as described above and on which Table 2.1 and Table 2.3 are based.

TABLE 2.2

Table 2.2 was abstracted from the *Census of Population* of Scotland and England and Wales for 1921, 1931, 1951, and 1961. The 'scientists and engineers' are composed of the following 1961 occupations: 288, 289, 290, 291, 292, 297, 311; 'draughtsmen' are occupation 312 (and exclude industrial designers); 'laboratory technicians' are occupation 313. Comparable occupations were used for 1921, 1931, and 1951.

TABLE 2.3

Table 2.3 was derived from Table 2A.1.

TABLE 2.4

The source of Table 2.4 is 'The World's Working Population: Its Industrial Distribution', *International Labour Review*, lxxiii (May 1956), p. 508, table 3.

The primary sector comprises agriculture. The secondary sector comprises: mining and quarrying; manufacturing; building; gas, electricity, and water. The tertiary sector comprises transport and communications, distributive trades, public administration and defence, professional services, and miscellaneous services.

TABLE 2.5

The figures in Table 2.5 are from the following sources: (a) For 1907, *Final Report of the First Census of Production of the United Kingdom, 1907*, p. 12. To obtain the figures for manufacturing industries the following industries were subtracted from the total given in the above *Report*: mining and quarrying; clay, stone, building, and contracting trades; public utility services; and factory owners—power only. (b) For 1924 and 1930, *Final Summary Tables of the Fifth Census of Production,*

TABLE 2A.I

The Occupied Population of Great Britain by Major Occupational Group by Sex, showing the Number in Each Group as a Percentage of the Total Occupied Population, 1911–61

Occupational group	Males					Females					Total				
	1911	1921	1931	1951	1961	1911	1921	1931	1951	1961	1911	1921	1931	1951	1961
1. Employers and proprietors	1,000 (7·7)	1,048 (7·7)	1,129 (7·6)	894 (5·7)	907 (5·7)	232 (4·3)	270 (4·7)	278 (4·4)	223 (3·2)	232 (3·0)	1,232 (6·7)	1,318 (6·8)	1,407 (6·7)	1,117 (5·0)	1,139 (4·7)
2. All white-collar workers	2,409 (18·6)	2,556 (18·7)	3,109 (21·1)	4,006 (25·7)	4,705 (29·4)	1,024 (18·9)	1,538 (27·0)	1,732 (27·7)	2,942 (42·5)	3,775 (49·4)	3,433 (18·7)	4,094 (21·2)	4,841 (23·0)	6,948 (30·9)	8,480 (35·9)
(a) Managers and administrators	506 (3·9)	584 (4·3)	670 (4·5)	1,056 (6·8)	1,072 (6·7)	125 (2·3)	120 (2·1)	100 (1·6)	189 (2·7)	196 (2·6)	631 (3·4)	704 (3·6)	770 (3·7)	1,245 (5·5)	1,268 (5·4)
(b) Higher professionals	173 (1·3)	186 (1·4)	222 (1·5)	399 (2·6)	648 (4·1)	11 (0·2)	10 (0·2)	18 (0·3)	36 (0·5)	70 (0·9)	184 (1·0)	196 (1·0)	240 (1·1)	435 (1·9)	718 (3·0)
(c) Lower professionals and technicians	208 (1·6)	276 (2·0)	300 (2·0)	492 (3·2)	697 (4·4)	352 (6·5)	403 (7·1)	428 (6·8)	567 (8·2)	721 (9·4)	560 (3·1)	679 (3·5)	728 (3·5)	1,059 (4·7)	1,418 (6·0)
(d) Foremen and inspectors	227 (1·8)	261 (1·9)	295 (2·0)	511 (3·3)	612 (3·8)	10 (0·2)	18 (0·3)	28 (0·4)	79 (1·1)	70 (0·9)	237 (1·3)	279 (1·4)	323 (1·5)	590 (2·6)	682 (2·9)
(e) Clerks	654 (5·1)	696 (5·1)	758 (5·1)	932 (6·0)	1,045 (6·5)	178 (3·3)	560 (9·8)	646 (10·3)	1,409 (20·3)	1,951 (25·5)	832 (4·5)	1,256 (6·5)	1,404 (6·7)	2,341 (10·4)	2,996 (12·7)
(f) Salesmen and shop assistants	641 (5·0)	553 (4·1)	864 (5·9)	616 (4·0)	631 (3·9)	348 (6·4)	427 (7·5)	512 (8·2)	662 (9·6)	767 (10·0)	989 (5·4)	980 (5·1)	1,376 (6·5)	1,278 (5·7)	1,398 (5·9)
3. All manual workers	9,516 (73·6)	10,031 (73·6)	10,522 (71·3)	10,685 (68·6)	10,378 (64·9)	4,169 (76·8)	3,889 (68·3)	4,254 (67·9)	3,765 (54·3)	3,642 (47·6)	13,685 (74·6)	13,920 (72·0)	14,776 (70·3)	14,450 (64·2)	14,020 (59·3)
4. Total occupied population	12,925 (100·0)	13,635 (100·0)	14,760 (100·0)	15,585 (100·0)	15,990 (100·0)	5,425 (100·0)	5,697 (100·0)	6,264 (100·0)	6,930 (100·0)	7,649 (100·0)	18,350 (100·0)	19,332 (100·0)	21,024 (100·0)	22,515 (100·0)	23,639 (100·0)

Note: Numbers in brackets are percentages. All other numbers are in thousands.

1935, p. 11, table 4*b*. (*c*) For 1935 and 1949, *Censuses of Production for 1950, 1949, and 1948: Summary Tables*, part I, table 1. (*d*) For 1958, *The Report on the Census of Production for 1958*, part cxxxiii, table 3. (*e*) For 1963, 'Census of Production Results for 1963', *Board of Trade Journal* (24 December 1965), pp. 2–4.

All figures are for the United Kingdom (England, Wales, Scotland, and N. Ireland) except for 1907 when the whole of Ireland was included.

The value of these figures is enhanced by the rather consistent definition given to the white-collar and manual groups in the successive Censuses of Production. In 1958 'administrative, technical and clerical employees' (the white-collar group) were defined to include:

> managers, superintendents, and works foremen; research, experimental, development, technical and design employees (other than operatives); draughtsmen and tracers; travellers; and office (including works office) employees. For Great Britain, but not for N. Ireland, they include directors, other than those paid by fee only.

Working proprietors are also included in the white-collar group except for 1949. 'Operatives', or the manual group, was defined to include:

> all other classes of employees, that is, broadly speaking, all manual wage earners. They include those employed in and about the factory or works; operatives employed in power houses, transport works, stores, warehouses and, for 1958, canteens; inspectors, viewers and similar workers; maintenance workers; and cleaners. Operatives engaged in outside work of erection, fitting etc., are also included, but outworkers [i.e., persons employed by the firm who worked on materials supplied by the firm in their own homes, etc.] are excluded.[1]

The definitions used by the Ministry of Labour are the same as those used in the Censuses of Production.

From the viewpoint of the present study, the main difficulty with the Ministry of Labour-Census of Production definition of a white-collar employee is that it excludes all foremen except works foremen and includes all grades of managerial personnel. Nevertheless, the figures give a relatively good idea of the increasing importance of the white-collar group over time.

The figures in Table 2.5 differ slightly from those given in Seymour Melman, *Dynamic Factors in Industrial Productivity* (Oxford: Blackwell, 1956), p. 73, table 10. Periodically, the Board of Trade (Census of Production) issues revised figures for former years and these have been used here. Melman used the figures which appeared in the Census of Production for the year in question. The differences in percentage terms, however, are negligible.

Table 2A.2 gives the number of white-collar employees in manufacturing industries in Great Britain from 1948 to 1964. The figures in Table 2.5 are for the United Kingdom and are from unpublished Ministry of Labour data.

TABLE 2.6

The figures for 1948 and 1959 are from 'Administrative, Technical and Clerical Workers in Manufacturing Industries', *Ministry of Labour Gazette*, lxix (January 1961), p. 9. All the figures for 1948 are not given because the differences between

---

[1] 'Introductory Notes', *The Report on the Census of Production 1958*, part i, p. 11.

the 1948 and 1958 Standard Industrial Classification were so great in respect of these industries that all comparability was destroyed. Even for those industries for which a 1948 figure is given, there are small differences in classification between 1948 and 1959. These differences, however, did not affect the percentages to any significant extent in 1959 when the figures were given according to both classification systems, and it has been assumed that this was also true for 1948.

TABLE 2A.2

Employment[a] *in Manufacturing Industries in Great Britain, 1948–64*

Year	White-collar (000s)	Manual (000s)	Total (000s)	White-collar as a percentage of total (%)
1948	1,286	6,749	8,035	16·0
1949	1,351	6,887	8,238	16·4
1950	1,397	7,067	8,464	16·5
1951[b]	1,462	7,141	8,603	17·0
1952	1,538	6,957	8,495	18·1
1953	1,586	7,126	8,712	18·2
1954	1,647	7,303	8,950	18·4
1955	1,741	7,422	9,163	19·0
1956	1,811	7,334	9,145	19·8
1957	1,852	7,318	9,170	20·2
1958	1,898	7,052	8,950	21·2
1959[c]	1,950	7,205	9,155	21·3
1959	1,801	6,709	8,510	21·1
1960	1,878	6,932	8,810	21·3
1961	1,957	6,892	8,849	22·1
1962	1,979	6,763	8,742	22·6
1963	1,976	6,702	8,678	22·8
1964	2,031	6,774	8,805	23·1

[a] These figures exclude the unemployed.

[b] The figures for 1948–51 inclusive are for December of each year; the figures for 1952–64 inclusive are for October of each year.

[c] All figures prior to 1959 are classified according to the Standard Industrial Classification 1948, while all those after 1959 are classified according to the Standard Industrial Classification 1958. For 1959 the figures are given on both bases.

The figures for 1964 are from 'Administrative, Technical and Clerical Workers in Manufacturing Industries', *Ministry of Labour Gazette*, lxxii (July 1964), p. 291.

The figures for 1948 and 1959 are for the end of October; those for 1964 are for April.

The Ministry of Labour uses the same definition of white-collar employees as the Board of Trade in the Censuses of Production (see notes to Table 2.5).

TABLE 2.7

The figures for foremen in Table 2.7 were abstracted from the *Census of Population 1961*, Industry Table 5, for both Scotland, and England and Wales. Foremen are defined as 'employees (other than managers) who formally and immediately supervise others engaged in manual occupations, whether or not themselves engaged in such operations'.[1] There is a three-year difference between the figures for foremen

[1] *Classification of Occupations 1960* (London: HMSO, 1960), p. xii.

and all other occupations in the table. This is unfortunate, but the 1961 figures for foremen are the only ones available. While the category has undoubtedly expanded since 1961, it is assumed that the relative importance of foremen between industries has remained the same.

The figures for all other occupations were derived from 'Occupations of Employees in Manufacturing Industries', *Ministry of Labour Gazette* (December 1964), pp. 492–502; (January 1965), pp. 11–19. These figures are for 16 May 1964 and relate to all firms with eleven or more employees in manufacturing in Great Britain. The details of the sampling techniques are given on p. 492. The Ministry of Labour's 'managers, work superintendents, departmental managers' group was excluded from Table 2.7.

All figures exclude the self-employed and the unemployed.

The occupational groups are defined as follows (all definitions taken from instructions to employers who were requested to complete the questionnaire forms):

(*a*) Scientists and technologists 'include persons engaged on, or being trained for, technical work for which the normal qualification is a university degree in science or technology and/or membership of an appropriate professional institute (e.g., A.M.I.Mech.E.)'. Managers and technical directors possessing such qualifications are excluded.

(*b*) All technicians 'include persons carrying out functions of a grade intermediate between scientists and technologists on the one hand and skilled craftsmen and operatives on the other, whether in research or development, production, testing, or maintenance'. Some of the main job titles are: draughtsmen, laboratory technicians, service engineers, production planners, testers and inspectors, technical writers, work-study specialists, and others.

(*c*) The draughtsmen category includes all people so designated. It does not include tracers who are included in the 'other white-collar worker' group.

(*d*) Other technicians include all the occupations specified in (*b*) except for draughtsmen.

(*e*) Clerks 'include shorthand typists, typists, office-machine operators, automatic data programmers, telephone operators, etc.'.

(*f*) Other white-collar workers 'include all other administrators, technical and commercial staff not included above, e.g., personnel and welfare assistants, occupational health nurses, safety officers, management trainees, tracers, salesmen and representatives, etc.'. In the paper, printing, and publishing industry this category also includes, in addition to the above, salaried reporters and journalists (not those working on a freelance basis), press photographers, circulation travellers, and advertising representatives.

The figures for shipbuilding and for marine engineering were given separately by the Ministry of Labour and no occupational breakdown of the administrative, technical, and clerical workers' category was given for shipbuilding (see table 6). Consequently, this over-all figure for shipbuilding was distributed on the same basis as the occupational distribution in marine engineering, and then the two sets of figures were added together to give Order VII, Shipbuilding and Marine Engineering.

For the printing and publishing sub-industry (see table 17) the 'designers and typographers' category was omitted as it was considered that they were manual employees and not covered by the scope of any of the unions under consideration.

The labour force figures relate to private employment except that Royal Ordnance Factories and railway workshops are classified under Engineering and Electrical Goods. The figures for foremen in Shipbuilding and Marine Engineering include those in Royal Navy Dockyards; employees in all other white-collar occupations in this industry are excluded if in Royal Naval Dockyards.

The actual numbers for Table 2.7 are given in Table 2A.3.

TABLE 2.8

Table 2.8 is based on the same sources as Table 2.7. The actual number of females in each white-collar occupation is given by Table 2A.4. The percentages in Table 2.8 were obtained by merely taking a figure in Table 2A.4 as a percentage of the corresponding figure in Table 2A.3.

The number of females in each white-collar occupation in Shipbuilding and Marine Engineering was determined in the same manner as total employment in each white-collar occupation in this industry (see *supra*, p. 194).

Obviously, the number of male white-collar workers can be obtained by merely subtracting Table 2A.4 from Table 2A.3.

TABLE 3.1

The trade union membership figures are those published annually by the Ministry of Labour. See, for example, 'Membership of Trade Unions in 1964', *Ministry of Labour Gazette*, lxxiii (November 1965), pp. 480–1. The figures from 1955–64 are only provisional and are subject to revision as additional information becomes available. For each year the latest revised figure was used.

These membership figures 'relate to all organisations of employees . . . which are known to include in their objects that of negotiating with employers with a view to regulating the wages and working conditions of their members'.[1] They thus include all trade unions and staff associations, whether they be registered or unregistered, affiliated or unaffiliated to the TUC, whose headquarters are situated in the United Kingdom. More specifically, they include all unions listed in the *Directory of Employers' Associations, Trade Unions, Joint Organisations, Etc., 1960*. Unfortunately, the figures also include the membership of British unions located in branches in the Irish Republic and overseas as well as members serving with H.M. Forces. Total union membership at the end of 1964 included 49,000 members in the Irish Republic and 89,000 in other branches outside the United Kingdom. It is not possible to adjust the revised total membership figures because the non-United Kingdom membership figures are not published on the revised basis. In any case, the numbers involved are relatively small and do not significantly affect the density figures.

The labour force figures for 1959–64 are from the 'Number of Employees (Employed and Unemployed) June 1964', *Ministry of Labour Gazette*, lxxiii (February 1965), pp. 61 and 64. The figures for 1948–58 were supplied from unpublished data and are comparable with the 1959–64 series. The figures exclude employers, self-employed, and members of the armed forces, but include the unemployed.

The labour force figures for 1891, 1901, 1911, 1921, 1931, 1933, and 1938 were derived as follows. The total occupied population of the United Kingdom was estimated by Professor Bowley for the above years as being 15,783,000, 17,648,000,

---

[1] *Ministry of Labour Gazette*, lxxiii (November 1965), p. 480.

TABLE 2A.3

Total White-Collar Employment in Manufacturing Industries in Great Britain, 1964

Occupational group	Food, drink, tobacco	Chemical	Metal manuf.	Metal N.E.S.	Eng. elect.	Ship. M.E.	Vehicles	Textiles	Leather, fur	Clothing, footwear	Bricks, etc.	Timber, furn. etc.	Paper, print, pub.	Other manuf.	All manuf.
1. Foremen	28,850	22,380	24,400	17,870	67,910	9,800	29,450	34,030	2,180	13,410	12,060	10,130	16,650	12,390	301,510
2. All scientists, technologists, technicians	7,560	43,030	19,630	10,110	156,700	7,516	51,800	11,680	370	2,540	6,660	2,230	4,670	7,620	333,116
(a) Scientists, technologists	2,770	17,100	4,950	1,610	33,220	570	7,000	3,000	150	200	1,800	50	1,560	2,080	76,060
(b) All technicians	4,790	25,930	14,680	8,500	123,480	6,946	44,800	8,680	220	2,340	4,860	2,180	3,110	5,540	256,056
(i) Draughtsmen	1,150	3,010	4,440	5,430	65,160	5,114	19,820	1,580	10	310	2,320	1,420	490	1,800	112,054
(ii) Other technicians	3,640	22,920	10,240	3,070	58,320	1,832	24,980	7,100	210	2,030	2,540	760	2,620	3,740	144,002
3. Clerks	84,380	74,000	59,020	55,830	275,050	10,004	101,770	50,820	5,590	32,610	28,770	27,660	80,940	34,290	920,734
4. Other white-collar workers	38,190	30,550	16,640	14,990	90,440	4,306	27,670	11,230	1,170	10,190	8,630	5,940	31,950	15,480	307,376
5. All white-collar workers	158,980	169,960	119,690	98,800	590,100	31,626	210,690	107,760	9,310	58,750	56,120	45,960	134,210	69,780	1,861,736

TABLE 2A.4

Total Female White-Collar Employment in Manufacturing Industries in Great Britain, 1964

Occupational group	Food, drink, tobacco	Chemical	Metal manuf.	Metal N.E.S.	Eng. elect.	Ship M.E.	Vehicles	Textiles	Leather, fur	Clothing, footwear	Bricks etc.	Timber, furn., etc.	Paper, print, pub.	Other manuf.	All manuf.
1. Foremen	5,520	2,010	360	1,510	4,330	20	390	4,340	360	7,370	850	400	2,740	1,660	31,860
2. All scientists, technologists, technicians	1,240	4,560	680	320	3,940	180	1,150	2,150	20	900	310	140	330	640	16,560
(a) Scientists, technologists	330	1,190	140	80	720	..	80	250	10	70	100	..	90	50	3,110
(b) All technicians	910	3,370	540	240	3,220	180	1,070	1,900	10	830	210	140	240	590	13,450
(i) Draughtsmen	..	10	40	70	1,310	128	280	10	..	110	30	30	20	20	2,058
(ii) Other technicians	910	3,360	500	170	1,910	52	790	1,890	10	720	180	110	220	570	11,392
3. Clerks	57,810	50,720	31,370	37,740	170,240	4,398	49,430	33,610	4,690	26,950	17,190	18,850	51,590	23,190	577,778
4. Other white-collar workers	5,130	4,450	2,810	3,680	18,240	1,137	5,290	2,900	40	4,730	1,390	760	4,800	3,330	58,687
5. All white-collar workers	69,700	61,740	35,220	43,250	196,750	5,735	56,260	43,000	5,110	39,950	19,740	20,150	59,460	28,820	684,885

19,615,000, 19,840,000, 21,620,000, 21,810,000, and 22,660,000, respectively.[1] To obtain the union potential, it was necessary to exclude the employers, self-employed, and the armed forces from the above figures. The number of employers and self-employed in Great Britain were obtained from an analysis of census data undertaken by Dr. Routh,[2] and the number in the armed forces was obtained directly from the Censuses of Population. The total of such occupational groups was 1,921,000 in 1911, 2,163,000 in 1921, and 2,238,000 in 1931. Out of the total gainfully occupied population of 18,347,000 in 1911, 19,333,000 in 1921, and 21,029,000 in 1931, the employers, self-employed, and armed forces represented 10·5 per cent, 11·2 per cent, and 10·6 per cent in the respective years. Professor Bowley's estimates of the total occupied population of the United Kingdom were then reduced by the same proportions. The 1911 ratio was used to reduce the 1891, 1901, and 1911 totals;[3] the 1921 ratio was used to reduce the 1921 total; and the 1931 ratio was used to reduce the 1931, 1933, and 1938 totals to give the figures shown in Table 3.1. These figures, like the 1948–64 series, include the number of unemployed.

TABLE 3.2

The employment figures for 1948 are based upon those appearing in 'The Employed Population, 1948–1952', *Ministry of Labour Gazette*, lxi (February 1953), pp. 39–47, and those for 1964 are from the 'Number of Employees (Employed and Unemployed) June 1964', *Ministry of Labour Gazette*, lxxiii (February 1965), pp. 59–64. The Standard Industrial Classification was changed between 1948 and 1964, and some of the 1948 figures had to be adjusted to make them even broadly comparable to the 1964 figures.[4]

The figures for the various industries were obtained in the following manner (the industries which are not mentioned below were considered to be broadly comparable and were simply abstracted unaltered from the above sources):

(*a*) *Professional and business services.* In 1948 this category was derived by subtracting 'Education' from 'Professional Services', and in 1964 by subtracting 'Educational Services' from 'Professional and Scientific Services'.

(*b*) *Distribution.* The 1948 figure was obtained by adding 'Wholesale Bottling' to 'Distributive Trades'.

(*c*) *Metals and engineering.* The 1948 figure was obtained by adding together 'Metal Manufacture', 'Engineering, Shipbuilding, and Electrical Goods', 'Vehicles', 'Metal Goods N.E.S.', 'Jewellery, Plate and refining of precious Metals', 'Scientific, Surgical and Photographic Instruments, etc.', 'Manufacture and Repair of Watches and Clocks', and then subtracting 'Motor Repairers and Garages'. The 1964 figure was derived by adding together the following: 'Metal Manufacture', 'Engineering

---

[1] The figures for 1891, 1901, and 1911 are from A. L. Bowley, *Wages and Income in the United Kingdom Since 1860* (Cambridge: Cambridge University Press, 1937), pp. 134–5. The figures for the other years are from his *Studies in the National Income 1924–1938* (Cambridge: Cambridge University Press, 1944), p. 56.

[2] Guy Routh, op. cit., pp. 4–5, table 1.

[3] The total number of employers and self-employed are not conveniently available in the 1891 and 1901 Censuses and hence the 1911 ratio was used for these years. Moreover, union membership figures only became available in 1892. No labour force figure is available for that year so the 1891 figure had to be used.

[4] For a brief summary of the major changes in the system of industrial classification see 'Standard Industrial Classification', *Ministry of Labour Gazette*, lxvii (February 1959), p. 55.

and Electrical Goods', 'Shipbuilding and Marine Engineering', 'Vehicles', and 'Metal Goods N.E.S.'.

(*d*) *Food, drink and tobacco.* The 1948 figure was obtained by subtracting 'Wholesale Bottling' from 'Food, Drink and Tobacco'.

(*e*) *Other transport and communication.* For both years this is simply 'Transport and Communication' minus 'Railways'.

(*f*) *Theatres, cinemas, sport, etc.* The 1948 figure was derived by adding together 'Theatres, Cinemas, Music Halls, Concerts, etc.', and 'Sport, Other Recreations, and Betting'. The 1964 figure was obtained by adding together 'Cinemas, Theatres, Radio, etc.', 'Sports and Other Recreations', and 'Betting'.

(*g*) *Furniture, timber, etc.* The 1948 figure is the one which appears for 'Manufactures of Wood and Cork'.

(*h*) *Footwear.* The 1948 figure is the one which appears for the 'Manufacture of Boots, Shoes, Slippers and Clogs (exc. rubber)'.

(*i*) *Clothing.* The 1948 figure was obtained by subtracting the 'Manufacture of Boots, Shoes, Slippers and Clogs (exc. rubber)' and 'Repair of Boots and Shoes' from 'Clothing'. The 1964 figure was derived by subtracting 'Footwear' from 'Clothing and Footwear'.

(*j*) *Textiles other than cotton.* The 1948 figure was obtained by subtracting 'Cotton Spinning, Doubling, etc.' and 'Cotton Weaving, etc.' from 'Textiles'. The 1964 figure was derived by subtracting 'Spinning and Doubling of Cotton, Flax and Man-Made Fibres' and 'Weaving of Cotton, Linen and Man-Made Fibres' from 'Textiles'.

(*k*) *Cotton.* The 1948 figure was obtained by adding together 'Cotton Spinning, Doubling, etc.', and 'Cotton Weaving, etc.'. The 1964 figure was derived by adding together 'Spinning and Doubling of Cotton, Flax and Man-Made Fibres' and 'Weaving of Cotton, Linen and Man-Made Fibres'.

In spite of the adjustments which have been made to the 1948 figures, there are still some differences in coverage between the figures of 1948 and 1964. Consequently, the percentage change in employment between 1948 and 1964 is subject to some error and should be used cautiously.

Most of the industry headings are self-explanatory regarding their scope. The ones which require special mention are:

(*a*) *Professional and business services.* This category includes accounting, legal, religious, and other services, as well as medical and dental services, i.e., personnel employed by the National Health Services.

(*b*) *Other transport and communication.* This category includes road, air, sea, and inland water transport, as well as the postal services and telecommunications.

The union density figures for 1960 were obtained from Keith Hindell, *Trade Union Membership* (London: Political and Economic Planning, 1962), p. 191, table 7. Hindell also gives (p. 156, table 1) the density figures for 1958 and the change in density between 1948 and 1958. It is therefore possible to determine what the actual density figure was in 1948 and then calculate the change in density between 1948 and 1960.

The method used by Hindell to calculate these density figures is given in the notes to table 1, p. 156, and also in the Appendix, pp. 199–200, of the above publication. These density figures are little more than rough approximations. In preparing their industrial analysis of union membership, the Ministry of Labour allocates the total membership of a union to the industry in which the majority of its members are employed. In the case of industrial unions such as **BISAKTA** and the National Union of Mineworkers, for example, this procedure involves little error. In the case of other unions such as the Amalgamated Engineering Union and the Electrical Trades Union, this procedure involves considerable error. The Ministry of Labour allocates the total membership of these unions to the Metals and Engineering indus-tries, but thousands of their members are employed outside this group of industries. Although Hindell has been able to remove some of the inaccuracies inherent in this procedure, it is not possible in most cases to correct the figures as the unions do not prepare detailed industrial classifications of their membership. The percentage change in density between 1948 and 1960 is subject to additional error because for 1948 Hindell used the labour force figures published in 1949 rather than the very much revised figures published in 1953.[1] Nevertheless, Hindell's figures are the most detailed and reliable ones published.[2]

TABLE 3.3

The membership figures of non-TUC unions were obtained from the files of the Ministry of Labour.

The membership figures of the purely white-collar unions affiliated to the TUC were abstracted from the TUC's *Annual Reports*. In general, these figures give a fairly reliable idea of the size of the various unions. Some unions, however, do not always affiliate their actual membership to the TUC; for various reasons they affili-ate more or less than the true total.

The white-collar membership of the partially white-collar unions was obtained from the the unions concerned. Only those partially white-collar unions which keep a record of their white-collar membership or could give a fairly reliable estimate of its size were included in this list. Nevertheless, the list includes all the major partially white-collar unions. In general, these figures slightly understate the actual totals. In some areas where there are very few white-collar members, these members will be placed in manual branches and no separate record kept of them. In addition, although many unions have separate supervisory branches, some newly promoted supervisors prefer to retain their membership in their old branch on grounds of class loyalty, tradition, etc. The totals of the Amalgamated Engineering Union and the Electrical Trades Union are likely to be particularly understated for the above reasons.

The membership figures for the purely and partially white-collar unions which are affiliated to the TUC are given in Table 3A.1, Parts A and B. The figures in Part C of Table 3A.1 were derived as follows:

(*a*) *Line 1*. This line was obtained by summing all the figures, except those in brackets, in each column of Part A of the table.

(*b*) *Line 2*. This line was obtained by summing all the figures, including the ones in brackets, in each column of Part A of the table.

(*c*) *Line 3*. The 1964 figure was obtained by summing all the figures in the 1964 column of Part B of the table. The 1955 and 1948 figures were obtained by assuming

---

[1] Cf. 'Estimated Number of Employees Insured Under the National Insurance Schemes at Mid-1948', *Ministry of Labour Gazette*, lvii (February 1949), p. 44, and 'The Employed Population, 1948–1952', *Ministry of Labour Gazette*, lxi (February 1953), pp. 44–7.

[2] Cf. Guy Routh, 'Future Trade Union Membership', *Industrial Relations: Contemporary Problems and Perspectives*, B. C. Roberts, editor (London: Methuen, 1962), p. 72, table 4.

that the white-collar membership of the partially white-collar unions grew at the same rate as the adjusted membership of the purely white-collar unions. In other words, the 1955 figure is 21·4 per cent less than the 1964 figure, and the 1948 figure is 36·2 per cent less than the 1964 figure. If anything, these figures understate the growth of the partially white-collar unions. It can be seen from Part B of the table that the white-collar membership of most of the partially white-collar unions for which growth figures are available grew by amounts substantially in excess of 36·2 per cent.

(*d*) *Line 4.* Since the number of partially white-collar unions affiliated to the TUC between 1948 and 1964 remained unaltered, line 4 is the same as line 3.

(*e*) *Line 5.* These figures were abstracted from the TUC's *Annual Report* for each year.

(*f*) *Line 6.* This line was obtained by adding line 2 to line 8.

(*g*) *Line 7.* This line was obtained by subtracting line 1 from line 5.

(*h*) *Line 8.* This line was obtained by adding to line 7 the membership figures of those manual unions which affiliated to the TUC since 1948 for the years they were unaffiliated; plus the membership figures of those unions which were temporarily expelled during the period (except the ETU) for the years they were expelled; minus the membership figures of those unions which left or were expelled during the period and have not reaffiliated. The membership figures of the following manual unions were added to line 7 for the years indicated (all dates inclusive): Card Setting Machine Tenters' Society, 1948; Amalgamated Union of Sailmakers, 1948–51; Nottingham and District Hosiery Finishers' Association, 1948–53; Leicester and Leicestershire Hosiery Trimmers and Auxiliary Association, 1948–54; Screw, Nut, Bolt and Rivet Trade Society, 1948–54; Watermen, Lightermen, Tugmen and Bargemen's Union, 1948–55; Northern Carpet Trades Union, 1948–57; National Union of Waterworks Employees, 1948–62; and the National Engineers' Association, 1955–7. The membership figures of the following manual unions were subtracted from the above total for the years indicated: National Amalgamated Association of Nut and Boltmakers, 1948–53; Nelson and District Preparatory Workers' Association, 1948–53; National Amalgamated Stevedores and Dockers, 1948–57. The figures of all these unions were obtained either from the union concerned or from the Registrar of Friendly Societies.

(*i*) *Line 9.* This line was obtained by adding line 1 and line 3.

(*j*) *Line 10.* This line was obtained by adding line 2 and line 4.

(*k*) *Line 11.* This line was obtained by subtracting line 9 from line 5.

(*l*) *Line 12.* This line was obtained by subtracting line 10 from line 6.

(*m*) *Line 13.* This line was obtained by taking line 1 as a percentage of line 5.

(*n*) *Line 14.* This line was obtained by taking line 10 as a percentage of line 5.

Since Table 3A.1 was prepared, five more purely white-collar unions have affiliated to the TUC: the Society of Telecommunication Engineers (7,154), the Customs and Excise Preventive Staff Association (2,600), the County Court Officers Association (4,725), the Association of Teachers in Technical Institutions (25,000), and the Prison Officers' Association (10,313).

TABLE 3.4

The union membership figures used in calculating the densities in this table came from the same sources as those used in Table 3.3.

The labour force figures for 1948 and 1964 are from the same source as those used in Table 3.1 and have been broken down into manual and white-collar categories using the proportion of white-collar and manual employees in the total occupied population (excluding employers) as given by the 1951 and 1961 *Census of Population*.

TABLE 3.5

Table 3.5 is largely an abridged version of Table 3.2. The derivation of the manufacturing figure is explained in the notes to Table 3.8.

Although the labour force of the 'Professional and Business Services' sector is predominantly white-collar, it was omitted from Table 3.5 because the Ministry of Labour classified both the AScW and the CAWU under this heading. As is shown in Table 3.6, however, a substantial proportion of the membership of both these unions was situated in manufacturing industries. Thus to have included this industry group along with the manufacturing group would have resulted in a considerable amount of double counting.

TABLE 3.6

All membership figures in this table are for the year 1963. The total membership figures of the AScW, ASSET, the CAWU, DATA, and the NUJ, and the total white-collar membership figures of BISAKTA, NATSOPA, and the TGWU are from Table 3.7. The total membership figure of BISAKTA is from its *Quarterly Report*, 31 March 1964, p. 7, and is its total contributing membership minus its retired members; NATSOPA's is from its *Annual Report*, 1964, p. 17; and the TGWU's is from its *Report and Balance Sheet*, 1963, p. 7.

The occupational and industrial composition of the unions' white-collar memberships was determined by the survey described in the notes to Table 3.8.

TABLE 3.7

All the membership figures in Table 3.7, with the exception of BISAKTA's, were supplied by the unions concerned. In all cases, they are the contributing or paying membership figure and generally exclude non-contributory and retired members. The figures in this table are more accurate than the ones given in Table 3A.1. As was explained in the notes to the latter table, unions do not always affiliate their true membership to the TUC.

The white-collar membership of BISAKTA was derived by analysing its quarterly list of individual branch membership. The list of the branch audits for December 1964 appear in the *Quarterly Report*, 31 March 1965, pp. 23–5. There are similar lists in earlier Reports. For 1964 it was possible to obtain a list of all the white-collar branches and to abstract their membership totals from the quarterly branch audits. This list was also used to help identify white-collar branches in earlier years. In any case, virtually all BISAKTA's white-collar membership is in separate branches and most of the branches are designated in such a way that they indicate the type of personnel covered, e.g., 'Britannia Clerical', 'Tees-side Chemists', etc. Not all the branches are audited every quarter. For each branch the audited figure closest to December of each year was used. Sample passers were included as white-collar, ambulance drivers were not. Although the annual totals are obviously subject to some error, they should nevertheless give a reliable idea of the growth of BISAKTA's white-collar membership between 1948 and 1964.

The figures of all the unions, except ASSET, are for December of each year. ASSET's figures are for March of each year and are therefore slightly understated relative to the others. This does not affect the relative size of its increase over the period.

TABLES 3.8 AND 3.9

The labour force statistics used to calculate the density figures of Table 3.8 are the ones which appear in Table 2A.3, and they refer to May 1964. A geographical analysis of these figures is not available.

The labour force figures used to calculate the density figures of Table 3.9 are from unpublished Ministry of Labour data sheets (H.Q.W. 474-200 4/64 EC). These data sheets give a geographical breakdown of the industrial and occupational analysis of the labour force which was published as: 'Occupations of Employees in Metal Manufacture, Engineering and Electrical Goods, Vehicles and Metal Goods', *Ministry of Labour Gazette*, lxxi (December 1963), pp. 474-80; and 'Occupations of Employees in Manufacturing Industries (Other than the Metal Group of Industries)', *Ministry of Labour Gazette*, lxxii (April 1964), pp. 132-42. The figures in these articles refer to May 1963 and exclude all employers, self-employed, and unemployed. They conform to the standard Ministry of Labour definition of a white-collar employee and include managers but exclude all foremen (except works foremen).

Unfortunately, the May 1963 survey does not include a regional analysis of the Shipbuilding labour force and, in addition, it includes the figures for Marine Engineering with those of Engineering and Electrical Goods. Thus in order to obtain comparable manpower statistics, the white-collar labour force of Marine Engineering had to be subtracted from that of Engineering and Electrical Goods (including Marine Engineering), and a geographical breakdown of the white-collar labour force of Shipbuilding and Marine Engineering had to be obtained. This was done in the following manner. In the May 1964 survey[1] the white-collar labour force of Marine Engineering was given separately as 10,240. This figure was distributed according to the regional distribution of *total* employment in the Shipbuilding and Marine Engineering industry in the United Kingdom as given by the Census of Production.[2] Then the regional white-collar labour force totals obtained by this procedure were subtracted from the Engineering and Electrical Goods (including Marine Engineering) regional white-collar labour force totals to leave the category Engineering and Electrical Goods. The May 1964 survey also gives the total white-collar labour force for the combined industrial order, Shipbuilding and Marine Engineering, as 26,890. This figure was distributed regionally using the same geographical distribution of total employment described above. The figure for Shipbuilding and Marine Engineering in Wales is not given because the Census of Production does not give the percentage of total employment in this industry in Wales as this would disclose information about individual establishments.

The scope of the regions is given by 'Definition of Standard Regions', *Ministry of Labour Gazette*, lxxiii (January 1965), p. 5. The Ministry of Labour's 'Midlands' and 'Yorkshire and Lincolnshire' regions are combined in Table 3.9. The union membership figures were originally classified according to the Standard Regions of the United Kingdom used by the Census of Production and the Census of Population.[3] At a later stage in the research it became necessary and desirable to use the manpower

[1] 'Occupations of Employees in Manufacturing Industries', *Ministry of Labour Gazette* (December 1964), pp. 492-502; (January 1965), pp. 11-19.

[2] *Report on the Census of Production 1958* (London: HMSO, 1963), table 8, pp. 134/8-134/9.

[3] Ibid., part 134, pp. 129-31; and *Census of Population 1951* Industry Tables, pp. x-xiii.

statistics of the Ministry of Labour. Unfortunately, the Ministry uses a different system of regional classification and the only way the two systems could be rationalized was to combine the union membership figures in the manner shown in Table 3.9. If the two systems of classification are compared, the need for the regional groupings used in Table 3.9 will become obvious.

The Ministry of Labour's system of regional classification and the manner in which it has had to be modified obscures much of the regional variation in union density. By grouping low-density areas with high-density areas (e.g., east midlands with west midlands and north Wales with south Wales) and by not giving separate labour force figures for the major conurbations, extremely broad and general average density figures result. The geographical analysis of May 1963 gives an occupational breakdown (except for Shipbuilding and Marine Engineering) but because of sampling difficulties the Ministry of Labour advised against using it.

The actual geographical labour force figures used in Table 3.9 are given by Table 3A.2.

In general, the union membership figures are for 1 January 1964 and exclude all retired and non-contributory members. The figures relate to Great Britain.

Unions keep their membership records in the most administratively convenient manner rather than in accordance with the official systems of industrial and regional classification. Consequently, in order to get membership figures which would be comparable with the government's labour force statistics, it was necessary to undertake a detailed analysis of the membership records of the major unions catering for white-collar workers in manufacturing industries. In general, this analysis was carried out in the following manner: (a) A list of the branches in the union and the names and addresses of the firm or firms covered by each branch were obtained from the union. (b) The membership in each firm or in each branch (if the branch covered only one firm) was determined. (c) The firm was then checked in *Kelly's Directory of Merchants, Manufacturers and Shippers* (Kingston-upon-Thames, Surrey: Kelly's Directories Ltd., 1963) to determine the type of product manufactured. This was checked against information supplied by the union. (d) The type of product manufactured was then located in the *Standard Industrial Classification: Alphabetical List of Industries* (London: HMSO, 1959) and the industry to which it was assigned was noted. (e) Finally, the membership of the firm was assigned to the industry as determined in (d) and the region as determined by its address in (a).

The specific details of the manner in which the membership of each of the major unions was regionally, industrially, and occupationally classified are given below:

(a) *AScW*. The AScW's membership records were decentralized. Each of the regional offices was visited and the membership files were analysed according to the general procedure described above. The AScW catered for two broad categories of personnel: qualified scientists and engineers, and laboratory technicians. The former were classified as Section I members and the latter as Section II members. The distinction between Section I and Section II members conforms very closely to the distinction the Ministry of Labour draws in its manpower statistics between 'scientists and technologists' and 'other technicians'.[1] The union stopped keeping an exact count of the two categories of membership in 1955 when Section I members comprised 31·4 per cent of the total. At that time the proportion of Section I members in the union was declining, and the AScW estimated that by 1964 only 25 per cent of

---

[1] Cf. notes to Table 2.7 and *AScW Rules*, 1964, p. 2, rule 5.

TABLE 3A.2

Total White-Collar Employment in Manufacturing Industries in Great Britain by Industry and by Region, 1963

Region	Food, drink, tobacco	Chemical	Metal manuf.	Metal N.E.S.	Eng. elect.	Ship. M.E.	Vehicles	Textiles	Leather, fur	Clothing, footwear	Bricks, etc.	Timber, furn., etc.	Paper, print, pub.	Other manuf.	All manuf.
1. Scotland	15,560	10,320	11,110	4,450	41,731	6,561	9,490	11,360	220	2,970	3,510	3,940	12,340	5,310	138,872
2. Northern	5,140	15,070	8,290	2,260	25,497	5,916	2,220	2,150	480	2,970	2,850	2,010	2,490	2,660	80,003
3. North-west	23,160	39,720	6,860	11,810	77,437	3,657	27,870	28,600	2,390	11,030	9,570	4,220	14,970	12,000	273,294
4. East and West Ridings of Yorkshire and East and West Midlands	33,890	26,940	59,550	53,380	152,119	1,076	74,410	47,640	3,530	19,590	22,100	10,990	20,020	16,210	541,445
5. Wales	4,320	5,300	17,720	3,470	11,200	n/a	2,700	4,320	380	1,220	1,040	1,360	2,180	2,170	57,380
6. Eastern and Southern	18,120	20,430	4,830	6,590	79,823	3,011	38,640	3,850	330	8,650	6,470	7,810	16,450	5,970	220,974
7. London and South-east	38,270	51,190	9,750	22,640	193,730	2,205	34,150	7,740	2,760	18,570	13,590	18,270	67,730	21,260	501,855
8. South-western	12,790	3,560	1,500	2,030	23,353	1,882	23,870	2,580	1,050	3,440	2,390	3,400	7,510	3,730	93,085
9. ALL REGIONS	151,250	172,530	119,610	106,630	604,890	24,308	213,350	108,240	11,140	68,440	61,520	52,000	143,690	69,310	1,906,908

its total membership was in Section I. Consequently, after the industrial and geographical analysis of its membership was completed, 25 per cent of the AScW's membership was assigned to the 'scientists and technologists' category and the remainder to the 'other technicians' group of Table 3A.3.

(b) *ASSET*. ASSET supplied a list of firms in each of its branches and the membership in each firm. The industrial and regional classification of the union's membership was then carried out according to the general procedure described above. Generally speaking, ASSET catered for two groups of personnel: 'foremen' and 'other technicians'. It also claimed to cater for executive grades but the number of such personnel in the union was negligible. Unfortunately, ASSET did not know the exact number of members in each occupational group. Consequently, the Industrial Officer in charge of each District of the union was interviewed and asked to estimate the proportion of his membership which was in the two groups. The national weighted average of all the estimates indicated that approximately 50 per cent of the union's membership was among foremen and 50 per cent among 'other technicians'. Thus after the industrial and geographical classification of ASSET's membership was completed, one-half of its membership was assigned to the foremen category and the other half to 'other technicians'.

(c) *BISAKTA*. As was explained in the notes to Table 3.7, a list of the white-collar branches in BISAKTA was obtained and then the membership figures for these branches were abstracted from the quarterly list of branch audits. Each branch's membership is not audited every quarter; for each branch the figure closest to 31 December 1963 was used (for the December 1963 audit see *Quarterly Report*, 31 December 1963, pp. 251–8). All of BISAKTA's membership is in the iron and steel industry, so industrial classification was no problem. Most of the branches have a geographical or company name and, in addition, are arranged according to the union's geographical divisions, so regional classification was relatively easy. Occupational classification was made possible by the union's practice, largely at management insistence, of keeping different types of white-collar personnel in different branches. The names of most of the white-collar branches indicate the type of personnel covered, e.g., 'Britannia Clerical', 'Tees-side Foremen', etc. The occupational composition of BISAKTA's membership as determined by analysing the branch audits was: clerks, 63 per cent; other technicians, 19 per cent; foremen, 16 per cent; other white-collar workers, 2 per cent. The membership of the few mixed white-collar branches was distributed on the same basis.

(d) *CAWU*. From the master membership file in the CAWU's head office it was possible to determine the names and addresses of the firms in each branch and the membership in each firm. Then the general procedure described above was carried out. The membership of the union is entirely composed of clerical and administrative workers so all of it was assigned to the 'clerks' category of Table 3A.3.

(e) *DATA*. DATA's membership was classified by analysing the returns the union received from its annual statistical survey. Between October and March the union sends out a questionnaire to each of its members requesting information on salaries. It also asks for the name, address, and product of the firm in which the member works. In the October 1963–March 1964 survey, 41,046 of the 61,446 members or 67 per cent of the total membership returned these questionnaires. These questionnaires were then classified industrially and geographically according to the general procedure described above. It was assumed that the 67 per cent return was a representative sample of DATA's total membership, and the total draughtsmen membership

TABLE 3A.3

Total White-Collar Union Membership in Manufacturing Industries in Great Britain by Industry and by Occupation, 1964

Occupational group	Food, drink, tobacco	Chemical	Metal manuf.	Metal N.E.S.	Eng. elect.	Ship. M.E.	Vehicles	Textiles	Leather, fur	Clothing, footwear	Bricks, etc.	Timber, furn., etc.	Paper, print, pub.	Other manuf.	All manuf.
1. Foremen	..	364	2,025	567	9,232	285	3,192	9,590	24	..	242	390	n/a	588	26,499
2. All scientists, technologists, technicians	130	4,120	5,184	262	44,112	4,023	19,676	308	2	24	556	280	21	1,073	79,771
(a) Scientists, technologists	33	2,136	148	..	1,280	77	162	50	..	6	79	..	4	69	4,044
(b) All technicians	97	1,984	5,036	262	42,832	3,946	19,514	258	2	18	477	280	17	1,004	75,727
(i) Draughtsmen	..	176	2,234	..	32,694	3,434	15,848	..	..	..	..	..	..	217	54,603
(ii) Other technicians	97	1,808	2,802	262	10,138	512	3,666	258	2	18	477	280	17	787	21,124
3. Clerks	4,592	1,735	12,595	1,337	33,749	556	22,701	1,715	..	180	1,508	112	12,310	3,498	96,588
4. Other white-collar workers	..	9	252	..	1,655	160	803	..	..	..	..	..	19,022	12	21,913
5. All white-collar workers	4,722	6,228	20,056	2,166	88,748	5,024	46,372	11,613	26	204	2,306	782	31,353	5,171	224,771

of 58,485 and the total tracer membership of 2,961 in 1963 were distributed on the same basis. The draughtsmen were assigned to the 'draughtsmen' category of Table 3A.3, and the tracers to the 'other white-collar workers' group. DATA also has a few 'other technicians' in membership, but the numbers in this group are not yet significant. Nevertheless, their inclusion in the draughtsmen category slightly inflates the density figures for draughtsmen and understates the density figures for 'other technicians'.

(f) NATSOPA. Among white-collar workers NATSOPA recruited only clerical and administrative grades and restricted itself entirely to the paper, printing, and publishing industry. Thus the occupational and industrial classification of its white-collar membership was straightforward. The union supplied a geographical breakdown of its membership.

(g) NUJ. A list of all the branches in the NUJ and their membership at December 1963 is given in the union's *Annual Report*, 1964, pp. 53–6. All the membership in Freelance, Radio and T.V., and Public Relations branches was excluded (the Ministry of Labour classifies these activities to professional and scientific services, and miscellaneous services), and then the remaining membership was assigned to the 'other white-collar workers' category in the paper, printing, and publishing industry. Most of the branches cover a specific geographical area and hence it was relatively easy to classify the membership regionally.

(h) TGWU. Approximately 30 per cent of the TGWU's white-collar membership was situated in the union's Region 1 (London and Home Counties). From the white-collar membership file in the regional office it was possible to determine the names and addresses of the firms in each branch and the membership in each firm. At the request of head office the other twelve regions of the TGWU analysed their white-collar membership and supplied the author with the names and addresses of the firms covered, the membership in each firm, and the product manufactured. The membership was then distributed industrially and regionally according to the general procedure described above. Among white-collar workers, the TGWU caters in the main for clerks and supervisors. Almost all its supervisory members are employed in public transport; the number in private industry is negligible. Consequently, all the TGWU's white-collar membership in manufacturing industries was assigned to the 'clerks' category of Table 3A.3.

The white-collar membership of the above unions accounted for almost 95 per cent of total white-collar union membership in manufacturing industries. In order to determine what other unions catered for white-collar workers in manufacturing, a questionnaire was sent to all unions organizing in the manufacturing area of the economy plus most of the major purely white-collar unions. The questionnaire asked the union if it had any white-collar workers in manufacturing industries in membership and, if so, to give an occupational, industrial, and geographical analysis of it. During the summer of 1964, 210 questionnaires were sent out and almost 60 per cent of these were completed and returned. Often, additional correspondence was engaged in to clarify aspects of the union's initial reply. Many of these unions restricted their white-collar recruiting to a single occupational group and/or a single industry and thus classification was relatively easy.

The following unions had white-collar members in manufacturing industries in 1964 and were therefore included in Tables 3A.3 and 3A.4: Amalgamated Engineering Union; Electrical Trades Union; National Union of General and Municipal Workers; National Union of Stove Grate and General Metal Workers; Heating and Domestic Engineers' Union; United Patternmakers Association; Philanthropic

TABLE 3A.4

Total White-Collar Union Membership in Manufacturing Industries in Great Britain by Industry and by Region, 1964

Region	Food, drink, tobacco	Chemical	Metal manuf.	Metal N.E.S.	Eng. elect.	Ship M.E.	Vehicles	Textiles	Leather, fur	Clothing, footwear	Bricks, etc.	Timber, furn., etc.	Paper, print, pub.	Other manuf.	All manuf.
1. Scotland	187	312	1,586	53	8,734	2,148	2,642	266	4	..	139	22	1,928	493	18,514
2. Northern	87	525	3,330	176	6,231	1,428	184	179	..	..	..	34	875	245	13,294
3. North-west	299	1,617	1,357	223	17,047	551	7,193	6,181	..	24	637	43	2,944	1,011	39,127
4. East and West Ridings of Yorkshire and East and West Midlands	2,282	1,004	6,299	595	25,572	288	16,317	4,213	22	72	503	67	2,691	1,631	61,556
5. Wales	64	132	6,836	369	2,715	19	1,387	503	..	50	46	299	533	240	13,193
6. Eastern and Southern	386	267	308	605	8,865	457	7,683	3	..	..	211	64	1,756	346	20,951
7. London and South-East	835	2,128	328	145	16,569	88	4,705	55	..	58	346	235	19,824	465	45,781
8. South-western	582	243	12	..	3,015	45	6,261	213	..	..	424	18	802	740	12,355
9. ALL-REGIONS	4,722	6,228	20,056	2,166	88,748	5,024	46,372	11,613	26	204	2,306	782	31,353	5,171	224,771

P

Society of Journeymen Coopers of Sheffield and District; National Union of Lock and Metal Workers; British Association of Chemists; Chemical Workers Union; Tobacco Workers' Union; United French Polishers' Society; Supervisory Staffs Federation of the Glove Industry; London Foremen Tailors' Mutual Association; Institute of Journalists; National Union of Printing, Bookbinding and Paper Workers; Civil Service Clerical Association (a few members in Royal Ordnance Factories); General Union of Associations of Loom Overlookers; National Federation of Scribbling Overlookers Association; Managers and Overlookers' Society; Yorkshire Association of Power Loom Overlookers; Textile Officials' Association; Scottish Lace and Textile Workers Union; Halifax and District Carpet Power Loom Tuners' Association; Trade Society of Machine Calico Printers; Amalgamated Society of Textile Workers and Kindred Trades; and the National Woolsorters' Society.

The following unions reported that they had a few white-collar members in manufacturing industries but were unable to determine the number: National Union of Leather Workers; Amalgamated Society of Woodworkers; Amalgamated Society of Boilermakers, Shipwrights, Blacksmiths and Structural Workers; National Union of Commercial Travellers; Union of Shop, Distributive and Allied Workers; Amalgamated Society of Lithographic Printers; National Union of Furniture Trade Operatives; Birmingham and Midland Sheet Metal Workers' Society; National Union of Boot and Shoe Operatives; Electrical Power Engineers' Association; and the Association of Supervising Electrical Engineers. The following public service unions reported that they had membership among white-collar workers in railway workshops and Royal Ordnance Factories: National Union of Railwaymen; Transport Salaried Staffs' Association; Society of Technical Civil Servants; Society of Civil Servants; Association of Government Supervisors and Radio Officers; and the Institution of Professional Civil Servants.

The Ministry of Labour's definition of a trade union, given in the notes to Table 3.1 (*supra*, p. 195) was followed in constructing Tables 3A.3 and 3A.4. However, the membership of three organizations of white-collar personnel listed in the *Directory* were excluded from the present survey. It was clear from the rules of the British Pottery Managers' Association and the Printers' Managers and Overseers Association and from correspondence with the general secretaries of these two organizations that they were not trade unions within the scope of the above definition. Their main purpose was to provide professional education and superannuation benefits. The British Iron and Steel Management Association caters for all managerial grades in the iron and steel industry and has been excluded because managers are outside the scope of the present study. BISMA was founded when the iron and steel industry was nationalized in 1951 but made little headway after the industry was denationalized in 1953. In 1964 it had approximately 400 members and has expanded since the industry was renationalized. As such, BISMA is not an exception to the general rule that managerial personnel in private industry tend to advance their interests by individual rather than collective bargaining.

Whether or not press telegraphists, proof readers, and lithographic artists are white-collar employees is a very debatable question. Fortunately, this question did not have to be resolved in this study. The memberships of the National Union of Press Telegraphists, the Association of Correctors of the Press, and the Society of Lithographic Artists, Designers, Engravers and Process Workers had to be excluded from Tables 3A.3 and 3A.4 on grounds of comparability. The Ministry of Labour does not include the occupations covered by these unions in its white-collar labour force figures.

The density figures in Table 3.8 are obviously subject to some error. Undoubtedly, the author's industrial classification of some firms, particularly those with joint products, does not always agree with that of the government statisticians. (Since the Statistics of Trade Act, 1947, prohibits the disclosure of any statistical information about individual enterprises, Ministry of Labour statisticians are not able to inform individual researchers how various firms are industrially classified.) Moreover, because it was not possible to classify USDAW's membership on an industrial basis, the density figures for food, drink, and tobacco are probably understated. Due to the difficulties in obtaining membership data for foremen (see *supra*, p. 200) the density figures for foremen are probably also somewhat understated. But, in general, it is felt that Table 3.8 gives a reliable account of the differences in the density of white-collar unionism between various occupations and industries in manufacturing.

The labour force figures used to construct Table 3.9 are subject to a wide margin of error and are not strictly comparable with the union membership figures, so this table should be used with great caution.

TABLE 4.1

This table is taken from 'The Size of Manufacturing Establishments', *Ministry of Labour Gazette*, lxx (April 1962), p. 145.

The unit measured in this table is not the firm or the enterprise but the establishment. 'In most cases the establishment is a single factory engaged in one type of industrial activity. Establishments have been counted separately and firms with more than one establishment are represented more than once in the figures.' But there are some exceptions to this, for these see the above reference.

TABLE 4.2

The figures for foremen were derived from Occupation Table 9 and those for all the other occupational groups from Occupation Table 2 of the 1961 *Census of Population*.

TABLE 4.3

This table was abstracted from Industry Table 13 of the 1961 *Census of Population*. These figures not only include foremen supervising manual workers but also those supervising white-collar workers. But in manufacturing industries the former make up approximately 90 per cent of total foremen so the inclusion of the latter is unlikely to affect the totals to any great extent. (Compare 'foremen and supervisors—manual' as given by Industry Table 5 with 'foremen and supervisors' as given by Industry Table 13.)

TABLE 5.1

This table was derived from Guy Routh, *Occupation and Pay in Great Britain 1906–60* (Cambridge: Cambridge University Press, 1965), tables 30, 33, 37, and 47. Where Routh gives quartiles, medians, or deciles for clerks, averages were calculated by giving a weight equal to one-third of the number of clerks in the relevant sector. Routh's skilled, semi-skilled, and unskilled manual categories were averaged together (using the weights given for 1951 in his table 1) to obtain the 'all manual workers' category.

TABLE 5.2

This table was obtained by converting the average annual money earnings figures given in Table 5.1 into index numbers with 1922–4 as the base year, and then taking the white-collar indices for each year as a percentage of the manual index for that year.

TABLE 5.3

The white-collar earnings figures for 1959–63 are derived from the annual October survey of white-collar earnings begun in 1959. See, for example, 'Earnings of Administrative, Technical and Clerical Employees, October 1963', *Ministry of Labour Gazette*, lxxii (March 1964), pp. 92–3. The Ministry of Labour supplied unpublished information which made it possible to separate the leather, leather goods, and fur industry from other manufacturing industries. They also supplied unpublished data which made it possible to compute the average annual earnings of all white-collar workers (column 7).

The average annual earnings of manual workers for 1959–63 were supplied from unpublished sources by the Ministry of Labour. They are comparable with the white-collar earnings figures. The figures for males include the earnings of men (21 years and over) and the earnings of youths and boys (under 21). The figures for females include the earnings of women (18 years and over), both full-time and part-time, and the earnings of girls (under 18).

In computing the 1954–63 relatives, the white-collar and manual earnings figures used for 1963 were obtained from the sources indicated above. For 1954, both white-collar and manual earnings figures were obtained from the Board of Trade, *The Report on the Census of Production for 1958* (London: HMSO, 1962), part 133, table 3.

For a definition of the term 'white-collar' as used in this table see the notes to Table 2.5.

TABLE 5.4

The white-collar earnings figures for each manufacturing industry are the same as those used in Table 5.3 for the period 1959–63. The earnings indices for male and female white-collar employees in the economy as a whole were abstracted from 'Index of Average Salaries', *Ministry of Labour Gazette*, lxxii (May 1964), p. 195. A similar index for males and females combined was obtained from *Statistics on Incomes, Prices, Employment and Production*, No. 13 (June 1965), p. 48, table B. 17.

TABLE 5.5.

Derived from *Occupational Pension Schemes: A Survey by the Government Actuary* (London: HMSO, 1958), p. 4, and *Occupational Pension Schemes: A New Survey by the Government Actuary* (London: HMSO, 1966), p. 12.

TABLE 6.1

The labour force figures used in computing these averages are those appearing in Table 2A.3, *supra*, p. 196. The number of establishments in each industry were obtained from *The Report on the Census of Production for 1958*, part 133, table 4, and are given in the following table.

TABLE 6A.I

Number of Establishments in Manufacturing
Industries in the United Kingdom, 1958

Industry	Number of establishments
Food, drink, and tobacco	9,233
Chemicals and allied	3,566
Metal manufacture	2,876
Metal goods N.E.S.	10,588
Engineering and electrical goods	14,992
Shipbuilding and marine engineering	1,255
Vehicles	2,289
Textiles	8,461
Leather, leather goods, and fur	1,945
Clothing and footwear	9,592
Bricks, pottery, glass, cement, etc.	5,252
Timber, furniture, etc.	9,976
Paper, printing, and publishing	9,371
Other manufacturing industries	3,389
All manufacturing industries	92,785

For a definition of the term 'establishment' as used in this table see the notes to Table 4.1.

FIGURE 7.1

Trade Unions and the Public in 1964 (London: The Gallup Poll, 1964).

FIGURE 7.2

The membership figures of the major white-collar unions in private industry are given in Table 7A.1. Those of ASSET, the AScW, the CAWU, DATA, and the NUJ were obtained from the Registrar of Friendly Societies. Those of the NACSS and NATSOPA were supplied by these unions. The membership figures of NATSOPA for the period 1920–43 are for the London Clerical Branch only. Those for 1944 onwards represent the union's total clerical membership. The manner in which BISAKTA's membership figures were obtained is described in the notes to Table 3.7. The membership figures given in Table 7A.1 do not always agree with those in Table 3.7 primarily because they are given for different months of the year.

APPENDIX A

TABLE 7A.I

The Membership of Major White-Collar Unions in Manufacturing Industries, 1890–1964

Year	AScW	ASSET	BISAKTA	CAWU	DATA	NACSS	NATSOPA	NUJ
1890				..				
1891				..				
1892				30				
1893				30				
1894				59				
1895				28				
1896				39				
1897				50				
1898				68				
1899				80				
1900				82				
1901				70				
1902				80				
1903				85				
1904				84				
1905				84				
1906				350				
1907				750				738
1908				1,000				1,004
1909				1,870				1,525
1910				3,166				1,925
1911				5,225				2,155
1912				8,840				3,338
1913				11,750	200			4,407
1914				10,206	350			3,232
1915				10,843	750			3,127
1916				12,738	2,500			3,095
1917				26,572	9,000			3,342
1918	545	..		36,302	10,911			3,629
1919	428	..		43,222	13,500			4,343
1920	681	2,905		33,949	14,570		2,000	4,888
1921	808	2,758		14,204	11,460		1,500	4,680
1922	809	2,159		11,044	10,764	6,129	1,590	4,190
1923	821	1,770		7,442	9,975	5,263	1,697	4,275
1924	725	1,938		7,056	10,176	5,272	2,134	4,484
1925	922	2,006		7,570	10,730	5,649	2,565	4,827
1926	930	1,749		7,303	10,785	5,047	2,729	4,579
1927	1,700	1,498		7,183	10,794	5,120	2,314	4,522
1928	1,500	1,443		7,397	10,690	5,056	2,335	4,638
1929	1,250	1,859		7,666	10,735	4,861	2,340	5,071
1930	1,216	1,762		8,146	11,670	5,270	2,572	5,486
1931	1,094	1,839		7,482	12,147	5,074	2,759	5,477
1932	1,154	1,803		7,362	11,188	4,891	2,886	5,226
1933	900	1,636		7,510	10,943	5,106	3,120	5,182
1934	1,109	1,654		8,100	11,400	5,335	3,412	5,441
1935	1,031	1,625		9,030	12,140	6,040	3,623	5,806
1936	800	1,585		10,335	15,147	7,960	3,976	6,090
1937	988	1,606	..	12,423	17,920	9,115	4,322	6,522
1938	1,177	1,674	..	14,217	20,179	9,214	4,738	6,978
1939	1,379	1,743	..	15,943	23,137	9,934	4,787	7,245
1940	1,764	1,829	..	18,478	27,350	10,038	4,513	6,984
1941	3,246	2,142	..	21,470	30,920	13,137	4,702	7,031
1942	9,474	5,833	..	29,422	34,383	17,020	4,888	7,357
1943	14,010	9,823	..	33,902	38,418	18,964	5,096	6,627
1944	16,275	11,495	..	30,093	40,752	20,746	5,977	7,897

TABLE 7A.I *(cont.)*

Year	AScW	ASSET	BISAKTA	CAWU	DATA	NACSS	NATSOPA	NUJ
1945	15,632	9,661	..	25,247	43,466	18,341	5,257	8,216
1946	17,158	10,618	..	31,370	47,038	22,428	5,995	9,277
1947	18,387	15,090	..	34,127	47,668	24,957	6,506	9,711
1948	15,623	15,069	4,774	37,071	46,734	27,620	6,846	10,256
1949	14,133	11,592	4,609	33,429	46,792	27,147	7,446	10,559
1950	13,206	10,934	4,797	31,781	46,712	29,133	7,879	11,267
1951	13,014	12,738	6,002	38,266	49,039	32,936	7,873	11,684
1952	11,190	13,971	6,154	43,014	49,994	34,391	8,627	12,013
1953	11,592	13,975	6,163	43,337	48,642	34,615	9,153	11,815
1954	11,289	14,199	6,226	46,113	54,325	35,202	9,855	12,175
1955	11,740	15,422	6,306	50,375	50,438	36,525	10,462	12,874
1956	12,446	16,532	6,433	52,993	52,725	37,044	10,911	13,499
1957	11,886	18,970	6,237	50,517	54,449	36,373	10,981	13,910
1958	11,474	19,930	6,479	47,990	55,664	37,143	11,066	13,917
1959	11,720	19,942	6,601	49,306	56,242	38,150	10,808	14,371
1960	11,888	22,945	7,167	56,501	58,945	44,491	10,800	14,737
1961	14,119	25,270	7,662	60,739	61,368	44,655	10,615	15,053
1962	16,170	28,636	7,430	65,336	62,513	47,571	11,308	16,034
1963	18,195	30,159	7,520	71,527	59,679	51,337	11,802	16,478
1964	19,796	33,880	9,039	75,558	60,381	56,541	12,250	17,030

APPENDIX B

A NOTE ON THE REGRESSION TECHNIQUES
USED IN THIS STUDY

THIS is not the place to give a complete exposition of regression analysis. The reader who does not understand this method of analysis and wishes to have more information regarding it than was provided in Chapter I should consult the sources referred to there (*supra*, p. 8 n. 1) as well as more advanced texts such as C. E. V. Leser, *Econometric Techniques and Problems* (London: Griffin, 1966), chaps. 2 and 3, and J. Johnston, *Econometric Methods* (New York: McGraw-Hill, 1963), chaps. 1–4. Only a few comments regarding the specific way in which the technique was used in this study will be made here.

The technique of simple regression analysis is used in this study to analyse the relationship between: (*a*) the density of unionization among foremen and the age distribution of foremen, *supra*, p. 47; (*b*) the density of white-collar unionism and the earnings of white-collar workers, *supra*, pp. 55 and 61; and (*c*) the density of white-collar unionism and the degree of employment concentration, *supra*, p. 79. Except where otherwise noted, the equation for each occupational group is fitted to fourteen industry observations; since the 'all manufacturing' observation is simply the total of these fourteen industry observations, it was excluded from the analysis.

Because of the relatively small number of industry observations, data from the various occupational groups has been pooled where possible and subjected to a multiple regression analysis. That is, a single equation was fitted to the seventy observations which result from pooling the data for the following occupational groups: (*a*) foremen, (*b*) scientists and technologists, (*c*) draughtsmen, (*d*) other technicians, and (*e*) clerks. The observations for (*a*) all scientists, technologists, and technicians, (*b*) all technicians, and (*c*) all white-collar workers, were excluded as they are simply the total of the observations for various of the occupational groups referred to above. The observations for other white-collar workers were also excluded because of the extremely heterogeneous nature of this category and the almost complete absence of unionism from it except among journalists in the paper, printing, and publishing industry. It proved possible to pool the data in analysing the relationship between: (*a*) the density of white-collar unionism and the proportion of women in the labour force, *supra*, pp. 41–2, and (*b*) the density of white-collar unionism and the degree of employment concentration, *supra*, pp. 79–80.

Pooling the data in this way implies that the relationship between the density of white-collar unionism and the various independent variables is the same for all occupational groups and all industries. But this need not be the case. The relationship may change systematically from one occupation to another and from one industry to another as a result, for example, of variations in employment distributions between different occupations and different industries (see *supra*, pp. 77–8). To allow for the possibility that the level as well as the slope of the equation may shift by occupation and by industry, dummy variables were included in each equation. These variables take the value of zero or one according to whether the particlar observation is from that specific occupation or industry.[1]

Allowing for only the level of the equation[2] to shift with occupation, then, for a five-occupation model, the linear equation $y = a + bx + u$ becomes:

$$y = a_0 + a_1\phi_1 + a_2\phi_2 + a_3\phi_3 + a_4\phi_4 + bx + u \tag{1}$$

where $\phi_i = 1$ in the ith occupation and o in all other occupations ($i = 1, 2, 3$, etc.). Allowing for only the slope of the equation to shift with occupation, then for a five-occupation model, the linear equation $y = a + bx + u$ becomes:

$$y = a_0 + b_1\phi_1 x + b_2\phi_2 x + b_3\phi_3 x + b_4\phi_4 x + bx + u. \tag{2}$$

Allowing for both the level and the slope of the equation to shift with occupation, then for a five-occupation model, the linear equation $y = a + bx + u$ becomes:

$$y = a_0 + a_1\phi_1 \ldots + a_4\phi_4 + b_1\phi_1 x \ldots + b_4\phi_4 x + bx + u. \tag{3}$$

Allowing for only the level of the equation to shift with industry, then, for a fourteen-industry model, the linear equation $y = a + bx + u$ becomes:

$$y = a_0 + a_1 I_1 \ldots + a_{13} I_{13} + bx + u \tag{4}$$

where $I_i = 1$ in the ith industry and o in all other industries. Allowing for only the slope of the equation to shift with industry, then, for a fourteen-industry model, the linear equation $y = a + bx + u$ becomes:

$$y = a_0 + b_1 I_1 x \ldots + b_{13} I_{13} x + bx + u. \tag{5}$$

Allowing for both the level and the slope of the equation to shift with industry, then, for a fourteen-industry model, the linear equation $y = a + bx + u$ becomes:

$$y = a_0 + a_1 I_1 \ldots + a_{13} I_{13} + b_1 I_1 x \ldots + b_{13} I_{13} x + bx + u. \tag{6}$$

Allowing for only the level of the equation to shift with both occupation and industry, then, for a five-occupation-fourteen-industry model, the linear equation $y = a + bx + u$ becomes:

$$y = a_0 + a_1\phi_1 \ldots + a_4\phi_4 + a_1 I_1 \ldots + a_{13} I_{13} + bx + u. \tag{7}$$

Allowing for only the slope of the equation to shift with both occupation and industry, then, for a five-occupation-fourteen-industry model, the linear equation $y = a + bx + u$ becomes:

$$y = a_0 + b_1\phi_1 x \ldots + b_4\phi_4 x + b_1 I_1 x \ldots + b_{13} I_{13} x + bx + u. \tag{8}$$

Allowing for both the level and the slope of the equation to shift with both occupation and industry, then, for a five-occupation-fourteen-industry model, the linear equation $y = a + bx + u$ becomes:

$$y = a_0 + a_1\phi_1 \ldots + a_4\phi_4 + a_1 I_1 \ldots + a_{13} I_{13} + b_1\phi_1 x$$
$$\ldots + b_4\phi_4 x + b_1 I_1 x \ldots + b_{13} I_{13} x + bx + u. \tag{9}$$

[1] This is a standard econometric procedure and is used, for example, by L. R. Klein *et al.*, *An Econometric Model of the United Kingdom* (Oxford: Blackwell, 1961), pp. 42–4, in adjusting for seasonal variation. The account of the procedure which is given below relies very heavily on this source. This technique is also used by Keith Cowling and David Metcalf, 'Wage–Unemployment Relationships: A Regional Analysis for the U.K. 1960–65', *Bulletin of the Oxford University Institute of Economics and Statistics*, xxix (February 1967), pp. 30–9, in adjusting for regional variation. See also Johnston, op. cit., pp. 221–8.

[2] The reader who does not find the following equations very illuminating may find that his understanding of this technique will be increased by studying the graphical description given by Klein, op. cit., pp. 45–6.

In analysing the relationship between variables, all these equations were fitted to the seventy observations. But, in each case, the results are cited only for those equations which possessed the correct signs and were most significant.

The above exposition has been given only in terms of linear relationships. But the following curvilinear relationships were also tested for: semilog, double-log, inverse, and log inverse (see Johnston, op. cit., chap. 2). The linear relationships always proved to be the most significant, and all results cited in the text are for such relationships.

All the computations were carried out by the Oxford University Computing Laboratory using their multiple regression programme FAKAD 2300 designed by Emiel van Broekhoven. The measure of correlation calculated by this programme is the $\bar{R}^2$ and has been adjusted for degrees of freedom.

APPENDIX C

BIBLIOGRAPHICAL NOTE

T H E sources which were consulted most frequently in the research for this study have been cited in the footnotes, and there seems little point in listing them once again here. Nor does there seem much point in compiling here a comprehensive bibliography on British white-collar unionism as this has been done elsewhere. See G. S. Bain and Harold Pollins, 'The History of White-Collar Unions and Industrial Relations: A Bibliography', *Labour History*, No. 11 (Autumn 1965), pp. 20–65. In addition, many of the more important foreign sources are listed in *Bibliography on Non-Manual Workers* (Geneva: ILO, 1959). But it might be of some use to the student who wishes to pursue this subject further to list here the major works in Britain and a few other countries.

The most important works on the subject in Great Britain include the following: F. D. Klingender, *The Condition of Clerical Labour in Great Britain* (London: Martin Lawrence, 1935); David Lockwood, *The Blackcoated Worker* (London: Allen & Unwin, 1958); J. R. Dale, *The Clerk in Industry* (Liverpool: Liverpool University Press, 1962); Geoffrey Millerson, *The Qualifying Associations* (London: Routledge & Kegan Paul, 1964); Kenneth Prandy, *Professional Employees* (London: Faber, 1965); and R. M. Blackburn, *Union Character and Social Class* (London: Batsford, 1967).

In the United States, as in Britain, histories of some of the more important white-collar unions have been written, and most of these are listed in Maurice F. Neufeld, *A Representative Bibliography of American Labor History* (Ithaca, N.Y.: Cornell University Press, 1964), especially pp. 74, 94–8, 111, 124–9. The more analytical studies include C. Wright Mills, *White Collar* (New York: Oxford University Press, 1951); G. Strauss, 'White-Collar Unions Are Different!' *Harvard Business Review*, xxxii (September–October 1954), pp. 73–82; B. Goldstein, 'Some Aspects of the Nature of Unionism Among Salaried Professionals in Industry', *American Sociological Review*, xx (April 1955), pp. 199–205; J. W. Riegel, *Collective Bargaining as Viewed by Unorganized Engineers and Scientists* (Ann Arbor: University of Michigan, Bureau of Industrial Relations, 1959); S. M. Lipset, 'The Future of Non-Manual Unionism' (unpublished paper, University of California, Institute of Industrial Relations, Berkeley, 1961); Richard E. Walton, *The Impact of the Professional Engineering Union* (Boston, Mass.: Harvard University, Division of Research, 1961); Albert A. Blum, *Management and the White-Collar Union* (New York: American Management Association, 1964); Archie Kleingartner, *Professionalism and Salaried Worker Organization* (Madison, Wisconsin: University of Wisconsin, Industrial Relations Research Institute, 1967); and by the same author, 'The Organisation of White-Collar Workers', *British Journal of Industrial Relations*, vi (March 1968), pp. 79–93. There is also a symposium on 'Professional Workers in Industry' in *Industrial Relations*, ii (May 1963), pp. 7–65.

The writing on the subject in Australia has been small in volume but generally analytical in nature. See, in particular, D. W. Rawson, 'The Frontiers of Trade Unionism', *Australian Journal of Politics and History*, i (May 1956), pp. 196–209; N. F. Dufty, 'The White Collar Unionist', *Journal of Industrial Relations*, iii (October 1961), pp. 151–6; R. M. Martin, 'Class Identification and Trade Union Behaviour: The Case of Australian White Collar Unions', *Journal of Industrial Relations*, vii (July 1965), pp. 131–48; and by the same author, *White-Collar Unions in Australia* (Sydney: Australian Institute of Political Science, 1965).

Finally, there are two sources which contain essays on white-collar unionism in the above countries as well as in Austria, France, Germany, Israel, Japan, Norway, and Sweden. See the symposium on 'Professional and White-Collar Unionism: An International Comparison' in *Industrial Relations*, v (October 1965), pp. 37–150; and Adolf Sturmthal, editor, *White-Collar Trade Unions* (London: University of Illinois Press, 1966).

INDEX

[The author is grateful to Kate Buckley who skilfully compiled this index.]

PRINTED IN GREAT BRITAIN
AT THE UNIVERSITY PRESS, OXFORD
BY VIVIAN RIDLER
PRINTER TO THE UNIVERSITY